DEPARTMENT OF EDUCATION A KV-197-829

EDUCATIONAL PRIORITY

VOLUME 3: CURRICULUM INNOVATION IN LONDON'S E.P.A.s

Edited by

JACK BARNES

Report of a research project sponsored by
the Department of Education and Science and
the Social Science Research Council

LONDON
HER MAJESTY'S STATIONERY OFFICE
1975

34618

ISBN 0 11 270297 X

Contents

Foreword

This is the third volume of the report of the three-year action-research programme in four English and one Scottish Educational Priority Areas. It deals with those elements of the London project in Deptford which were evaluated by the research team. The context and contents of the volume need a brief word of explanation and comment from me as National Director of the programme.

The origin of the five projects is to be found in the circumstances in which, in 1967, Plowden offered the last report of the Advisory Council to the Department of Education and Science. Anthony Crosland was Secretary of State, I was his Adviser, while Michael Young was Chairman of S.S.R.C. and the economic situation was, as usual, inauspicious for new spending proposals. In this situation Mr. Crosland was remarkably successful in securing a £16m. school building programme for the E.P.A.s. Soon afterwards there was also a response to the Plowden suggestion for increased teachers' salaries in E.P.A. schools. The other significant response, not so much financially but rather in terms of a style of policy development, was our action-research programme. Indeed, it may be plausibly argued that this third response was in the long run the most significant of the three.

If this is so, it is fundamentally because action-research is a means of intelligent and self-conscious social change. That sounds, of course, a loud claim to make for a financially miniscule intervention in the vast apparatus that we call the education system. It is not intended to imply that there are no other methods of critical self-consciousness or monitoring used or to be used by organisations. It is, however an assertion of the potential power of action-research to link social science directly to the politics and administration of government. There are serious problems of co-operation and confrontation involved in such a relationship, but our experience, we would claim, illustrates and confirms its value.

There are also problems internal to the action-research project as such. One of them is the inevitable outcome that some experiments will *fail*. If caution were taken to the point of never trying uncertain ideas there would be little experiment and less excitement. The voluminous Report which we submitted to D.E.S. and S.S.R.C. on the last day of the programme (31st December 1971) was indeed a long story of both success and failure. Our next step was to plan and prepare the material for general publication. Two broad outcomes were looked for; an account of successful and unsuccessful innovations in the chosen districts in London, Liverpool, Birmingham, the West Riding and Dundee; and an evaluation of success and failure according to acceptable criteria of validity and reliability.

Our first volume, *Educational Priority: Problems and Policies*, was published in the late summer of 1972. In it we presented a synoptic view of the English project but with a special emphasis on the implications of our work for a national E.P.A. policy—national, that is, in the sense of being generalisable and translatable from one district to another and worthy of attention from Government, administration, schools, colleges, community organisations and teacher unions. In other words, the first volume offered a summary of a national programme of action-research designed in the aftermath of the Plowden Report to explore practical ways of raising standards of educational living in districts suffering from multiple deprivation, which are labelled Educational Priority Areas. Substantively, this book described a programme of intervention divided roughly in its energies between pre-schooling and primary schooling. It will be recalled, however, that our activities took us outside the traditional and formal bounds of the educational system in our attempts to make a reality of the principles of positive discrimination and the idea of the community school.

The synoptic description of the first volume is, then, the context for an understanding of the particular projects, experiments and innovations which are reported and discussed in more detail in the later volumes. Thus, in Volume II, edited by Joan Payne, we have concentrated on research in the form of an analysis of our surveys in the several E.P.A.s and on further details of our experiments with a structured pre-school programme. Meanwhile, a detailed account of the Liverpool project has been written and published by Eric Midwinter—*Priority Education*, Penguin Education Specials, 1972.

The third and present volume in the H.M.S.O. series continues the emphasis of Volume II with respect to some elements of the Deptford project. The reader will be aware of a relatively pessimistic and negative tone in it, by comparison with the first, as well as with Volume IV and V on the West Riding and Dundee, and even more with Eric Midwinter's account of the Liverpool project. This is not an accident, nor does it represent a conflict within the national team as to the truth about our experience in the E.P.A.s. Our organisation has been far from monolithic, as may be gathered from Volume I, and especially the discussion of action-research in Chapter 13. Each local project organisation developed its own peculiar organisation according to the characteristics of the district and the personalities in the action-research team. In the case of Deptford there was the special feature of an existing and strongly organised research division in the Inner London Education Authority, the large and therefore elaborately organised Authority itself and the background of the Action Director as a successful primary school teacher who had previously experimented along Plowden lines in his own school and who was, by training and experience, strongly teacher-oriented. Jack Barnes and his research colleagues were firmly rooted by training and career in the social science disciplines. The welding of an effective action-research programme was accordingly difficult. What Jack Barnes has made of it from the point of view of evaluation makes up the body of Volume III. Reports on the projects which are reported here inevitably reflect different conceptions of what kind of intervention in the Priority Areas would be most valuable, as well as how it could best be planned and how the result could most appropriately be measured. Inevitably, too, and for complex reasons, some activities proved more successful than others. The part of the story which is told here by Jack Barnes and his colleagues is one of relative failure. Much can be learnt from these failures as well as from the successes. They present a sharp outline from the point of view of particular and well-established social science methods. The peculiar difficulty, which the authors bring out at several points, is that, in describing and analysing social action, measured outcomes are often ambiguous. This difficulty is fundamental. It arises not only because of the problems of measurement but also because the participants may, and usually do, define the purpose and significance of action differently from the social scientists. Action-research does not escape this problem any more than older approaches to social study, more pure or more applied.

I would make two comments. First, the evaluation of the London project has showed how very important it is in action-research to arrive at a clear statement of goals and to explicate the theory of how intervention will achieve the stated goals. Second, the reader should be reminded that the criteria which the authors have brought to bear in the London evaluation would be ones which elsewhere have shown remarkable successes in different elements of the various programmes.

This volume, then, puts some elements of one of the E.P.A. projects into sombre light. But it is our duty and our interest to try to encompass the successful and disappointing, the cheerful and sad, outcome of the programme as a whole.

The authors of all the papers which make up this volume would like to thank the children and teachers who took part in the experimental studies. In situations where learning and teaching were in any case difficult, it was extremely rare not to have a friendly reception and whole-hearted commitment to the success of the schemes.

Last, the I.L.E.A. encouraged, tolerated and financed a substantial proportion of the work reported here. Without their support the schemes would not have been possible. But opinions expressed in the reports are those of the authors and not of the I.L.E.A.

A. H. HALSEY
Nuffield College, Oxford,
1.2.74

Acknowledgements

Five of the reports in this volume record attempts by a large number of people to find ways of raising the school performance of children in educational priority area schools in Inner London. Parts 2 and 3 are reports of innovations promoted directly by the Inner London Education Authority and evaluated by Mrs. Janet Woods, an officer of the Research and Statistics Group of the I.L.E.A. Parts 4, 5 and 6 are reports of schemes developed during the London E.P.A. Project as part of A. H. Halsey's National Programme. I would like to thank all the people who worked on the London E.P.A. Project, in particular Jim Stevenson who concerned himself with all the Project evaluations until the end. I wish to pay special tribute to Charles Betty, the London Project Director, whose hard work and enthusiasm made the Project possible and gave it its particular character, but whose achievements are under-represented in the volume. Besides members of the Project staff, essential help was given by Miss Wendy Fader, of the National Foundation for Educational Research, over the computing and data analysis for Parts 5 and 6; and Dr. Alan Little, as Director of the Research and Statistics Group, was always available with encouragement and ruthlessly impartial criticism. Part 7 is a re-analysis of data collected by the I.L.E.A. in the 1968 and 1971 surveys of literacy standards in London primary schools. The analysis was completed after the E.P.A. Project had finished, while I was a Fellow of the Centre for Studies in Social Policy, and was presented to the Social Science Research Council's seminar on Sociological Theory and Survey Research. I am grateful to my colleagues at the Centre and to the members of the S.S.R.C. seminar for their comments on the work.

Part One

Approaches, Lessons and Questions
J. H. Barnes

Approaches, Lessons and Guidance

Approaches, Lessons and Questions

Each of the parts in this volume is a separate and self-contained record of particular events in primary schools in Inner London during the period 1968–71. But there are themes common to all of them. They are all concerned with social and educational disadvantage, and with positive discrimination and work in educational priority area schools to tackle it. Five of them are accounts of curriculum innovations: three of which were promoted by the London E.P.A. Project and two directly by the Inner London Education Authority.[1] For these the method of approach was the same in all cases but one[2]; it was, in fact, a London hybrid of the combination of local diagnosis and action-research found to be successful in the National E.P.A. Programme.[3] The subject of Part 7 is still educational and social disadvantage; but the focus has changed from small scale pilot exercises in a few schools to analysis of data on one age cohort of 30,000 primary school children in 600 schools.

What people will find in this book, therefore, is a collection of essays on various perceived aspects of the educational priority area problem and attempts to do something about it. But they will not find any comfort in it. Nor will they find a list of things to do next. These essays raise questions about what it is appropriate and realistic to expect from schools as they are currently organised. And we hope that the reader will gain more insight from them into what not to expect, and how not to go about educational innovation: more accurately perhaps, how to improve our knowledge of educational innovation by knowing what will prove to be inadequate. Many people will question, and perhaps then come to disagree with, our methods and our findings. We hope they will be questioned and discussed. At the same time, those who wish to reject either must be prepared to replace them with realistic and credible alternatives.

The Need for Discrimination

The Plowden policy of positive discrimination in favour of educational priority areas is a proposed solution to a number of different problems,

---

[1] Parts 2 and 3 are accounts of work promoted directly by the Inner London Education Authority (the I.L.E.A.); and Parts 4, 5 and 6 are records of innovations sponsored directly by the London E.P.A. Project.

[2] Part 2—the aids to reading—is in many respects different from all the other innovations. The teaching materials were created by outside "experts" and the local teachers were simply asked to arrange for their use. But the concern, as with all the others, was to find ways to improve the quality of education and so the school performance of children in Educational Priority Areas.

[3] See the other volumes of this E.P.A. series, H.M.S.O., London; and Eric Midwinter, *Priority Education*, Penguin, 1972.

rather than to any single set. Let us accept for a moment that the primary concern was to help disadvantaged children (although the meaning of this is problematical): there was, in 1966–67, the political question of getting *something* done to help them. There was then the question of how to do it cheaply.[1] There was the question of resource disparities between different local education authorities; and then the question of the allocation of resources within local authorities, between schools.[2] And overriding everything else, there was the constraint that the Plowden Council was an educational body with terms of reference which, in a formal sense, limited it to making educational recommendations.[3]

In the first volume of the E.P.A. series Dr. Halsey developed some of the dimensions to this tangle of problems. The main thrust of his argument was directed, as was the Plowden Council's, towards what we might call the politics of change. He recognised, and rejected, the position that an E.P.A. policy was essentially a device for doing nothing.[4] He saw the policy as legitimately within the tradition of educational attacks on social inequality; but he pointed out that the substance and tone of the discussion had changed since the publication of the Plowden Report. Local diversity rather than national uniformity should now be the policy objective. At the micro level this meant that the content of education and the curriculum of schools should be more responsive to local (community) social situations.[5] At the macro level Halsey showed how the four English E.P.A. study areas differed from each other and he recommended local variations to any national policy.[6] In the second volume of the series Mrs. Payne has documented, more systematically than was possible in the first, what we might call the sociology of the needs of educational priority areas. The dominant picture here is of an accumulation of difficulties to be faced by people living and working in them.[7]

Much of the London work creates tensions for the Plowden Council style of analysis and, as it were, for the majority reports of the National E.P.A. Programme. Currently the prognosis is at three levels. Past periods of economic growth, of social change and of real improvements in living standards have not substantially altered the relative position of poor people in our society. Particularly oppressed are those poor people who live in poor areas; and educational reform can, at least, bring assistance to their children. The

---

[1] See "The Plowden Committee on Primary Education" in Richard Chapman (ed.), *The Role of Commissions in Policy-Making*, Allen and Unwin. In this essay Maurice Kogan, who was the Secretary to the Plowden Council, stresses "The conscientious attempt to make (the Council's) recommendations uncostly".

[2] The Plowden Council recommendations for an E.P.A. policy were primarily concerned with the need to distinguish between schools and areas *within* local authorities. But clearly those authorities with disproportionate numbers of poor areas or schools would need more than an equal share of national resources: see the *Plowden Report*, Chapter 3 *passim*.

[3] The Council's terms of reference were "to consider primary education in all its aspects, and the transition to secondary education". In a formal sense, therefore, they were excluded from making recommendations for a policy to tackle child poverty in other than its educational manifestations.

[4] A. H. Halsey (ed.), *Educational Priority. Volume 1: E.P.A. Problems and Policies*, Chapter 13.

[5] *Educational Priority,* Vol. 1 Chapters 9 to 12.

[6] *Educational Priority*, Vol. 1 Chapters 5 and 14.

[7] Joan Payne (ed.), *E.P.A. Volume II: Surveys and Statistics*.

curriculum innovations in Parts 2 to 6 of this volume are field trials of the last proposition. But we can also say something about the first two, placing the problems of educational priority areas in perspectives of time and of social geography.

The early 1950s was a period of interest in the intelligence and reading standards of London's school children.[1] The concern seems to have been to establish the proportions of backward and retarded children, and a number of surveys were conducted among the population at the time.[2] Similarly in 1968, and again in 1971, surveys of literacy standards were conducted among one cohort of junior school children in Inner London.[3] From the evidence that is still available on the proportions of backward readers in London in the early 1950s, it is possible to compare the situation at two points in time—sixteen years apart. It is very important to be clear that the comparisons are crude: different tests were used; the definition of poor readers changed from survey to survey in the early 1950s; all the data are standardised with reference to national norms, which themselves improved over the period[4]; and there is, in fact, no remaining comprehensive account of the data from the early surveys. Nevertheless, assuming that the distributions of score were normal for all the data, it is possible to transform the 1968 and 1971 results to make them comparable with those of the earlier period.[5]

The major survey in the early 1950s was conducted in the school year 1953–54, across a sample of children from the whole of the London County Council area who were in their last year in junior school. It was found, according to the definition used,[6] that 14 per cent of the London group were backward readers (see Table 1). This is a smaller proportion than could be expected from a normal distribution (16 per cent), a fact which is noted in the report of the survey. The proportion of similarly defined backward readers found in the 1971 survey of 11 year old children in Inner London was almost twice as high as that found in 1953–54: 27 per cent as opposed to 14 per cent.

As it happened, a further survey of reading was conducted, in 1952, among

---

[1] This interest was, at the time, seen to be within the traditions set by Burt before the Second World War. See Burt, *The Backward Child*, University of London Press.

[2] Two are significant for our purposes. The first in *1952* measured, among other things, the reading performance of second year junior children in schools in the Metropolitan Borough which, in 1968, contained the E.P.A. Project Schools. The second survey, during the school year *1953–54*, measured the reading ages of a representative sample of children from the whole of the London County Council area who were in their last year in junior school.

[3] These were surveys of all the children present at school from one age cohort of I.L.E.A. children: which in 1968 was in its second year in junior school, and in 1971 was in its last year in junior school. See *Literacy Survey: 1971 follow up—Preliminary Report*. I.L.E.A. 203.

[4] See *The Plowden Report*, Volume II, Appendix 7, "Standards of Reading of Eleven-year-olds, 1948–1964".

[5] See Blalock, *Social Statistics*, for the properties of a normal distribution. It needs to be stressed again that these comparisons should be taken as illustrative rather than in any sense definitive.

[6] The definition of backward reading used here was: "a level of attainment *85* per cent or less of the average attainment of a child of that age". (It becomes clear from the report that this means children scoring below one standard deviation from the average for a test with a standard deviation of 15; it is pointed out, for instance, that 16 per cent of a normal population could be expected to do this.)

Table 1

Proportions of Backward Readers in 1952–54 and 1968–71

	Proportion of backward readers %
A. In junior schools in the *Metropolitan Borough*, which in 1968 contained the E.P.A. Project junior schools	
Backwardness defined as scoring below 80	
1952 Survey of 8 year olds	16
1968 Survey of 8 year olds	19
Assuming a normal distribution	
Expected proportion	9
B. In *L.C.C.*: a stratified sample of schools to give a representative sample of children	
Backwardness defined as scoring below 85	
1953–54 Survey of 11 year olds	14
In *I.L.E.A.*: all children at school in the age cohort at the time of the test	
(1968 Survey of 8 year olds)	(27)
1971 Survey of 11 year olds	27
Assuming a normal distribution	
Expected proportion	16

children in their second year of junior school (aged between eight and nine) in schools in the Metropolitan Borough which, in 1968, contained the E.P.A. Project junior schools. The definition of backward reading used in the presentation of results from this survey gives a smaller expected proportion: 9 per cent.[1] Nevertheless, 16 per cent of the age cohort in the Borough at this time were found to be backward readers (see Table 1). Using the same definition, the proportion of nine year old children who were backward readers in the same group of junior schools in 1968 was even higher: 19 per cent. But significantly, the proportion had increased by far less than the proportion of backward readers across the whole of Inner London (where the less rigorous definition was used).

Table 2 gives even more interesting evidence. It is impossible to identify specific schools from the data on the 1952 survey; but Table 2 shows the schools with various percentages of backward readers among their second year junior school children in 1952 and in 1968. Remember that the percentage of poor readers for the whole area increased over time. But the percentage in the median school decreased; and the range of schools, ranked with reference to the proportion of backward readers in them, grew smaller.[2] In other words, although the proportion of backward readers in the area increased over the period, such children became more evenly spread across the schools.

What follows? We live in a world of relativities. Over time national standards improved. But standards in Inner London, expressed as proportions of

---

[1] The definition of backward reading used here was: "a level of attainment 80 per cent or less of the average for a child at that age". Again a normal distribution can be assumed.

[2] One school in the Borough in 1968 had a selective intake of children and an unusually low proportion of backward readers for the area (5 per cent). If we exclude this school then the range is even narrower.

Table 2

Proportions of Backward Readers in Junior Schools in the Same Metropolitan Borough 1952 & 1968

	Schools with various percentages of poor readers (%)							Total schools
	<5	6–10	11–15	16–20	21–25	26–30	30+	
1952 Survey of 8 year olds Median school = 22% Range = 29	—	2	2	1	4	—	2	11
1968 Survey of 8 year olds Median school = 16–17% Range = 26 (excluding school with lowest percentage = 16)	1	—	3	2	—	3	—	10

backward readers defined with reference to the improving national standard, certainly did not: indeed they became relatively worse. Standards in a disadvantaged London Borough[1] also deteriorated over time relative to the national norm; but by relatively less than those for the whole of the inner city school population. And within the Borough the range of school scores would have narrowed over time. In other words, the educational problem (in this case of backward readers) is less concentrated in a particular group of inner city schools than it was, say, twenty years ago. The educational problems of the inner city have become more severe, but also more general and more widespread.

All this suggests that the focus for our thinking should not be small areas within the inner city but the inner city as a whole. In Part 7 we develop this line of reasoning. The 1968 I.L.E.A. Literacy Survey was conducted with the intention of providing the education authority with descriptive information on its schools and children. But during 1972–73 (after the National E.P.A. Programme had finished) the data were re-analysed to establish the spread and the consequences of social disadvantage throughout the twelve Inner London Boroughs. The results of the analysis show the problems of social and educational disadvantage in a new light. If we accept the original Plowden criteria for identifying disadvantaged children,[2] then we must conclude that they are not as concentrated in educational priority areas as has been thought. Indeed we must face an apparent paradox: most disadvantaged children are not in the educational priority areas, and most of the children in educational priority areas are not disadvantaged. Further, the substance of educational and social disadvantage is extremely heterogeneous. In fact the concepts seem to describe many different situations of need; and we would contend that

---

[1] The Metropolitan Borough is classified in the poorest third of L.C.C. Boroughs and in the third with the highest proportion of backward children, in the Burt studies soon after World War I and in the L.C.C. study soon after World War II. The schools in it were (with two exceptions) in the most disadvantaged third on I.L.E.A.'s 1967 index of relative disadvantage; and the schools in the London E.P.A. Project (6 out of 10) were relatively more disadvantaged than those in the rest of the Borough.

[2] The Plowden Council were interested in identifying areas and schools. In Part 7 we have used criteria identical to those which identified *areas* to identify *individual children* at risk of being disadvantaged.

effective policies should be tackling the different needs that children have rather than some general, and possibly misleading, notions of disadvantage.

Nevertheless, the average educational performance of E.P.A. schools is lower than that of more privileged schools. But again we must face a paradox. Poor or low social class or immigrant or disadvantaged children do badly at school, whatever sort of school they are in. And most of such children are not in the E.P.A. schools. The children who do badly *because* they are in E.P.A. schools are groups who, in terms of their "objective" home circumstances, are relatively privileged.[1] Thus, the children who have most to gain from a straightforward improvement of schools are those children who are currently disadvantaged because of the schools they attend: children whose home circumstances are relatively privileged.

What then should we be trying to do? Should we improve schools and improve opportunities for all children expecting, from the evidence presented in Part 7, a consequence to be that the disparities in performance between privileged and disadvantaged groups of children will increase? Or should we transform schools, in order to avoid reinforcing the effects of ascribed status, or of the various benefits that children are lucky enough to inherit without, in effect, knowing the consequences of such a policy for any group of children?

Before pursuing this line of reasoning, it is instructive to examine the curriculum innovations reported in this volume. They constitute only a fraction of the work in London's E.P.A.s over the period. But there are strong similarities of method, of content and of conclusions to be drawn from all of them. The principal components of method are local diagnosis of educational problems and situations, and action-research field trials of remedies for them; and much of what happened can be seen within the context of these.

Local Diagnosis

In principle the methods of local diagnosis are very close to those of social anthropology. A particular situation is examined in great first-hand detail, and diverse bits of information are drawn together into a unified interpretation of it. There is intense investigation and integrated interpretation. Its attractiveness and its strength as a method of advancing policy comes from a belief that, when seen in their local context, social problems are multidimensional and defy neat categorisation into areas of administrative responsibility. The "local man", it is argued, is better equipped to see and to respond to this than is the "man at the centre", who must rely on information filtered through precisely those channels which obscure the interconnected nature of

---

[1] In a sense, therefore, we might say that all children who attend E.P.A. schools are disadvantaged: by a changing combination of school and home circumstances. But it is important to be clear that home circumstances affect performance more than school circumstances, and most children who are disadvantaged in this respect are not in E.P.A. schools.

social situations. In this way, it is hoped that generalisations can be established about the interrelationship of institutions in certain types of context: and more particularly, that policies can be tailored more precisely to local circumstance. Thus as an idea, the anthropological approach to policy development is free from the constraints of any one discipline or administrative responsibility.

In practice, the local diagnosis in London was more limited than this. The specific concern was always with education, and almost always with educational institutions (in fact with primary schools). Some of the work was promoted directly by a local education authority, and the E.P.A. Project worked closely with the teachers and officers of the local authority. In consequence, the main thrust of the work was to enable schools to do better what they were already doing.[1]

At the same time decisions were made through the interaction of a complex of interested parties. Although most of the people concerned were educational practitioners, this did not mean that they all necessarily wanted the same thing.[2] The eventual directions of any programme often corresponded directly to the purpose of no one group. They might be seen rather as "aggregate intentions", or resultants, from perhaps conflicting interests. The consequences of this are extremely important. One way of making progress was to construct a plan or a design, which accommodated many different points of view and with which all might come to terms. Such a plan would embrace as much as possible, so that all those who needed to ratify it could see something of their position in it. But what really happened corresponded neither to what any party originally intended nor, in fact, to the agreed plan. And the dominant factor in all cases was what the teachers actually did with their children. In view of this, we need to see the educational innovations within a broad context of the climate of teacher opinion at the time on the problems and opportunities facing E.P.A. schools.

The Teachers' Point of View

During the school year 1968–69 forty-seven head teachers of educational priority area and "immigrant" schools in Inner London were interviewed.

---

[1] Various other activities were promoted by the London E.P.A. Project. A social worker was appointed to work with a small group of children—see K. H. Lyons, *Social Work and the School: A study of some aspects of the role of an education social worker*, H.M.S.O.—and a number of efforts were made to initiate community schools: which were activity based junior clubs running one evening each week with an open invitation to parents to attend. But both of these were seen by the majority of the local teachers to be tangential to the main concern, which was with in-school curriculum matters.

[2] At the most abstract level, it is possible to see a series of functions being performed as the Project evolved: sponsorship, production, implementation, affected party, etc. Involvement with each function entailed different sorts of demands for any activity. But even supposing all parties were ostensibly engaged with the same purpose—say planning a scheme's implementation—once again demands could vary. An obvious clash of interests here was between those who saw things in the long term, beyond the life of the E.P.A. Project, and those whose purpose was to reach an assessment within the life of the Project. This was by no means simply a question of differences between Project personnel and implementing teachers. Actually within the local schools, head teachers tended to stress the long-term and participating class teachers the shorter-term view; there were exceptions to this generalisation.

They were asked two sets of questions: first of all how they saw the "E.P.A. problem", and secondly what they thought could be done about it.[1]

The heads had no difficulty identifying the problem. The children were the problem. Thirty of the forty-seven heads stated that the backwardness or low ability of the children was the major problem they perceived in their school. Further, the children were seen to be in poor physical and mental health; and there was an abnormal incidence of fatigue, apathy and aggressive or destructive behaviour. Immigrant children were nearly always seen to have special problems, and were often seen to be a problem. But interestingly there was no relationship between the situations where immigrant children were thought to be a problem and the proportion of immigrant children in the school. Thirty-two of the heads specifically identified immigrant children as "a problem"; ten specifically said they were not. But the proportion of immigrant children in the "no problem" schools ranged from 4 per cent to 52 per cent, and the proportion in the "problem" schools ranged from 4 per cent to 56 per cent.

The difficulties faced by the children were all believed by the head teachers to result from social conditions outside the school, and poor housing was cited most frequently. Overcrowding, multi-occupation and shared amenities were thought to result in social tension and illness.[2] Nearly one-third of all the heads mentioned the effects of isolation and lack of playspace for children who lived in high rise dwellings. Apart from poor housing, various combinations of other social problems were seen by the head teachers to cause the "E.P.A. problem": economic insecurity, both parents working long hours, neglect (in some cases cruelty), criminality (of the parents and more generally of the area), lack of open space, lack of a middle-class "leaven" and the concentration of poor families together were all frequently mentioned. One head expressed a dominant view: "There's everything wrong with this place to bring up kids."

Although the head teachers perceived the cause of their problems to be "social", they all envisaged "educational" solutions to them. Further, the solutions they thought possible were all relatively unambitious. When asked if there was anything else the education authority might do to help them, nine of the forty-seven thought there was not. In spite of their list of formidable and acute problems, they thought that everything possible was being done. Those heads who made suggestions largely wanted "more of the same": minor building improvements (18 heads), more teachers (6 heads), more ancillary help (5 heads), etc. Only two respondents made original suggestions, and both were expressing concerns seen to be specific to their school. One wanted to stop the planned concentration of problem families on an estate

---

[1] Fifty-three primary schools from four contrasting divisions were selected at random from the I.L.E.A.'s ranked list of educational priority area schools. Forty-seven head teachers agreed to be interviewed. The interviews were conducted by experienced educational practitioners, who were on the London Institute of Education's course of training for educational administration. The returns were analysed by Pam Smith of the Research and Statistics Group of the I.L.E.A.

[2] In the E.P.A. Project area, all children who entered school during the 1970–71 school year were given an extended medical examination, and questions were asked about their home circumstances. It was found that 97 per cent of the children were living in overcrowded conditions according to the census definition. Equivalent proportions of overcrowding for households in the 1961, 1966 and 1971 censuses for the Metropolitan Borough were respectively 5·8, 6 and 4·3 per cent.

next to her school, and she wanted London Transport to divert a bus route nearer to the school. Another wanted to see television used to build up "informed" support among parents.

Most of the head teachers expressed concern about their teachers (only five did not). But the perceived problems seemed to vary widely. Ten heads found it difficult to obtain teachers; twenty-one experienced greater difficulty in retaining them. Twelve considered that several of their staff were not suited to work in E.P.A. schools. All were asked what attributes they considered most important for E.P.A. teachers. Significantly, more emphasis was placed on personality factors (like self-confidence and warmth) than on training or intellect; and a majority preferred older teachers for this reason. Fifteen of the forty-seven pointed out specifically that teachers in their first post ought not to work in E.P.A. schools—largely because they were thought to have difficulties over discipline and classroom organisation One observation was common to all the head teachers interviewed: no matter how difficult they saw their staffing position to be, it was always a consequence, and not a cause, of their educational and social situation.

Towards the end of the interview all the head teachers were shown a list of the Plowden Council's recommendations for help to E.P.A. schools, and were asked to rank them in terms of their helpfulness in the situations they perceived in their school. Table 3 shows the ranked priorities of the head teachers.

It is clear that the Plowden Council envisaged "educational" solutions to the "E.P.A. problem", and in this respect the head teachers were in sympathy with the Council. For instance, the least strictly educational recommendation —number 13—was generally held by the head teachers to be the least helpful, and in any case impracticable, and was ranked accordingly.

The heavy emphasis given by the head teachers to more educational resources as solutions, or at least anodynes, to their problems, is also clear from Table 3. Smaller classes in schools, more schooling, more adults and more

Table 3

Head Teachers' Ranking of the Plowden Council's Recommendations in Terms of Their Helpfulness

Order	Mean rank
1. No class should have more than 30 children	1·9
2. Children in E.P.A.s should be given a nursery class experience	4·2
3. It should be easier for E.P.A.s to get teachers	5·7
4. There should be one teachers' aide for every two classes in E.P.A.s	5·8
5. There should be extra books and equipment allowances in E.P.A.s	6·0
6. Teachers in E.P.A. schools should have a £120 salary allowance	6·3
7. E.P.A. school buildings should be extensively modernised	6·3
8. There should be more money generally made available to E.P.A. schools	7·2
9. Educational Social Workers should work in E.P.A. schools	7·6
10. There should be more research into the needs of E.P.A.s	8·5
11. E.P.A. schools should have better links with the Colleges of Education	9·4
12. Teachers' centres should be provided in E.P.A.s	10·3
13. There should be changes in the social composition of the intake of E.P.A. schools	10·5

equipment in schools were all given the highest priority. At the same time, it is clear what was not wanted—teachers' centres and links with Colleges of Education. The heads unanimously thought that these would result in one way flows of information: that they would be told what they should be doing, and that relationships would not be reciprocal.

In summary then: what the head teachers of a sample of E.P.A. schools in London saw, in the period immediately after the publication of the Plowden Report, was an extremely difficult educational situation. The difficulties were caused by the "poor environment"[1] of the children; the head teachers were only moderately optimistic over what they could do about it; but they thought more educational resources might help. From their point of view more effective schooling was needed.

The Curriculum Innovations

All of the innovations described in this volume were designed, mostly with the intimate participation of the teachers concerned, to improve schooling. The dominant purpose was to use some of the time the children were in school to overcome particular disadvantages they were seen to have by their teachers. The schemes were all in this sense remedial. They were all designed to be operative in schools in educational priority areas; and all but one of them were short-term demonstration projects in preparation for the possible larger scale adoption of such schemes.[2]

An impressive feature is their diversity. One of the I.L.E.A. schemes (reported in Part 2) concentrated exclusively on reading. Two sequenced reading programmes—the Science Research Associates Reading Laboratory and Rank's Talking Page—were made available to a number of schools, to be used experimentally by as many children as possible. The other I.L.E.A. scheme (reported in Part 3) also concentrated on teaching reading skills, but both the methods employed and the range of work undertaken were more flexible than in the reading programme innovations. A half-day centre was set up for children with "social, cultural and linguistic deprivation" to attend. These children were seen to be a residual group which conformed to none of the conventional categories of subnormality, emotional disturbance or retarded development. Two teachers were employed to work at the centre. They were chosen because of their experience and skill; and were instructed to teach reading, but also to cover as wide a range of experiential areas as possible. The teaching methods to be employed were left open, but teacher-child contact was to be on as near an individual basis as possible. Two of the London E.P.A. Project's schemes of work concentrated on language development—that reported in Part 4 on pre-school work, and that in Part 5 on

---

[1] A "poor environment" was seen to be a mixture of poor physical conditions (like old, bad, overcrowded housing), of a corrupting social environment (like being surrounded by criminals and violence) and, for some, a pathological family environment. The mixture for any one individual might change. But one consequence was commonly perceived: an "E.P.A. child" could be expected to have difficulty at school.

[2] This was specifically the case with the innovations promoted by the E.P.A. Project (Parts 4, 5 and 6). Any assessment of the two schemes promoted by the I.L.E.A. was less closely tied to a decision as to their viability.

creating an "oral curriculum" for eight and nine year old children. The approach was similar in both cases. Regular meetings were held between employees of the E.P.A. Project and teachers from the local schools to discuss children's acquisition and use of language; these meetings generated teaching ideas which were subsequently formulated into small programmes of work. In the case of the pre-school scheme an attempt was made to classify classroom situations in terms of their usefulness for verbal interaction between teacher and child, and to monitor some of that interaction. The other innovation of the E.P.A. Project (described in Part 6) was designed to promote an environmental studies curriculum. Through having the regular and frequent opportunity to study a country environment, it was hoped that the subject children's perceptions of their own urban environment would be made more acute and their study habits, skills and attitudes to school improved.

In addition, all the schemes were unique—with the possible exception of the reading programmes. They were all idiosyncratic mixtures of circumstance, intention and personalities; and they were consciously so. There will never be an environmental studies scheme, a language programme or a half-day centre quite like those reported here.

But at the same time all the innovations had certain important and broadly common features. To begin with they were all manipulations of the existing curriculum. Three of them (the language work and the reading schemes) took place within the constraints imposed by normal classroom and school situations. The two schemes which challenged those constraints did so by removing children from their normal schools for a period of time. In one case —that of the environmental studies work—classes of children and their teacher were removed to spend one day each week in the country. In the other, particular children left their class teacher and school for remedial attention in the half-day centre. The point is that all the innovations added to the normal school curriculum. They were placed in competition with the extant curriculum for time and emphasis; and so, in effect, the curriculum needed revision to accommodate the innovations.[1]

In an obvious and traditional sense some of the schemes were very costly. The environmental studies project, for instance, cost eighty times more than could normally be spent by a school on outside visits.[2] The cost of some of the capital equipment necessary for the reading schemes was substantial, and the pupil–teacher ratios at the half-day centre were half those current in traditional E.P.A. primary schools.[3] Even where the traditional resource costs appeared minimal, there were significant investments of time in all the schemes. The language work, for instance, required the teachers taking part to attend discussion groups and to create their own work programmes. People's time

---

[1] Mario Fantini in "Alternatives for Urban School Reform", *Harvard Educational Review*, Volume 38(1), Winter 1968, makes a similar observation about compensatory education programmes in the United States. He argues, for instance, that "more trips, more remedial reading, etc." . . . are . . . "essentially an additive or 'band aid' approach that works by augmenting and strengthening existing programs. It builds layers onto the standard educational process in order to bring the strays into the fold . . . the assumption is that the schools need to do somewhat more for disadvantaged pupils . . ."

[2] See Appendix 2 of Part 6 for a breakdown of the costs.

[3] The ratio of pupils per teacher in primary schools nationally at the time was 27·7:1. In I.L.E.A. it was 26·5:1. In the London E.P.A. Project Schools it was 26:1. At the half-day centre it was 12·5:1.

was never costed; but it should not be discounted in an appraisal of what happened.

All the innovations made substantial demands on the E.P.A. classroom teachers who implemented them, and in all cases the nature of these demands was insufficiently foreseen. The two reading schemes were in a sense "teacher free": the idea being that they should release the teacher from certain routine chores so that she could give individual children specialised help. In principle, therefore, all the teacher need do was to ensure that they took place; inter-action with the programmes themselves would raise levels of reading skill. But in practice considerable planning was necessary to ensure that all children used the schemes at the required frequency, without disturbing the normal timetable. For the environmental studies scheme (Part 6), there were also ostensibly very few requirements of the teachers; they took their children to the country and were advised to adopt an environmental studies curriculum. But for the scheme to be implemented effectively, requirements were actually quite substantial. Contact with a new sort of educational provision—a country environment—was obligatory; and something had to be done at the country centre. To continue with work which had been appropriate for the London E.P.A. environment would have been impossible in the new situation. Advice and materials were offered but there were few practical demonstrations of how to implement these. The warden played a primarily service role, re-garding herself as an extra facility rather than as an on-the-spot demonstrator of environmental studies work. For the language work (in Parts 4 and 5) and for the half-day centre, the explicit demands on the teachers were high: indeed the teachers were the main vehicle for the work programmes. In practical terms, however, what an individual teacher did in his or her class-room was subject to no control and hardly any help. For the second year language work, for instance, intricate problems of implementing suggestions for language work in particular classroom contexts were infrequently dealt with, and the organising team hardly ever worked with an individual teacher to resolve a classroom problem.

There was one further set of common denominators to all of these schemes. Without exception they were seen to be successful by the teachers who im-plemented them. Almost without exception they were continued after the trial period, and in some cases were expanded. Also without exception, the measured effects on the school performance of the subject children were disappointing. Indeed, the more careful the evaluation of these the more dis-appointing were the results. But these issues are best discussed in the context of the role of research.

Action-Research

It seems that action and research are profoundly attracted to each other: with research "getting some of the action", and at least observing some of its propositions working out in practice; and with action in theory, again at least, gaining knowledge and discipline. And it seems that all kinds of activity which bring research workers into day-to-day contact with practitioners are liable to be called action-research. Currently it is difficult to be neutral towards the combination. On the one hand there are observers who argue that practitioners and research workers cannot sustain their relationship for any length of time.[1] But the experience of the E.P.A. Programme denies this on the whole; and, as Halsey observes, there is much to be gained from the attempt.[2] In this respect the counsel of David Donnison, admittedly over the benefits of collaboration between research workers and policy makers on a broader front than in particular action-research teams, would be echoed by action-researchers. "Each has different skills and experience to offer, and each can learn more than he teaches."[3]

In order to understand more clearly what happened, and what is at issue from the London experience of action-research in curriculum innovations, it is expedient to begin with a rather different but more mature, and more consciously developed, example of the action-research method: that of the Tavistock Institute.[4] Here, as with the E.P.A. Programme, both research workers and practitioners collaborate in creating situations of relatively small scale social change.

Rapoport, for instance, defines the Tavistock action-research aim as "to contribute to the practical concerns of people in an immediate problematic situation and to the goals of social science, by joint collaboration within a mutually agreeable ethical framework".[5] More particularly this method was developed when "psycho-analytic ideas and methods were transferred to the social context". The two principal groups involved are "the client system and the scientific community"; Rapoport calls these the two "taskmasters". The client has a problem and is prepared to pay for help in solving it. The scientific community are Tavistock personnel who undertake to provide that help. The client's problem is taken "as data, not as a mandate"; and the problem may change its character during the course of the action-research, as the client is helped to see his social situation with new insights. Ultimately the client is responsible for helping himself; he is responsible for "mutually agreed initiatives" (for the action). But the "contract with the client has always been based on an understanding that the effort would be a collaborative one to help work through a problematic situation". Rapoport identifies three "dilemmas"

---

[1] P. Marris and M. Rein in *Dilemmas of Social Reform*, Routledge and Kegan Paul, 1967, writing about the relationships between research and action in American Community Action Programmes, summarize this view. They write, for instance—"Research requires a clear and constant purpose, which both defines and precedes the choice of means. . . . Action is tentative, non-committal and adaptive. Each seeks to limit the ignorance of which it must take account, the one by shortening its time span, the other by arbitrarily excluding factors and purposes which may be irrelevant."

[2] *Educational Priority*, Chapter 13.

[3] David Donnison, "Research for Policy", *Minerva*, Volume X, Number 4, October 1972.

[4] Lippitt, Watson and Bendix, *The Dynamics of Planned Change*, Harcourt Brace and World Inc. And see A. B. Cherns, "Models for the Use of Research", *Human Relations*, Volume 25, Number 1; M. Foster, "An Introduction to the Theory and Practice of Action-Research in Work Organisations", *Human Relations*, Volume 25, Number 6; and R. N. Rapoport, "Three Dilemmas in Action-Research", *Human Relations*, Volume 23, Number 6.

[5] Rapoport's article is probably the most concise and directly relevant for our purposes; the quotations in the text above are all taken from this.

which result from the interaction of research and action in such contexts: those of *ethics*, of *goals* and of *initiatives*.[1] In each case, Rapoport argues, "the resolution in one direction leads away from science (i.e. towards the sort of action which is not theoretically informed and does not have a cumulative scientific character) while resolution in the other direction leads away from action (i.e. to the sort of research which is 'purist'/'ivory tower' in character and lacks relevance to the important current problems of mankind). In each case 'good' action-research selectively combines elements of both." And always the bias is expressed in terms of how far the researcher will involve himself: risking his detachment in order to gain involvement and, through that, a new kind of knowledge.

From this brief account there are four distinct differences between the Tavistock method and the London experience of action-research in educational priority areas: and each contributes to an understanding of the character of the London work. To begin with action-research is, for the Tavistock, a *method* engaged in by research workers when they help practitioners. In the London E.P.A. Project, on the other hand, there was an action-research *team* of people recruited from the fraternities of both research and educational practice. And so the tensions (or dilemmas) identified by Rapoport were acted out within the team, as well as between the action-researchers and those who were to implement any programme of activities. Secondly, and perhaps in consequence, the E.P.A. Project action-researchers were less detached from the situation being analysed than are Tavistock Institute personnel. The Director of the London Project, for instance, was an ex-headmaster: who shared the commitment, the pre-conceptions and the frame of reference of the local E.P.A. teachers.[2] Thirdly, in any analysis of the London Project, there are difficulties identifying a "client system" of the kind identified by Rapoport. In the Tavistock model approach, the client is the sponsor, and the "scientific community" (Tavistock personnel) work with him to clarify the nature of his problem and to find solutions to it. The action-researchers in London were paid by the sponsors to work with a different group (of clients). These might be seen variously as teachers, parents or children. But one characteristic was common to all of them: they would not have been prepared to pay for the action-research experience.[3] Lastly, there are striking differences between the Tavistock and London methods over how decisions were made. For the former of the two, the client's perceptions of his problems are "data"; interpretation of these remains the prerogative of the the researcher. For the

---

[1] The issues associated with the question of *ethics* are as follows: "Whether or not a client is acceptable to the researcher"; "confidentiality and protection of respondents" in an ongoing situation; "personal involvement in the client organisation's affairs". The issues associated with *goals* arise when "scientific goals" are pursued "in situations ordinarily funded by clients with practical goals", and concern whether the action is too "service oriented" or too "ivory tower". And *initiatives* concern questions of who wants the particular work to be done and who decides what happens during it.

[2] This was more or less true of all the Project Directors in the National Programme. A basic principle in the selection of personnel was that the Project Directors should be "experienced educationalists".

[3] And thus the action-research teams needed to be advocates of their method, and of their point of view. For instance, a diagnosis had to be "sold" to the local teachers. This involved a heavy retreat from the traditional research prototype of impartiality; and it is clearly difficult to advocate a proposition without cynicism, but at the same time retain the impartiality necessary to evaluate what is happening.

E.P.A. Project, the expressed opinions of certain groups were virtually mandatory.[1]

We might state these differences briefly as follows: one approach to action-research (that of the Tavistock Institute) is for relatively high status social scientists to be paid by an agency to diagnose the true nature of difficulties it is facing, to advise and to assist in accomplishing a solution. In the London method, the diagnosis was heavily weighted in favour of local teacher and practitioner perceptions. The work was pragmatic and eclectic rather than generated from any developing theory of managed social change. We might almost say it was parochial. Certainly a paramount concern was to get something done at a particular place and time, in particular circumstances, and the problems of generalising from this were only dealt with as a secondary issue.

The Contribution of Research

Why then was research necessary at all? Research is not considered an indispensable, not even a usual correlate of local teacher diagnosis and problem solving in education. It is indeed thought by some people to be unnecessary; and in these London field trials it was seen by some to be a positive hindrance. Perhaps, therefore, we should rephrase the question: what can research add to local practitioner diagnosis and solution through curriculum reform? In principle it can make the action more rational and the report of it more credible. And it can achieve this by successful performance of three tasks: first of all providing information internal to the programme, then an evaluation of it and lastly an overall estimation which is informed but is not committed to a proof of success.

The first research contribution is supplementary to the action, but adds to its rationality. The needs of external audiences are here subordinate to the internal development of the work programme. Obviously research knowledge contributes in an indirect way to this by helping to create a climate of opinion about current educational issues. For instance, all discussion of the London work took place before a backdrop provided by Bernstein's research on the relationship between socio-cultural patterns and different spoken language contexts,[2] of the Plowden research on the relative importance of school and home variables in accounting for educational attainment,[3] and of experience in the United States of educational programmes for "disadvantaged" children.[4] But the contribution can be more direct. It can be to "feed back"

---

[1] Clearly only those activities which were acceptable to the teaching force were remotely possible. And at a higher level the local Steering Committee had powers of sanction, and in this respect the local authority was important. It sponsored the London Project directly in two senses: it contributed resources, and it "placed" the Project in the local social system by giving it legitimate access to a number of its schools. But the sponsorship also established what activities it would be regarded as appropriate for the Project to undertake. And so the London Steering Committee of the Project, which was comprised substantially of officers of the local authority, scrutinised all proposals in the light of this and was certainly capable of proscribing them.

[2] See B. Bernstein, *Class Codes and Control*, Routledge and Kegan Paul.

[3] See The Plowden Report, *Children and their Primary Schools*, Volume 2, for analysis of data from the 1964 National Survey.

[4] See H. Passow, *Urban Education in the 1970's*, Teachers' College Press.

detailed intelligence on the implementation of a scheme to those organising and planning it. The assumptions behind such "feed-back" activity are that we need information to improve what is, in fact, already being tried out, rather than to decide or to select between a number of different schemes. And the questions asked tend to be of the type: what works, and how, and under what sort of conditions? At the least research "feed-back" can hope to delineate areas of possible activity and show those parts of a scheme which are patent failures. At best it may include participation in the formulation and reformulation of a scheme.[1]

Understandably, perhaps, teacher observations tend to cluster in this area; and in many respects teacher and researcher "feed-back" data are analogous. But there are differences of perspective; and the most useful research contribution is distinct. For teachers the question "how to improve" mostly means how to improve the implementation. The educational worth of a proposed innovation needs to be assessed by them *before* they can agree to try it out. If its educational credentials are not acceptable then it will be rejected.[2] These credentials are already available before any field trial: indeed the teacher decision to take part in a field trial gives *de facto* approval to them. Subsequent re-evaluations of those credentials by teachers, therefore, are evaluations of their professional judgement and of their teaching performance.[3] For the research contribution then, if it is to do more than confirm teacher opinion, the question "how to improve" must be more than an exploration of the process of implementation. At the very least, however well the programme appears to be going, the possibility of further improvement should be kept open; and output as well as input and process criteria should be brought to bear.[4]

A basic difficulty for research concerns how to achieve the balance between

---

[1] Examples of "feed-back" activity in the innovations reported in this volume are numerous. In a general sense, whenever children were tested, their teachers were told the scores achieved by individual children, their school scores and the aggregated area scores. But perhaps the best and most prolonged examples are in the pre-school work and the second year junior language work (Parts 4 and 5). These were both based on the principle of information "feed-back" to a constantly evolving work programme; in particular, the course of the second year junior programme was radically altered by "feed-back" evidence.

[2] For instance, the Peabody Language Development Kit (the P.L.D.K.)—the example of a structured learning kit used in the National Pre-School Experiment—was rejected *a priori* by the London nursery teachers; and the reasons for this were that it was seen to contravene their teaching principles of free play and child initiated activity. See Part 4 of this Volume and Volume II: *Statistics and Surveys.*

[3] The argument can be expressed in the form of a syllogism: Professionals make *a priori* decisions about an innovation: they can decide to reject it if it does not conform to their perception of an appropriate code of practice. Practitioners are sustained by myths: they need a code of practice which contains beliefs about the worthwhileness and efficacy of what they are doing, in order to continue doing it. And yet in their very nature many of these beliefs remain untested. Therefore, to test an *a priori* decision in favour of an innovation, necessarily puts professional myths to the test.

[4] See H. Freeman and C. Sherwood, *Social Research and Social Policy*, Prentice Hall, for a synoptic account of the various issues. The danger always exists that a view which accords relevance only to input criteria will prevail, without regard to other factors. As the I.L.E.A. put it. "The children are more cared for because there are more people caring for them." (See Part 6.) The distinctive research contribution is to stress the rationality of connecting inputs with outputs, ends with means.

effective performance of the "feed-back" role and roles which are geared more to the needs of sponsors and other groups that want to know about the field trial. Flexible "feed-back" provides quick on-the-spot information; and often complete reliability can be sacrificed for speed and immediate relevance. Research technology, which gives us reliable results and which in consequence is necessary for generating information for external assessment, is often too laborious to provide "feed-back" data. By the time the research worker has analysed his material to understand what is happening, the situation in question is a part of history. And so fully to understand the potential research contribution to locally diagnosed curriculum innovations, a distinction must be made between being a research worker in a development project and the research process that leads to a complete and comprehensive report. A great deal of research time in the London work was devoted to internal "feed-back", particularly in the schemes promoted by the E.P.A. Project (Parts 4, 5 and 6). The reports of this aspect of the work are perhaps (necessarily) sketchy and inconclusive; but we should be clear that the planning and intelligence for the schemes was richer than could normally be assumed for curriculum innovations involving a number of schools.

The second research contribution—attempting to meet the needs of audiences external to an innovation—cannot be supplementary to the action. It must be independent of it. Once the need for external audiences to have information with which to judge the viability of a scheme is admitted, then it necessarily follows that the effort to meet that need be given some autonomy. In some cases the issue of autonomy is not a crucial one. For instance, other teacher groups may need no more information than was available to the pilot teachers before they committed themselves to an activity. Further knowledge here can be an accumulation of experience on how to implement the work programme, and therefore a report relying substantially on "feed-back" evidence would be satisfactory—indeed most desirable; and research autonomy would be unnecessary. But suppose, even though the educational credentials and the character of the resource inputs are right, the ultimate viability of the particular innovation remains an open question: then qualitatively different sorts of knowledge are needed. And further, if the decision about what needs to be known is made by those (teachers and practitioners) who had already decided in favour of it, then the danger exists that data are generated to confirm previous commitments.

For its second contribution, therefore, the initiative lies with research. The assumption is that policy options are open and knowledge is needed with which to make rational choices: of whether to adopt or reject a particular innovation, taking account of improvements that have been possible over the trial period. The substance of much of the reports in this book relies on that sort of research contribution. Assuming the policy choices were still to be made, it was decided that some understanding of what happened to the children who were exposed to the various innovations would be most valuable. The question that was asked in all cases therefore, with more or less comprehensiveness and tenacity, was whether the children in question benefited from their experiences.

The notion of benefit was defined educationally. The method chosen to find an answer to the question was an approximation to controlled experimentation, using recognised and reliable tests of school skills, language development, attitudes and motivation to do well at school. The method can be criticised on a series of grounds by determined critics, who disagree with the findings. Results obtained from standarised tests are given priority over teacher observations.[1] This gave us precision, but necessarily meant that the spectrum of possible consequences had to be narrowed and isolated. The relevance of the areas of skill and attitude chosen, and the tests used, to the purposes of the innovations and to displacements of those purposes might be questioned. For instance, the tests tend to be specific while the objectives of the intervention programmes were often multiple and ambiguous, and they evolved and became re-emphasised over time. We attempted to accommodate this by "going behind" ostensible and stated purposes to broad background goals; and using broad based measuring instruments. It can be pointed out that the evaluation periods were short;[2] that the experimental methods were crudely applied;[3] and that not enough can be said about why such results were found.[4] All such criticisms have some validity, and should be used by the reader in weighing-up the evidence.

But the results are systematic and precise and relatively stable across all the evaluations. If the question "what happened to the children" as a consequence of these schemes is seen to be pertinent, then these answers are salutary. At best there were no consistent observable effects on the measured behaviour of the children. At worst there are some signs that manipulations of the E.P.A. school curriculum of the sort described here have harmful effects on children's school performance.

---

[1] Consider the complexity of the comparisons necessary to ascertain the effects of any intervention scheme (leaving aside the questions of impartiality, and whether the unit of observation is to be individual children, or groups or the whole class). Children can be expected to gain in school skills as they become older; therefore they will in any case improve in skills over a school year. (But some groups of E.P.A. children, in fact, did not—see Part 6). There is then the question of the "natural" rate of relative change. There was some evidence that E.P.A. groups lost ground relative to national norms over time: for instance, particularly in school attainment skills (see again Part 6). Therefore, although most groups will improve over a year, it will be by smaller amounts than their national counterparts. Real performance may improve, relative performance may deteriorate. From this the effect of the intervention must be isolated. For teachers, comparisons can be made with reference to their memory of what happened to past children, their beliefs about other children and their expectations of current children. We decided that an experimental method, measuring real and relative changes over time and comparing these to control (non-treatment) groups, would make these comparisons more rigorous and reliable.

[2] They were usually one school year; but remember that a year is still a substantial proportion of the school experience of a child in an educational priority area. The brevity of the evaluation period limits what can be said in another sense. Most of the work was in a relatively early stage of its development. But remember again that, if we accept a high turnover of teachers in inner city schools, a two or three year development period for teacher innovations is all that can realistically be expected before teachers move from the programme to new schools. Clearly then retraining and development programmes might, hopefully, have a long term cumulative effect as they are disseminated. But the evaluations reported here would be realistic accounts of the likely short term effects in the schools where they are taking place.

[3] Both the experimental and control groups were either self or more or less arbitrarily selected. The evaluations were substantially "tagged on" to an extant scheme.

[4] For instance, in most cases there were variations in the rate of measured change between different experimental schools or classes; variations which, on the whole, cannot be explained with the research data available. But the significant point is that, while the research could not find or explain reasons for differential change, the intervention could not generalise any significant overall level of reform.

The Nature of the Problem

The third research contribution is to map out what follows, and perhaps to establish more fruitful or more realistic ways of seeing some of the issues which have been uncovered by the experience.

We should begin with the labyrinth of problems: with the needs of the people. In these reports, indeed in the whole E.P.A. series, they are shown to be both serious and profound. But our work also shows them to have been crudely and misleadingly classified. And as a matter of urgency we must now begin to refine the ways in which we think about them.

In as far as the concern is for children in need: then the great heterogeneity of needs should be recognised. We should no longer be talking in general terms of concepts like disadvantage. We should be explicit about which problems we wish to tackle. In as far as the concern is for needs as such, we should look to causes and not to consequences. For instance, poor housing and low income are evils that should be tackled in their own right—by tackling poor housing and low income: unless we require an educational excuse for it. Even if we do, then it is a nonsense to expect very much from a policy which identifies a problem in terms of poor housing and low income, and then offers better schools: unless we assume that social insecurity and economic underprivilege will continue, while we attempt to refract some of their consequences by improving education. If this is what we want, then our expectations of such policies must be very moderate indeed.

But suppose for the moment we ignore the issue of social and educational outcomes, and continue to speculate on the possibility of bringing some relief, or simply more enjoyment, to poor children through a discriminatory schools policy. Even then we must recognise the severe limitations to what we can expect. For instance, unless we discriminate in favour of all schools (a logical impossibility) then some poor children will be left out. And so, even at the level of its ability to reach the groups who are thought to need its ministrations, positive discrimination in favour of schools, or groups of schools in specific areas, is a policy which can only be viable as a supplement to (some) other means of reaching the population at risk.

In as far as the concern is for poor school performance, and poor performance which appears to be caused by social situations (and this was the concern of the teachers we interviewed): then again our work advances the analysis, but again in ways that create disconcerting problems. We would perhaps now all recognise that social situations explain more of the variation in educational performance than do school situations. (Although it can certainly be argued from the evidence in these reports that we have not yet explored the full implication of such a recognition. At least, for instance, we should improve social situations rather than school situations if we wish to act on school performance; yet the teacher-initiated activities reported here were attempts to improve schools.) Nevertheless, after a decade of speculation about the best proxy measures for the non-school factors which most affect performance (during which disadvantage, deprivation and underprivilege were the most favoured candidates), we are driven back to the measure which was available before. The social class of a child's home, as measured by the occupation of its father, still has the most powerful explanatory importance. With one exception it overwhelms the other factors which were thought to contribute to some condition of social disadvantage as an explanation of poor school performance.

The consequences of this for policies directed at poor performance are profound. We are not talking about a phenomenon (disadvantage) which marks off a small section of the population. We are, once again, talking about something in which the whole population is involved: the system of socio-economic stratification. If they have any meaning, then the terms social and educational disadvantage—as they are used in the debate about educational priority areas—refer to a situation to which we all contribute rather than to a condition to which a minority are subject. And the numbers of children being helped by a policy of positive discrimination therefore tells us more about the political will, and the amount of money thought to be available, than it does about the children and families in need.

At the same time, the exception should also be recognised: the immigrant status of groups of children appears to operate in a way which is at least partially independent of other factors, including social class. Immigrant children are seen to cause school-level problems (although we had difficulty finding more than circumstantial evidence for this). In any case, from our research the problems they cause are outweighed by the different and distinct difficulties these children face. To recognise this may confront many groups with some awkward dilemmas, but it certainly increases the prospect of schooling becoming more relevant for these children.

Lastly, in listing the major ingredients to the problem, we must recognise its time dimension. It was probably easier in the 1950s than it is in the 1970s to identify particular inner city "problem" primary schools and areas as targets for discriminatory policies. Our evidence on this is admittedly inadequate and was acquired as a by-product of the main work programme. But it points to a pattern of changing social and educational geography in Inner London at least. Looking at poor reading performance, we found a greater concentration in the city with a greater dispersion across it.

When we move on to consider what educational policies can and should be doing about these problems, we should perhaps begin by confessing our sense of ignorance and of impotence. And the work reported in this volume has expanded the area of uncertainty rather than provided us with firm prescriptions. The paramount need now is for a realistic clarification of what to expect from our schools: and for this to happen at the level both of policy and of educational practice. At the policy level we have been working through a period of over-expectation in what to expect. Perhaps we should recognise that schools currently are marginal institutions in the lives of a majority of our population; and be very moderate in what to expect from attempts to improve them in the face of a mass of problems faced by poor families. If we want to help poor families, then improving the schools their children attend should be a long way down the shopping list of policy options. At this level our expectations of education ought probably to be more temperate.

At the level of educational practice, on the other hand, a more ambitious programme might be considered. Our London experiences in this respect were frustrated. Across the whole range of Inner London schools, as they were operating at the end of the 1960s, we found that it made a significant difference to children's performance whether they were attending one school rather than another. But attempts to change that pattern in the pilot innovations were singularly unsuccessful. Our case here rests almost entirely on a fairly narrow band of school performance tests: we considered these to be the core cognitive skills that children must learn and we tested for them in fairly conventional ways. Clearly these skills are by no means all that must be considered, and the expectations of the different groups potentially involved with education may be quite diverse. If this is so, then there should be open discussion of it. But in the meantime we can say something about what follows from our failure to find ways of changing the effect of educational priority areas and schools on the skills of the children in them.

One response, a leit motif which runs through most of the reports, is to assert that innovations in priority area schools are not and should not be designed to improve the school performance of the children. Positive discrimination is about compensating the teachers for working in difficult schools, and compensating the children for experiences they are missing in their non-school life. Thus successful innovations result in happier, more harmonious schools. Undoubtedly this belief influenced the development of London's educational innovations. We doubt whether this is a sufficient rationale for schooling or for attempts to improve schools; but it is one that should be considered.

Another response, while admitting that schools should attempt to improve the cognitive skills of children, is to argue that the endeavour must fail. It must fail because the educability of children is a finite quantity. Children's educational performance is like their weight; we might affect it marginally up or down in the short term, but the effort needed will always be large and the returns disappointingly small. A more specific expression of this belief also affected the results obtained from the London work: and it amounted also to a conclusion in terms of social determinism. Many people believed that children in educational priority area schools performed badly *because* of the social and intellectual environment of their homes. Thus the children's problems were too profound to be affected by manipulations of their school experience, and therefore were intrinsically insoluble by anything that schools could do. Now we have argued that schools serving children who come from poor homes can achieve little on their own; and therefore the expectation of educational policy must be moderate in this respect. But how much schools can do for children is unknown, because it has not effectively been put to the test. Whatever truth there is in the intrinsic insolubility of the children's educational problems, these certainly interact with other blocks to change coming from the beliefs of their teachers and the organisation of their schools. And so, while recognising the children's difficulties, we should be considering these other factors: ones which, at the level of educational practice, we might hope to operate on in the short term.

The E.P.A. teachers were concerned at the children's low performance; but were not optimistic over what they could do about it in their working day. Considering only teacher expectations, it seems to us that our finding of almost as much variation within schools as there is within the London population is profoundly important. Even in the most severely under-privileged educational priority area school there is heterogeneity of both performance and social circumstance. Might not teacher perceptions which focus on this, rather than on a depressed average, result in some more optimistic appraisals of the children's potential?

In some of our work teacher expectations of the children they taught were in fact raised; but even then we could not overcome a series of organisational difficulties within the pilot schools. At first sight it looked as if primary schools were inefficient. For instance, if teaching can be defined in terms of interaction in some purposive way with children, then our initial, casual observation was that for a considerable proportion of their time teachers were not teaching! The National Foundation for Educational Research's study of the "Teacher's Day" has examined this more systematically, and their findings confirm our first impressions. They found, for instance, that two-thirds of a teacher's day was devoted to "teaching sessions" and, of this, slightly less than half was actually spent teaching.[1] But subsequently the picture in the E.P.A. Project schools appeared to us more complex: one teacher was responsible, full-time, for each class and she was, therefore, totally engaged with her class. The class regime was thus highly integrated, and it was extremely difficult to change it without affecting everything else that had already been established. And so, while the regime of one class might differ from another, within any particular class there was considerable uniformity. The E.P.A. Project's innovations failed to recognise the interlocked nature of activities in the pilot classrooms, and for this reason were rarely integrated into the normal classroom routines. But the problem cannot be seen simply as a question of inadequately conceived innovation. It is intrinsic to the way the schools are organised. At the very least then, if we can establish more realistic expectations of schools, we must ask school teachers themselves to appraise more openly the extent to which their own practices preclude educational change.

---

[1] J. Hilsum and B. Cane, *The Teacher's Day*, National Foundation for Educational Research, 1971.

Part Two

The Study of Reading Aids
Janet Woods

The Study of Reading Aids

The intrinsic importance of reading and its basic function in developing other skills means that the level of literacy in schools is a cause of much concern. Suggestions for raising the standard of literacy abound, ranging from schemes to improve a child's environment (home and school) and thereby improve his linguistic ability and his level of literacy to the introduction into the school of programmed aids to the teaching of reading.

The S.R.A. Reading Laboratory and Rank's Talking Page are two such aids to the teaching of reading. Two independent projects were carried out between September 1969 and June 1971 to assess the effects of these instruments on the reading standards in the schools in which they were introduced. The projects were carried out in a similar manner and therefore this report presents both sets of results but it should be emphasised that they were not designed specifically to draw comparisons between the two teaching aids.

I   A Description of the Teaching Aids

The S.R.A. Reading Laboratory Series

The Reading Laboratory Series is designed to develop a child's reading ability once the child has mastered the preliminary skill of reading. Each kit consists of reading material which is graded to allow each pupil to work at his own level. It is made up of units, each of which is contained in a box and each of which is termed a Reading Laboratory. Each box is designed to take into account both the reading age and interest age of the children. The boxes contain three main types of material: Power Builders, Listening Skill Builders and Rate Builders. The Power Builders are short stories or articles followed by exercises on comprehension and vocabulary; the Listening Skill Builders are stories read to the class and on which the children then have to answer questions from memory; the Rate Builders are short stories on which questions have to be answered within a given time limit. The Power Builders and Rate Builders are graded by colours so that a child is placed at a certain colour level by a preliminary exercise. He then works through cards at that colour level until he has successfully completed a certain number of cards at each level—at which stage he moves on to the next colour level. The Reading Laboratory Series is supplemented by a Word Games Laboratory containing phonic games and longer stories in the Pilot Libraries.

The aim of the Series is that each child should develop his comprehension, vocabulary, listening ability and ability to work accurately and at speed and that his development should take place at his own rate. As the children work

27

through the material on their own, the teacher is left free to assist individual children with their particular problems.

The Talking Page

The Talking Page[1] is a system which aims to teach the child to read. It consists of a machine and software in the form of books and records. The machine synchronises visual material (the book) with audio instructions (the record). It is of a size which fits on to a child's desk. The child operates the machine by notching a lever at the side into position in line with a mark on the side of the book. The record is then picked up at the point which corresponds to that page and the child receives his instructions. The child then works through the books on his own. The reading programme is divided into two stages (first and second stage reading programme). The first is designed to teach nonreaders the basic skills of reading, the second to develop those skills once learnt.

The Talking Page is designed so that the child operates the machine himself and works at his own pace so that the teacher is free to attend to the rest of the class and the children's individual needs.

II The Research Project

Aims

The aims of both projects were:

   (i) To assess the effects on the children's reading level of introducing the aids to the classroom.

  (ii) To assess the effect of the introduction of the aids on the children's other skills.

 (iii) To assess the ease with which the aids could be incorporated into the ordinary school and classroom situation.

 (iv) To obtain the teachers' and head teachers' reactions to the aids.

The Selection of Schools to Take Part in the Project and the Establishment of Control and Experimental Classes

(i) The S.R.A. study

Schools were selected so that the project would include children of as wide a range of age, ability and home background as possible. Selection was based

---

[1] Since this project was carried out Rank have withdrawn the Talking Page from the British market.

on information on the reading level and socio-economic composition of the schools and on recommendations from the inspectorate of schools which of them would be willing to co-operate for at least a year. The final experimental sample consisted of four infants' schools, fifteen junior schools, four secondary schools and one College of Further Education; in addition five junior schools agreed to administer the required tests to their children as a control group.

A major problem in this study was the establishment of control and experimental groups. It was decided that it would be desirable to have a sample of schools in which there was a control class in each year in the school which used the S.R.A. materials and that there should also be a sample of schools which did not have the S.R.A. materials in the school at all. In this way it was hoped that some estimate of the effect of the presence of the materials in the school could be obtained.

The majority of head teachers did not wish to have one class in each year not using the materials and only five schools were found which were willing to have such control classes. A further five schools were added in as control schools not using S.R.A. materials. A total of 57 experimental classes and 32 control classes were set up in the junior schools. No control classes were set up in the infant or secondary schools.

(ii) The Talking Page study

In the first year the project was confined to first year junior children; however, in the second year the age range was extended to include infants, all junior children and those secondary children in need of remedial help. Selection of the schools was similar to that for the S.R.A. study, in that schools were selected to include children with as wide a range of ability and home background as possible and the inspectors recommended schools which would be willing to co-operate in the study.

Control classes were established in the first year classes, parallel to those using the machines. No control classes were established for the other age groups, as older children using the machines were in remedial groups and no parallel classes were available.

For both the S.R.A. and Talking Page projects a study of the socio-economic factors of each group and their initial reading level showed that the control and experimental groups were similar in composition. Any differences which did occur did not operate uniformly to the advantage of either the experimental or control group.

Equipping the Schools

(i) The S.R.A. study

Each school was given assistance in deciding which kits would be most suitable for it A total of 73 Reading Laboratory Kits, 21 Word Games Kits and 28 Pilot Libraries were placed in the schools in addition to 11 kits of other kinds.

(ii) The Talking Page study

Five machines were allocated to each class of approximately 35 children and enough books and records were supplied to ensure that no group of children selected to participate in the experiment would be unable to do so owing to a shortage of equipment.

Training the Teachers

A preliminary training course and a follow-up seminar were arranged for each project. The publishers also arranged to visit any school which requested any further assistance and visits were made to the schools to ensure that the materials were being used correctly. The amount of training each teacher received was greater than if the schools had purchased the aids for themselves and not as part of a project.

III   The Evaluation of the Teaching Aids

The evaluation of the teaching aids took two forms. The first was by the administration of tests to the experimental and control groups, the second was the assessment of teachers' and head teachers' attitudes and opinions about the equipment through questionnaires and interviews. The scale of the project necessitated that the tests selected were tests which could be administered by the teachers and also that the test battery should not be too large. Each child in the experimental and control groups was therefore given a reading test, a vocabulary test and a non-verbal test. It was decided that the effect of the use of the aids on other subjects should be assessed by the teachers.

The Tests Used

The reading test

The Southgate reading test was given by the class teachers to the first year junior children in both studies in the first year of the project. This test has two versions, the first of which is a word recognition test and is designed for children with a reading age of 5 years 9 months to 7 years 9 months, the second is a sentence completion test for children with a reading age of between 7 years and 9 years 7 months.[1] It was not possible to find a single up-to-date group test to cover the entire reading age range of the first year children. When the children were tested at the beginning of the project (October) the teachers were asked to give each child the test they thought appropriate and if in doubt they were asked to give a child both versions of the test. On the basis of the results obtained in October the teachers were sent instructions as to which children should be given each version of the test in June. Children who had

---

[1] The reliability coefficient of the Southgate test is 0.9545 ± 0.009; that of the Southgate 2 is 0.965.

obtained a reading age of below 7 years on the Southgate 1 version of the test were given the same version again. If they had scored over that level the teachers were asked to give them both versions of the test. All children who had been given the Southgate 2 test in October were given the same version again. In addition teachers were asked to retest on Southgate 2 all children who obtained the maximum score on the first test. However, this second testing was not carried out in all cases.

In the second year, the Neale Analysis of Reading Ability[1] was given by trained testers to the first year children. This test gives the child an accuracy reading age and a comprehension reading age. It is an individually administered test.

The second, third and fourth year children using the S.R.A. kits were given the two versions of the sentence reading test devised by the National Foundation for Educational Research for their streaming project; test S.R.B. in October and S.R.A. in June. This test gives the child a standardised score with a mean of 100 and a standard deviation of 15.

The vocabulary test

The vocabulary test was only used in the first year of the study as at the end of this time the value of the results obtained was considered insufficient to justify its administration in the second year. The test used was the English Picture Vocabulary Test—version 1 was given to the infant children and version 2 to the older children. This test provides a measure of the child's listening vocabulary. The tester gives a stimulus word and the child has to decide which of four pictures best fits that word.

The non-verbal test

The non-verbal test used was the Raven's Progressive Matrices. This is a group test consisting of patterns with a piece missing. Each pattern is completed by choosing one piece from a selection of six. The manual for the test describes it as a test of "observation and clear thinking" and as providing "an index of (the child's) intellectual capacity whatever his nationality or education". The coloured version of the test was used for the infants and first and second year junior children, the standard version for the older junior and secondary children.

IV   Results from the S.R.A. Study

Test Results

Comments on the Southgate reading test

As stated above, the reading test used for the first year children was the Southgate reading test. The use of a test with a limited range of reading ages

---

[1] The reliability of the Neale test is 0·99 for accuracy and 0·96 for comprehension.

led to a problem in the analysis of the results. Several children obtained a score which placed them at the upper or lower limit of the test at one of the testing times. A true reading score was therefore not obtained for these children. It could only be said of them that their score was, e.g., less than 5 years 9 months or more than 7 years 9 months. It was therefore decided that two means should be calculated for each group of children. The first mean included the scores of only those children who did not obtain a ceiling score at either testing session. The second mean included those children whose scores were at the ceiling level at either one or both testing sessions.

The main aim of this project was to assess the change in reading ages over the period of the project. The effect of the inclusion of the ceiling score on this change in reading age is not the same for each type of score. If a child obtained a ceiling score on the first test which was at the upper limit of the test then the inclusion of this ceiling score in the mean artificially increases the mean change in reading age, i.e., if a child's reading age is only known to be more than 7 years 9 months on the first test but is known to be a definite age, e.g., 8 years 6 months on the second test then the inclusion of ceiling scores will mean that a change in reading age of 9 months will be recorded for that child. This will in fact be more than the actual change in reading age. Conversely, if a child obtained a reading age at the lower end of the test in the first testing or at the upper end in the second testing, then the change in reading age will be underestimated. (It should, however, be noted that the teachers were asked to use their judgement to decide which test should be given to each child. It is therefore unlikely that a child's reading age is either considerably above or below the ceiling level of the test.)

The sentence reading test (S.R.A. and S.R.B.) given to the second, third and fourth year children provided no such problem of analysis. As the raw score achieved by the child on the test is then related to the child's age to calculate the standardised score, any increase in the standardised score shows an improvement in the child's reading level as compared to his previous level, both being related to his age.

A comparison of reading results for all experimental and control children

In the following results statistical tests of significance have only been carried out on the reading results which are expressed in terms of standardised scores. The educational significance of the reading results which are given in terms of reading age can more readily be assessed in relation to the increase in chronological age of the children.

(i) Infants

Table 1 shows the reading scores obtained by children in the four infants' schools taking part in the study. As stated above, no controls were provided in the infants' schools because of the difficulties of matching groups of children at this age.

The increase in reading age of the infant children was 6·9 months when the ceiling scores were excluded and 6·6 months when they were included.

Eight months elapsed between the two testing sessions.

(ii) First year junior school children

Table 2 shows mean reading scores for two groups of control children. The first were only the children in schools where the S.R.A. Reading Laboratories

Table 1

Change in Reading Age of Infant Children Using the S.R.A. Laboratories

Mean reading age Ceiling score children excluded (mean October chronological age: 6·6)				Mean reading age All children (mean October chronological age: 6·6)			
October	June	No.	Change in R.A. (months)	October	June	No.	Change in R.A. (months)
6 y 9·3 m	7 y 4·2 m	158	+6·9 m	6 y 7·4 m	7 y 2·0 m	89	+6·6 m

Table 2

Change in Mean Reading Age: First Year Junior Children

	Ceiling score children excluded Mean chronological age: 7·6			All children Mean chronological age: 7·6			
	Oct. Mean R.A.	June mean R.A.	No.	Change in R.A. (months)	Oct. mean R.A.	June mean R.A.	No.	Change in R.A. (months)
Experimental group	7 y 2·6 m	7 y 9·3 m	445	+6·7 m	7 y 3·4 m	7 y 10·0 m	625	+6·6 m
S.R.A. controls only	7 y 2·3 m	7 y 9·0 m	168	+6·7 m	7 y 3·2 m	7 y 10·2 m	212	+7·0 m
All control children	7 y 1·9 m	7 y 8·2 m	311	+6·3 m	7 y 3·1 m	7 y 10·9 m	437	+7·8 m

were being used, the second were all control children whether or not they were in schools where the S.R.A. materials were being used.

It can be seen from the table that there was little difference in the amount of progress made by the experimental and the control children. The group for which the inclusion of the ceiling scores had the most effect was the total control group. Of the 126 control children in this group who obtained ceiling scores, 58 obtained scores which artificially increased the mean change, 48 obtained scores which decreased it and for 20 the effect could not be calculated. Therefore, when the ceiling scores for this group are included, the mean change in reading age is higher than the actual change in reading age.

(iii) Second, third and fourth year junior children

Table 3 shows that the group of control children in the schools where the S.R.A. materials were being used made a greater gain in reading score than the children using the S.R.A. materials or those in schools where the materials were not being used. When all the control children were combined into one group their progress was equal to 2·52 points: slightly less than that made by the experimental group. However, a test on the significance of difference between means showed that the increase in score for both the experimental group and the total control group was significant at the 1% level.

Table 3

Mean Change in Reading Score—Second, Third and Fourth Year Children

Experimental group				Control group S.R.A. in school			
Oct mean reading score	June mean reading score	No.	Change in reading score	Oct mean reading score	June mean reading score	No.	Change in reading score
95·42	98·24	1134	+2·82	96·77	100·22	316	+3·45

Control Group No S.R.A. in school

Oct mean reading score	June mean reading score	No.	Change in mean reading score
93·22	95·16	508	+1·94

(iv) Secondary school children

The mean reading age of the secondary school children was calculated from the raw scores obtained on a reading test standardised for a younger group of children. The standardised reading test for their age level was found to be too difficult so that it did not discriminate at the lower level and therefore the same test as that used for the junior children was given. Table 4 shows

Table 4

Change in Mean Reading Scores, Secondary Children

Mean raw score, October	Reading age equivalent	Mean raw score, June	Reading age equivalent	No.	Mean chrono-logical age, October	Change in R.A. (months)
22·6	9·0	26·7	9·10	246	12·3	+10

the mean raw score at each testing period and the mean reading age equivalent at that time. It can be seen from this table that the reading age of the secondary schools increased by an equivalent of 10 months in the 8 months of the study. No control group was available for the secondary children.

A comparison of reading results by class and school

An analysis was made of the change in reading age in each class of the experimental and control schools. Within each school neither the experimental nor the control group made a consistently better gain in reading age, i.e., in some schools the control classes made greater progress than the experimental classes, in others the reverse was the case. In addition, in schools where there were a large number of experimental and control classes, there was no indication that consistently better progress was made by either category of class.

The most noticeable feature of the results for the junior schools was that an increase in score was shown in all but six of the classes. It should be remembered that on a test with standardised scores an increase in score shows an improvement in the level of reading in relation to the age of the children. Therefore, in all but six of the junior classes (i.e., 51 classes) the reading standard at the end of the project was higher than that at the start.

As considerable class differences in changes in reading level were shown—both within schools and between schools—an analysis was made of the features of the classes which had made progress of over four standardised points. No common features were found in these classes. High class progress was not related to whether the class was an experimental or control class, nor was it related to the intelligence level of the class, the class reading score at the start of the project, or the teaching experience of the teachers or their attitude to the S.R.A. materials.

A comparison of the mean increase in reading level of the children by their sex, non-verbal intelligence level and socio-economic background

The increase in reading level of the above groups was compared to see if children of a particular category benefited more or less when using the S.R.A. materials. Analysis of reading progress by the non-verbal intelligence level of the children showed that the brighter control and experimental first year children made more progress; for the older children, although more progress was made by the brighter experimental children than the other experimental children, the control group made more progress the lower its score on the non-verbal test. The patterns of progress, however, were such that there was no indication that the S.R.A. materials consistently stimulated either the more or less bright children to greater progress. Similarly the analysis by sex, ethnic group, parental occupation and school experience showed that there was no indication that either boys or girls, children of any particular ethnic origin, from manual or non-manual homes or with any particular school experience (reading series used, remedial help or not) benefited to a greater or lesser extent from the use of the S.R.A. materials.

Although there was very little difference in the progress made by children in E.P.A.[1] schools whether they used the S.R.A. materials or not, there was a slight tendency for children in non-E.P.A. schools to make greater progress when using them. In addition, in London some schools were designated as being in "special need", on the basis of the high proportion of immigrants in the school. Two schools taking part in the study were placed in this category. One of these schools had no control classes, all had parallel experimental and control classes in each year. It was found that the children in the special needs schools using the S.R.A. materials made better progress than the children in the same schools not using the materials. But it should be noted that the number of schools and children involved was small (231 experimental and 86 control children).

---

[1] The criteria used to designate a school as E.P.A. when the London E.P.A. index was compiled were the social class composition of the catchment area of the school, the number of large families, amount of overcrowding and housing stress in this area (using census data): and within each school, the proposition of children receiving free meals, the amount of absenteeism, the proportion of immigrants in the school, the proportion of pupils of low ability, the amount of teacher turnover and the amount of pupil turnover.

Reading results from the College of Further Education

Only 59 students were tested both in October and in June, which makes interpretation of their change in mean reading score very difficult. A sentence completion test similar to that given to the older junior children and the secondary children was given to the Further Education students (the N.F.E.R. test N.S.6). Test results were given in terms of raw scores which were then converted to reading age equivalents. Using this method the mean increase of the students was 7 months, in the 8 months between testing periods.

Vocabulary test results

The results given below are those from the English Picture Vocabulary Test given to the infants and junior school children.

Table 5

Vocabulary Results

(a) *First year children*

S.R.A. Group			Control Group		
Mean score, October	Mean score, June	No.	Mean score, October	Mean score, June	No.
97·51	97·27	396	97·67	96·00	362

(b) *Second, Third and Fourth year children*

95·06	95·57	1150	95·35	98·66	798

Table 5 shows that the first year children showed no improvement over the year of the study. The older children improved by 2·51 points for the experimental group and 3·31 points for the control group. The 144 infant children were given the individual form of the test and showed an improvement of 2·23 points from 98·49 to 100·72.

Analysis of the Questionnaire Data

Questionnaires were sent to all teachers and head teachers who had taken part in the study in order to assess their attitudes to the S.R.A. materials, the ease with which they had been able to use them and the effect they considered it had had on the children in their school. The comments given here are only a brief summary of the responses received to the questionnaire.[1]

A total of 53 questionnaires was received from 12 of the 15 Junior schools which took part in the study, 10 questionnaires were received from all 5 of the

---

[1] A full analysis of the questionnaire response is available in the main report obtainable from the I.L.E.A. Research and Statistics Group.

infants' schools and 4 questionnaires from 2 of the 4 secondary schools—this information was supplemented either by completed questionnaires or general comments from 6 head teachers.

The use of the S.R.A. materials and teaching experience of the teachers taking part

Nearly half the teachers taking part in the study (41·8 per cent) had had over 11 years teaching experience and more than half the teachers had spent over 3 years at their present school. The high proportion of experienced teachers in the sample, therefore, means that the comments made on the S.R.A. kits are probably made in the light of considerable experience of other items of equipment.

Although the teachers' manual recommended that the kits be used for a concentrated period of approximately 12 weeks, the schools were allowed to make their own decisions on the frequency and length of use of the materials. The majority of the schools used the kits all year. The schools varied considerably in the amount of time each week they used the kits. Most of the schools used the Power Builders for three sessions or more a week (the sessions being on average 30 to 40 minutes in length); the Rate Builders and Listening Skill Builders were generally used for only one session a week.

Comments on the content of the laboratories

Of the 45 junior school teachers who commented on the Power Builders in the kits, 24 said that they were good or excellent and 15 that they were enjoyable or popular. Criticisms made were that they were "too American" (18 teachers), too factual (3 teachers) and that they were dull or that the interest was slanted too much towards boys (4 teachers). The Listening Skill Builders were received least favourably of the three types of content but these were still received favourably by the majority of teachers. However, the phonic games in the Word Games Laboratory were not received well by the junior school teachers, although less criticism of them was received from the infants' schools.

General comments on the S.R.A. materials

The use of the S.R.A. materials had had little effect on the content of the curriculum, although in several schools work covered by the kits had been excluded from the timetable. The children's work in other subjects was seen to be influenced by their Reading Laboratory work in terms, e.g., of greater enjoyment in reading and use in other subjects of facts learnt from the laboratories.

All the junior and secondary teachers were unanimous in the view that the S.R.A. principle of individualisation of the reading programme is useful, and thirty-seven thought that the principle was effective through the S.R.A. techniques. The majority of teachers said that the children enjoyed the S.R.A. work and had worked with interest. Nineteen of the junior teachers and one secondary teacher stated that the materials had given them more time to work with individual children; eight said that they had had more time to work with less able children, although fifteen said that they had had no effect on the amount of time available to help individual children.

Although the reading test was administered to all the children it was considered that it would be worthwhile asking the teachers for their opinions on the children's progress in particular aspects of reading. Approximately half the teachers thought that the materials were very effective in increasing the children's phonic knowledge and half that they were moderately effective. Only half saw them as having even a moderate effect on the children's ability to read aloud, although slightly more than half thought that they were very effective in increasing the children's rate of reading with comprehension and their listening ability; the remainder found them moderately effective in teaching these skills.

In the Spring term, following the end of the supervised period of the project, the schools were asked which kits they were now using and with which classes; and whether they had purchased any additional student record books and kits from their own school allowances. Although several schools had been supplied with sufficient materials for all the classes it was thought that the purchase of additional materials would provide some indication of the schools' enthusiasm for the materials.

It was found that all but five schools had purchased additional student record books and that eight schools had purchased additional kits.

Only one school (an infants' school) was no longer using the material that had been supplied to it by the Authority. In four schools one less class was using the materials in the second year than in the first year, although in nine schools additional classes had been introduced to the material, so that twenty-three additional classes were using the materials in the second year. It was also found that for the small group of children (495) who had been tested again, as part of the literacy survey at the end of 1971, while part of the gain in reading score achieved by these children had been lost, it had not dropped by the same amount as that of the control classes, although the few control children in this group had not originally made the same progress as the overall control group. This is shown in Table 6.

Table 6

Change in Reading Score over Two Years

	Mean reading score, October 1969	Mean reading score, June 1970	Mean reading score, June 1971	No.
Experimental Group	95·66	99·68	97·48	346
Control Group	95·99	97·62	96·03	149

It was apparent from the replies to the questionnaires and the comments made by the teachers at meetings that where the teachers had learned to use the materials they found them useful aids in the classroom. This was reinforced by the number of schools which not only continued to use the materials bought for them for use in the project but also bought additional material for themselves.

V   Results from the Talking Page Study

Test Results

Comments on the tests

As the Southgate test was used in the first year and with all the remedial and infants' children in the second year of the study, the test results have been given in two forms—with the ceiling scores included and with the ceiling scores excluded. No such problem was encountered for the Neale test as the test covered a wider range of reading ages.

A comparison of reading results for all experimental and all control children—first year junior children

Table 7(a) shows that the mean reading age of the experimental children increased by 5·2 months when the children who obtained ceiling scores at

Table 7(a)

Year 1 (1969–1970)—Southgate Test

	Mean reading score—ceiling score children excluded				
	October 1969 mean R.A.	June 1970 mean R.A.	Change in R.A. (months)	Mean chronological age, October	No.
Experimental Group	7 y 0·3 m	7 y 5·5 m	+5·2	7 y 4 m	296
Control Group	7 y 0·8 m	7 y 7·4 m	+6·6	7 y 7 m	235

	Mean reading scores—all children				
	October 1969 mean R.A.	June 1970 mean R.A.	Change in R.A. (months)	Mean chronological age, October	No.
Experimental Group	7 y 1·0 m	7 y 7·3 m	+6·3	7 y 0 m	386
Control Group	7 y 2·6 m	7 y 11 m	+8·2	7 y 6 m	357

either testing session were included and by 6·3 months when they were excluded. The corresponding increases for the control groups were 6·6 months and 8·2 months. The number of months that elapsed between the two testing periods was eight. It would therefore have been expected that the children should have made 8 months reading progress. However, only the control group of children with ceiling scores included made this progress. The other groups all showed a lower increase in reading age.

Table 7(b) shows that the mean accuracy age of the experimental and control children increased by the same amount (8·7 months) in the 9 months between the two testing sessions. The comprehension increase was higher for both groups and for the experimental group was slightly more than for the

Table 7(b)

Year 2 (1970–1971) Neale Analysis of Reading Ability

	Experimental			Control		
	Accuracy	Compre-hension	Chrono-logical age	Accuracy	Compre-hension	Chrono-logical age
September 1970	7 y 4·1 m	6 y 10·8 m	7 y 6·4 m	7 y 2·8 m	6 y 10·8 m	7 y 5·3 m
June 1971	8 y 0·8 m	7 y 8·8 m		7 y 11·5 m	7 y 8·4 m	
No.	138			149		
Changes in R.A. in months	+8·7	+10·0		+8·7	+9·6	

control group. The increase in comprehension was greater than the increase in chronological age and the increase in accuracy age was only slightly less than the increase in chronological age.

Change in reading test results—remedial situations

Table 8 shows that there was a considerable difference in the increase in reading age in each year. However, the small number of schools meant that

Table 8

Reading Test Results—Remedial Situation*

	Mean reading age all children		Change in R.A. (months)	Mean chron. age October	No. of children	No. of schools
	Oct./Nov.	June				
Year 1	7 y 2·2 m	7 y 3·1 m	+0·9 m	8 y 1 m	98	2
Year 2	7 y 0·2 m	7 y 6·3 m	+6·1 m	8 y 8 m	123	9

* No separate columns have been included in this table for a mean reading age with the ceiling scores excluded as there were too few children in this category.

there were also considerable differences in the mean increase made by the children in each school. In the second year, the mean increase made in each year varied from 4·3 months to 12·9 months (the latter being the one school in the sample which drew children from a predominantly middle class area).

Change in reading results—infant and secondary schools

In the one infants' school in which testing was carried out there were only 12 experimental and 12 control children. The experimental children showed an increase in reading age of 5·4 months, the control children of 4·5 months. In the controlled situation in one secondary school the 41 experimental children showed an increase in reading age of 4·4 months and the 37 control children of 5·7 months.

Analysis of class results

Analysis of the reading progress made by each class showed that there was no consistent pattern of greater progress being made by either the control or experimental classes. In some schools the experimental classes made greater progress, in others greater progress was made by the control classes. Therefore, the factors affecting reading progress were more closely related to the characteristics of each class (the teacher, social composition of each class, etc.) than to whether or not that class used the Talking Page.

Analysis by sex, socio-economic background and non-verbal intelligence level of the children

Analysis showed that for both experimental and control groups greater progress was made by the "advantaged" children, i.e., those with a higher non-verbal I.Q., with a higher reading age at the start of the project and from non-manual homes. Although there was no clear trend to show that "advantaged" or "disadvantaged" children benefit more or less from the use of the Talking Page, there were some indications that the "advantaged" children in the junior schools who used the Talking Page increased their comprehension level by a greater amount than comparable children who did not use the machine, and that the "disadvantaged" children increased their reading age by a greater amount when not using the Talking Page.

Some confusing results were obtained when analysis was carried out according to whether the children were in E.P.A. or non-E.P.A. schools. Six of the experimental schools taking part in the first year were E.P.A. schools and eight non-E.P.A. schools had a first year class tested at both testing sessions. Only three of the E.P.A. schools but seven of the non-E.P.A. schools had a first year control class.

The results in Table 9 show that the E.P.A. schools which used the Talking Page made 3 months less progress in the 8 months of the study than the experimental children in the non-E.P.A. schools. By contrast, however, the 99 control children in the E.P.A. schools made more progress than their counterparts in non-E.P.A. schools and in fact made progress which was slightly greater than their increase in chronological age. The control children in E.P.A. schools made more progress than the experimental children in non-E.P.A. schools. Although these results indicate that children in E.P.A. schools do not make as much progress when using the Talking Page as when being taught by other methods and that children in non-E.P.A. schools make better progress when using the Talking Page, the high reading progress made by children in E.P.A. schools is surprising. It is possible that it is accounted for by the small number and that only three schools and four classes are represented in this group. As with the reading laboratories experiment, considerable differences were found between classes.

The actual mean reading age of the children in non-E.P.A. schools was higher at the beginning and end of the year than the reading age of the E.P.A. children. However, as the total analysis showed that children with higher reading ages at the start of the project made more progress throughout the year than those with low reading ages, this makes the results of the E.P.A control children even more unexpected.

Table 9

Reading Results First Year of the Study
Children Using the Talking Page
E.P.A./non-E.P.A. Schools
(*All results in years and months: Southgate reading ages*)*

	Ceiling and floor scoring children excluded				All children			
	Mean R.A., Oct.	Mean R.A., June	Change in R.A.	No.	Mean R.A., Oct.	Mean R.A., June	Change in R.A.	No.
	y m	y m	m		y m	y m	m	
Experimental Group								
E.P.A. schools	6 11·4	7 4·5	+5·1	114	6 11·0	7 4·3	+5·3	140
Non-E.P.A. schools	7 1·3	7 8·3	+7·0	182	7 3·2	7 11·4	+8·2	246
All schools	7 0·3	7 5·5	+5·2	296	7 1·0	7 7·3	+6.3	386
Control Group								
E.P.A. schools	6 10·0	7 6·4	+8·4	69	6 10·7	7 7·3	+8·6	99
Non-E.P.A. schools	7 3·3	7 8·3	+7·5	166	7 4·3	7 11·6	+7·3	258
All schools	7 0·8	7 7·4	+6·6	235	7 2·6	7 11·0	+8·2	357

* The mean chronological age of all children in October was seven years four months.

In the second year only one of the five schools using the Talking Page under controlled conditions was an E.P.A. school. Again the children in E.P.A. schools made less progress than those in non-E.P.A. schools and the control children in E.P.A. schools made slightly greater progress than their experimental counterparts, although there was little difference in the progress made by children in non-E.P.A. schools.

The general trends reinforced the analysis by home background, I.Q., etc., that more "advantaged" children made greater progress when using the machines and less "advantaged" children progressed better without them.

The subjective assessment

The subjective judgements on the Talking Page were collected from teachers and head teachers in the first year by means of questionnaires, and in the second year by the Inspectors visiting the schools and interviewing the staff concerned. The Inspectors also made their own assessment of the equipment.

Summary of comments made by the head teachers and teachers in the first year

(i) Although the manufacturers had stated that each child should have a minimum of five 20 minute sessions per week and a maximum of nine per week, the majority of schools used the machines for less than five sessions. This was partly due to the difficulties experienced by the teachers in organising more frequent sessions and partly due to the failure of books to be delivered as needed, which meant that some children had to wait before they could continue to the next book. The intermittent use of the machines may have had implications for the first results but there are no indications that the mean reading age increase made by each class was related to the number of sessions for which the machines were used each week.

(ii) Sixty-two per cent of teachers supervising the machines during 1969–1970 had had more than 6 years' teaching experience, so organisational problems cannot be attributed to inexperience.

(iii) Most teachers said the children reacted positively towards the machines—although even after 8 months some said the novelty had worn off, particularly for poor readers who became frustrated with it. Teachers of "remedial" and "deprived" children had mixed views— some felt the Talking Page provided good motivation for these children, others felt it was too depersonalised to be a success.

(iv) Most teachers said the Talking Page did not affect the time they were able to devote to the individual child. No teacher was able to give more time to the teaching of other subjects.

(v) Twelve teachers felt the Talking Page had a positive effect on the children's attitudes and attainment in other subjects (in terms of an increase in confidence, enthusiasm, ability to concentrate, etc.). However, ten other teachers said the Talking Page had no effect at all.

(vi) Eighteen of the 26 teachers who returned questionnaires thought the machine would be useful in a primary school (only two teachers said it definitely would be of no use at all). Eight of the above 18 teachers thought it was best used with remedial children.

(vii) Half of the teachers felt the money spent on the Talking Page could be more usefully spent—particularly on extra part-time teachers and additional reading schemes.

Summary of comments in the second year

(i) Fourteen of the 17 head teachers interviewed considered that the Talking Page improved the reading standards of the children.

(ii) No head teacher said he would be prepared to buy the Talking Page from his school allowance, although eight said they would have it in their schools if the cost was fully borne by the Authority and a further six said they would have it if the Authority partially subsidised its cost. Only three said they did not want the Talking Page or would prefer to have the money spent on something else.

(iii) Head teachers considered the Talking Page to have been more successful than the class teachers. Just over half the class teachers wanted the Talking Page made available, but only if placed in a special reading workshop rather than the classroom.

(iv) Three-fifths of teachers agreed that the Talking Page increased the child's confidence, enjoyment and interest in reading and also that it helped to improve the child's concentration—all these being important factors in the development of reading skills.

(v) The Talking Page was generally regarded by both the head and class teachers as being of most benefit to "remedial" children. However, the infants' teachers regarded children of infants' age who were "slow starters" as being in need of more pre-reading activities and activities which did not demand quite so much mechanical operation.

(vi) When asked about the advantages and disadvantages of the Talking Page teachers were more critical than uncritical of it. Disadvantages most commonly mentioned were—"it is excessively time-consuming; it involves too much organisation and tends to dominate all other classroom activities, and the software is poor".

(vii) Most teachers felt their teaching with the Talking Page could have been assisted by more supplementary material and more guidance as to which children were most likely to benefit from using the Talking Page. However, as one of the project's aims was to find out which children would benefit most from the use of the Talking Page no such guidance could obviously be given to begin with.

(viii) Most children were able to cope with the understanding and correcting of Talking Page work, although the problem was reported of children continuing to work through books and records despite the fact that they had not understood or successfully completed previous work. The mechanical aspects of the machine presented very few problems.

(ix) Despite criticism half the teachers preferred the Talking Page programmes to other reading schemes because they introduced another approach and therefore increased interest.

Assessment by the Inspectors

A wide variety of comments were received from the Inspectors. In general, these comments stated that, although some teachers worked well with the Talking Page, others found the machine demanded considerable organisation and was time-consuming, especially when checking of work was involved. Several Inspectors said the Talking Page introduced rigidity into an otherwise flexible situation. Teacher-training on how to make the best use of the equipment was also thought to be very important by the Inspectorate. It was the weaker teacher who, although needing the extra help in the classroom, had the greatest difficulty using the machine. It was not felt to be a success in the infants' schools and it was recommended that it should only be made available in the secondary schools in certain selected cases. Its most effective use was generally thought to be in a language laboratory situation.

General comments

Over the 2 years the experiment was carried out, the experimental group did not show any greater gain in reading level than the control group. There were individual children who made considerable gains in their reading age, although it is quite possible they would have made this progress anyway. It cannot be generally stated that the inclusion of the Talking Page in a class will necessarily raise the reading standard of that class.

VI   Summary of Results

The S.R.A. Results

The most important findings can be summarised as follows:

(i) The reading age increase made by both the experimental and control groups was similar. The infants' reading age increased by 6·9 months when the ceiling scores were excluded and 6·6 months when they were included. The first year junior children showed increases of between 6 months and 8 months. Both the experimental and control children in the second, third and fourth year junior classes showed an increase in reading level significant at the 1 per cent level. The mean reading age equivalent increase made by the secondary children was 10 months and by the students at the College of Further Education was 7 months, although two classes in the latter made progress of over a year.

(ii) Analysis by sex, ethnic group and school experience of the children showed that there was no consistent pattern of greater increase in level by experimental or control groups for any category of children.

(iii) An individual reading test, the Neale Analysis of Reading Ability, was given in one school. A greater increase in reading age was made by the control children for both accuracy and comprehension. For both the control and experimental groups the comprehension reading age increased by twice the amount of the accuracy reading age. The increase in the rate of reading age varied considerably by class.

(iv) Considerable variation was shown by each class in the amount of progress made, but this was not found to be related to whether or not that class was an experimental class, or to the intelligence level of the class, the teacher's attitude towards the S.R.A. materials, or the teacher's years of teaching experience.

(v) An increase in vocabulary level was seen for the infants and the second, third and fourth year children but not for the first year junior children.

(vi) Comments made by the teachers who used the S.R.A. materials were generally favourable. The organisational problems of introducing the materials into the classroom situation were not found to be too great by the majority of teachers. Over half the teachers saw the equipment as being very effective in increasing the children's rate of reading with comprehension and half saw it as effective in increasing the children's phonic knowledge. All but one of the schools chose to continue to use the equipment after the year of the experiment, when the purchase of additional workbooks had to be financed by the schools themselves.

The Talking Page Results

The following summarises the test results given in the text and the other major findings of the total analysis.

(i) In the first year the control group made a greater gain in reading age than the experimental group in the eight months of the project. The experimental children made an increase in reading age of 5·2 months and 6·0 months (ceiling score children included and excluded) and the corresponding groups of control children made increases of 6·3 months and 8·2 months.

(ii) In the second year using assessment on the Neale test, the control and experimental children both increased their accuracy ages by 8.7 months in the 9 months of the project. The experimental children showed a slightly greater increase in comprehension age.

(iii) In the one school in which the Southgate and Neale tests were given there were indications that the Neale test gives a slightly higher reading age than the Southgate test. This could explain the slight differences in progress made in the two years.

(iv) There was a slight indication that children from more socially and academically "advantaged" backgrounds made better progress than those from more "disadvantaged" backgrounds.

(v) The progress made by children in remedial classes who use the Talking Page varied very much from school to school. In the absence of controls it is not possible to draw conclusions on the use of the Talking Page with remedial groups.

(vi) The progress made by infants and secondary children who used the Talking Page was similar to that made by comparable control groups.

(vii) A vocabulary test given in the first year of the study showed that neither the experimental nor the control group increased their score over the year of the study.

(viii) The teachers who used the Talking Page reported that there had been difficulties in incorporating the Talking Page into the classroom time-table. There had been an initial good reaction on the part of the children to the machine but in some cases the novelty wore off after a few months. The class teachers regarded the Talking Page as a more suitable instrument for use with remedial children in a language laboratory situation although it should be noted that the reading test results indicated that the results were more positive with the brighter children. The Talking Page was viewed as more successful by the head teachers than the class teachers but no head teacher was prepared to buy the machine from his own school allowance.

General

It should be remembered that both projects took place in the "normal" school environment. No attempt was made to ensure that the educational experience of the experimental and control children was identical except in their use of the materials. It was decided that the schools should incorporate the materials into their classroom timetables as they would have done if they had not been taking part in an experiment. The materials have therefore been examined as if they had been bought by schools for their use in a non-experimental situation.

Part Three

The Case Study of a Half-Day Centre

Janet Woods

The Case Study of a Half-Day Centre

The Purpose of the Centre

The centre described in this paper was opened in September 1966 in an inner urban area to provide specialist attention for children described as "socially, culturally and linguistically deprived". It was specifically stated that the centre was not intended for E.S.N. children, the retarded reader of average intelligence or for the emotionally disturbed child needing treatment at a Child Guidance Clinic or education in a Tutorial Class or School for the Maladjusted. Provision was already made by the Local Education Authority for these children. The purpose of the centre was therefore to assist a "residual" category of children for whom special provision was not already made by the Authority.

The Aims of the Study

The aims of the case study were:

(i) to describe what happened at the centre;
(ii) to describe the children attending the centre and how they were selected to attend;
(iii) to examine the effectiveness of the centre in helping the children sent to it;
(iv) to consider the implications of these findings for remedial and special education in general.

The study was carried out by observation, interviews with the staff, head teachers and educational psychologists involved and the administration of standardised tests to the children.

I A Description of the Centre

The General Organisation of the Centre

The centre was run by two experienced teachers who had had special training in the teaching of English to immigrant children. A maximum of fifty children could be registered at the centre at any one time divided into two independent groups of twenty-five in the morning and twenty-five in the afternoon. The children spent 4 half-days a week at the centre. The other 6 half-day sessions were spent in their primary schools. Friday was set aside as a day on which medicals could be held, interviews between the two teachers and the parents could be arranged, interviews with the head teachers could be arranged and on which courses could be held at the centre.

The half-day system exists in all the remedial reading classes in this Authority. The rationale behind this is that the children should be able to follow the normal curriculum of their school whilst receiving specialised help in particular areas, e.g., reading. By this method they are not excluded from the benefits of being part of a larger community, such as participation in a play or membership of a football team. The half-day system also makes it possible for more children to be given special help while at the same time maintaining a low ratio of students to teachers.

The Teaching Arrangements at the Centre

The centre was housed in a one storey building containing three rooms of classroom size, a hall and facilities such as toilets and a medical room. The timetable was originally planned so that each teacher took a class of approximately twelve children and the third room was used as a staff-room. However, the teachers felt that the wide range of reading ability in each group led to a situation in which the children were not receiving sufficient individual attention. The children were therefore re-grouped so that one teacher took a small group of children (approximately two to four children) for reading tuition and the other teacher took the remaining children for other activities, such as a group story, writing or art. In this way it was planned that each child should receive at least 5 minutes individual reading help each day. The rooms were, therefore, furnished so that one room was used as a classroom, another as a reading room as well as the staffroom furnished with a carpet, armchairs and a bookcase, the third as a jungle gymnasium and the hall was used for art work, dressing up and other activities requiring space.

The centre had the services of an assistant who prepared the hall for art work and cleared it after use. She was also responsible for escorting some of the children to their primary schools at lunch time. The centre had no other staff and all work of a secretarial and administrative nature had to be done by the teachers.

The Aims and Teaching Programme of the Staff of the Centre

The staff considered the main aim of the centre was to provide a compensatory language programme to equip children to learn to read and write and in addition to assist their social development. The staff of the centre adopted a teaching programme which aimed to widen the experience of the children with the object of enriching their language. The teachers saw an important part of this programme as being visits to such places as Brighton, the zoo, parks and to go fishing. Many of the children had never previously visited the places mentioned. An outing was developed into a project involving reading about the place to be visited, and discussing and drawing pictures about it both before and after the visit took place.

The day-to-day activities were not always identical but the description of the programme given below may be considered to be that of a fairly typical day at the centre.

When the children arrived they all went into the reading room where they took any book they wished from the book display to read or look through. Both teachers were in the same room but the children's reading was not supervised at this time. Children were also at this time allowed to use games such as alphabetical and picture games and jigsaws.

Following this, one of the teachers took the majority of the children into the classroom and left two or three children with the other teacher. (The teacher who took the small group of children in the morning took the large group in the afternoon.) The number of children left in the small group depended on the activities planned with them. Only one or two children would be left if the children were to read to the teacher, in which case while one child was reading to the teacher from the book he had reached at that time, the other child would either read or look through his own book or he would be set some form of activity. A larger group (three or four children) remained with one teacher if phonic work was to be done with them or if special work was to be done with a group of non-English speaking children. In the latter case all the non-English speaking children would remain with the teacher. Although some phonic work was done with all the children, the main emphasis was not on phonics but on ensuring that the children understood what they read. The teachers made a point of talking to the children when they were teaching them individually and perhaps tape-recorded their version of the story.

The larger group of children frequently began the day with a story which would then be followed up by a variety of methods. The children might discuss it and write about it, act it, record it or illustrate it. Frequent use was made of the tape recorder with the large group. At the end of the session the children might be allowed to dress up, taught to sew and knit, play games, use "Lego" and "Meccano" and other pieces of equipment, and also use the jungle gymnasium. Children who arrived early for the afternoon session would also be allowed to dress up before the session began. Several of the children had previously had few toys or opportunities for dressing up and these were seen as valuable means by which the child could mature. During the course of the story and follow-up activities and the activities at the end of the session the children would be called out of the class-room or hall in ones and twos to go and read to the other teacher.

The above general description might be varied by both the teachers working together with all the children. This could occur when a book was chosen for detailed study or in preparation for an outing. When such a book was chosen for detailed study the teachers sometimes wrote the book out on large sheets of paper card or paper which the class then read together or individuals read to the class. Each child in the class would then take a part and the story would be acted and tape recorded.

The main feature of the programme at the centre was that the children were encouraged to actively participate throughout their half-day's attendance. This active participation was intended to lead to opportunities for conversation and hence language development.

II   The Children Attending the Centre, their Selection and the Schools from which They were Drawn

The Schools from which the Children were Drawn

Nine junior schools sent children to the centre during the year of this study. The head teachers of the schools in the area were able to decide whether or not they wished to send children. An indication of the schools' characteristics can be seen by considering the rank position given to each school on the Authority's index of educational priority drawn up in 1971. Of the 644 primary school sites in the Authority the 9 schools were ranked from position 1 (the school most in need of help) to position 214. Six of these schools were ranked in the top 104 positions. The proportion of immigrants in each of the schools ranges from 14·3 per cent to 70·7 per cent[1] (in five of the schools over one-third of the pupils were immigrants—the criteria used by the authority to designate schools as being in special need). In six of the schools over half the teachers had been in the schools for less than 3 years and in no school had more than two-thirds of the staff been there more than 3 years. In the seven schools for which the information was known the percentage of children with a father whose known occupation was in a manual job ranged from 66·7 per cent to 100 per cent in 1968.[2]

The Selection of Children for the Centre

The selection of children for the centre took place in two stages. The head teacher put forward the names of the children he or she considered would benefit from attendance at the centre. These children were then interviewed and tested by one of three psychologists who were responsible for the selection of children for the centre. A policy agreed upon by the educational psychologists, inspectors and teachers concerned was not to select first year children on the basis that these children may not have had sufficient time to settle in their junior school and therefore should not be subjected to the additional stress of having to attend a further new school. Fourth year children were also generally excluded as it was considered profitable for these children to be accustomed to the routine of a whole day in one school before transferring to a secondary school. As a result children were normally selected from the second and third year of the junior school.

The head teachers of the nine schools concerned were interviewed regarding the basis on which they asked the psychologist to see a child. There was no general agreement between the head teachers as to the type of child they should send to the centre. One head teacher specifically chose children with reading problems whereas another sent children with reading problems only

---

[1] Figures taken from the 1967 returns for the D.E.S.
[2] Data from 1968 Literacy Survey carried out in the Authority—in all the Authority the percentage was found to be 75·6 per cent.

to the district remedial class and those with other problems as well to the centre. A third head teacher wished to send children with behaviour problems to the centre but had been told that the centre was not intended for such children. Some head teachers were uncertain as to which children to send and in two schools the centre staff were asked to visit the school and select the children from a list of children and their reading ages presented to them.

The three psychologists were asked to define the type of child they were looking for when they made their selection for the centre. Two said they were looking for children in need of a compensatory language programme. One of these saw the centre as a method of approaching the "immigrant problem" in the area and consequently the majority of children referred were West Indian. The third psychologist looked for children of low reading ability and below average intelligence with minor behaviour problems. All three psychologists selected children on the basis of an interview, a reading test and intelligence test. However, they did not all use the same tests. Two used the Schonell test (one in conjunction with the Burt test) and one used the Holborn. All three used part or all of the W.I.S.C. intelligence test and all three used the Goodenough–Harris "Draw a man" test. These tests were supplemented by a spelling test on occasion and one of the psychologists also used an assessment of laterality. The psychologists' main purpose in using the tests was to assess whether the child would be better placed in an alternative form of special education, such as an E.S.N. school or a district remedial class. All three psychologists also sent to the centre children for whom they were uncertain what would be the most suitable form of special education, so that the children could be closely observed for a period. None of the psychologists used any tests to assess the child's social adjustment, although one psychologist said that if a child's reading ability was average he could usually consider the child's problem to be one of social adjustment and therefore recommend placement in a tutorial class or child guidance. However, children with mainly problems of social adjustment were also admitted to the centre; as one psychologist said, this was frequently the only place to send them as waiting lists for tutorial classes and schools for the maladjusted were so long and parental permission for child guidance could not always be obtained. However, the tests used by the psychologists were basically used as confirmation of the head teachers' selection as only one psychologist had rejected any of the children put forward in the previous year.

The lack of rejection or alternative placement by the psychologist of the children put forward by the head teacher meant that the selection was in fact made by the head teacher. As the interviews with the head teachers showed, they did not all use the same criteria for selection, which resulted in a hetero- geneous group of children being placed at the centre. The problems of selection seem to be partly related to the difficulties in interpretation of the phrase "socially, culturally and linguistically deprived" and partly to the desire to place children in some form of special education but for whom there was no obvious or immediate placement. It is possibly erroneous to assume that children are either E.S.N. or maladjusted or retarded in reading. Children may in fact suffer from a combination of problems and therefore it would be expected that any school which catered for a residual category of children would receive those children which did not clearly fall into any other category. The result, however, of the difficulties of defining which children should be sent to the centre means that the staff who ran the centre and the head teachers of some of the schools had differing expectations of the effect of the centre on the children.

The usual reason for a child's resumption of full-time attendance at his own school was that the centre staff decided that the child had made sufficient improvement at the centre or that although he had not made much improvement he was unlikely to gain further from prolonging his attendance at the centre. In addition children left the centre if they were placed in an alternative type of special school. The final decision as to whether a child should resume full-time attendance at his own school was made by the educational psychologists who tested the children put forward by the centre staff.

A Description of the Children at the Centre

Information was collected on all the children who were at the centre in January 1969 and who were admitted to the centre from that date up to the end of the Spring Term 1969. A total of 49 children were included in the study in this way. Background data on the children (age, race and sex) and information on their educational performance (reading level, vocabulary level, nonverbal ability and behaviour as seen by their teacher) was collected.

Three-quarters of the children at the centre were boys (73·5 per cent) and over half were West Indian (55·1 per cent). Except for one Greek Cypriot the remaining children were all of British origin. All but three of the forty-nine children were from the second or third years of the junior school.

Two reading tests were used. The Neale Analysis of Reading Ability (which gives an accuracy reading age and a comprehension reading age) and the Daniels and Diack test (which in addition to a reading test gives the child a diagnostic test to assess his weaknesses in various types of reading related skills, e.g., letter and sound recognition).

In February 1969 only eight of the children had a sufficiently high reading age on the Daniels and Diack test to be able to obtain a score on the Neale test (six years or over). Twenty children failed to obtain a score of over 5 years 4 months on the Daniels and Diack test and nine of these children failed to complete successfully the diagnostic tests of visual discrimination indicating that they could not yet see the patterns of letters sufficiently to begin to read. The mean reading score of all the children on the Daniels and Diack test was 5 years 7 months and their mean chronological age was 9 years 1 month. Their reading level was therefore retarded by 3 years 6 months.[1] The eight children who were also given the Neale test had a mean accuracy age of 8 years 1 month and a mean comprehension age of 7 years 6 months.

A similar severe retardation in terms of vocabulary was found when the children were given the English Picture Vocabulary Test. This test measures the child's listening vocabulary by asking him to match a picture to a stimulus word. It is a standardised test with a mean score of 100. The mean score of all the children at the centre was 79·0, that of the boys being 81·9 and the girls 71·9.

Results on the Raven's Coloured Progressive Matrices test, a test of non-

---

[1] Scores on the Daniels and Diack test are given in terms of year and decimal fractions of a year. These have been converted into years and months for greater clarity.

verbal ability, showed an approximately normal distribution with only a slight skew towards the lower end of the scale. Since this study two other pieces of research have been carried out by the same research team which have suggested that the norms on the Raven's test are out of date and produce a pronounced skew towards the upper end of the scale indicating that the test is biased towards giving children high scores.[1] It may be, therefore, that the children at the centre were also at a lower level in terms of non-verbal ability.

One other measure was obtained. This was a behaviour rating made by both the child's class teacher in his own school and by the staff at the centre using the rating scale devised by Dr. Rutter.[2] This scale was created as a screening device but it allows for comparison between the proportion of children with abnormal scores in a particular population, e.g. the centre, and the general school population.

It was found that when rated by the staff at the centre 72·7 per cent of the children obtained an abnormal score. Of these 16·1 per cent were classified as neurotic and 77·4 per cent as anti-social.[3] The class-room teachers' ratings placed seven less children in the abnormal category so that a total of 55·8 per cent were placed in that category. These scores are extremely high. In the group studied by Dr. Rutter only 9·7 per cent of the boys and 4·6 per cent of the girls in the general population obtained abnormal scores.

In addition to the children at the centre, information was obtained on 48 children randomly selected from the same schools as those from which the centre children were drawn. These were not a control group, but the purpose of obtaining information on these children was to see how the children at the centre differed from those in the general school population in the same school. It was found that the main points of difference were that there were a greater proportion of West Indian children at the centre, the centre children had a higher incidence of school absence, and although information on home background was only minimal it was apparent that more of the children attending the centre came from unsettled home backgrounds, e.g., did not live with both parents. Little difference was found between the children at the centre and the comparison group on the English Picture Vocabulary Test and the Raven's Coloured Progressive Matrices but considerable differences were found on the reading test (only nine children failed to obtain scores of over 6 years on the Neale test) and on the behaviour scale. On the latter, 27·1 per cent obtained an abnormal rating which, although it was only half the proportion of the centre children who did so when rated by the same teachers, was three times the proportion found by Rutter in his normal population. This indicates that the behaviour problems in this area were considerably greater than those in the area studied by Rutter. The vocabulary level was also so low (comparison group mean 85·5) that it would indicate that the term

---

[1] Alan Little and Janet Woods, *A Study of the Science Research Associates Reading Laboratories.* Alan Little, Janet Woods and Annette Gray, *A Study of Rank's Talking Page 1969–71.*

[2] Dr. M. Rutter, *Child Behaviour Scale B.* Obtainable from the Institute of Psychiatry, Denmark Hill, London.

[3] Boys obtained abnormal scores more frequently than girls (74·1 per cent of the boys and 66·6 per cent of the girls), and whereas only 8·7 per cent of the boys with such scores were classed as neurotic, the remainder being anti-social, 62·5 per cent of the girls were classed as neurotic and only 37·5 per cent as anti-social.

"linguistically deprived" could be applied to the majority of the children in the area.

III   The Effectiveness of the Centre in Helping the Children sent to it

Problems of Assessing Effectiveness

A major problem of the evaluation of effectiveness was the creation of a definition of what the centre was trying to do which could be translated into objectively measurable criteria and which would also be consistent with the expectations of those who sent children to the centre and the staff of the centre. They take into account the views expressed and the selection of children. The evaluation was divided into three sections on the educational effects, the social effects and the observation function of the centre.

A research project involving evaluation should include a control group. However, no such control group was available as it was not possible in an existing education institution to assign children selected for the centre either to the centre or to a control group and, as shown above, the children in the ordinary primary schools showed considerable differences in background and reading ability to those at the centre and therefore were not directly comparable.

Educational Progress made by Children at the Centre

(i) Linguistic development

Two approaches were made to the assessment of the linguistic development of the children. The first was by testing their vocabulary scores using the English Picture Vocabulary Test[1] at the beginning and end of the year; the second was by tape recording each child telling a story from a series of pictures at the beginning and end of the year. However, as the problems involved in the analysis of the tape recordings were too complex these have not been included in the evaluation.

The results given in Table 1 show the change in scores on the English Picture Vocabulary Test. It can be seen from this table that the change in scores over this period was only negligible—an overall increase of 0·9 points. (The comparison group of children were also given this test in March and December and the mean score of the 45 children tested on both occasions fell from 86·2 to 84·2.) However, for neither group was the increase or decrease in scores statistically significant.

It was noticeable that the individual changes in scores of the children varied

---

[1] A Test of listening vocabulary in which the child has to identify which word goes with one of four pictures. The reliability of the test is 0·92.

Table 1

Change in Mean Standard Scores on the English Picture Vocabulary Test*

	Boys	Girls	All
February 1969	81·8	71·8	79·4
December 1969	82·5	72·9	80·3
Total number	31	9	40

* Only the 40 children who were at the centre throughout
the period of the study have been included in this table.

considerably. Nine of the children obtained increases in their scores of over nine points—higher than the change in score that could be attributable to error. (Six of these also obtained high reading age increases and six had obtained high scores on the non-verbal test.) Slightly greater progress was made by the 22 children who had been at the centre throughout the year (2·9 standardised points) than by the 18 who had left before the end of the year (0·8 points) but neither change was significant. In addition, more progress was made by the children of British origin than by those of West Indian origin but the numbers in each group were very small. Although overall the children made very little progress, it should be remembered that the test used was a standardised test and therefore the maintenance of the same score indicates that in relation to their age, their vocabulary level did not deteriorate further.

(ii) The change in reading levels of the children

All the children were given the Daniels and Diack reading test at the beginning of the Spring term and at the end of the Autumn term. The group of children who obtained high scores in February on the Daniels and Diack test were also given the Neale test in February, July and December. In addition because of the differences noticed between the two tests and the more detailed information received from the Neale test on children who could read all the children were given this test as well in July and December. In all the tables in this section only children who were tested at all the relevant testing sessions have been included.

Table 2 shows that over the 10 months between the two testing sessions the children at the centre showed an increase in reading age of 7 months, the girls' increase being 9 months, the boys' 7 months. This progress may be

Table 2

Mean Reading Ages—Daniels and Diack Test

	Boys	Girls	All
February 1969	5 yrs 6 mths	5 yrs 10 mths	5 yrs 7 mths
December 1969	6 yrs 1 mth	6 yrs 7 mths	6 yrs 2 mths
Number	31	9	40
Mean chronological age February	9 yrs 1 mth	9 yrs 0 mths	9 yrs 1 mth

educationally significant when it is considered that these children were those who showed the greatest reading and educational difficulties in the schools from which they came and were already very retarded in terms of reading before they were admitted to the centre.

Table 3 shows that the children who were given the Neale test on three

Table 3

Mean reading ages: Neale analysis of reading ability. Six Children Tested at Three Sessions (mean February chronological age, 9 years 0 months)

	Mean accuracy reading age	Mean comprehension reading age
February 1969	8 yrs 0 mths	7 yrs 7 mths
July 1969	8 yrs 7 mths	8 yrs 2 mths
December 1969	8 yrs 9 mths	8 yrs 2 mths
Number	6	

occasions made greater progress both in terms of their accuracy in reading the passages and their comprehension of those passages between February and July than they did between July and December. However, the numbers in this group were very small and individual changes in score varied considerably.[1]

All 40 children were given the Neale test in July and December. Their results are given in Table 4. This shows that the reading age of these children

Table 4

Mean Reading Ages: Neale Analysis of Reading Ability. All Children.

	Accuracy reading age	Comprehension reading age
July 1969	7 yrs 3 mths	7 yrs 3 mths
December 1969	7 yrs 4 mths	7 yrs 2 mths
Number	40	

increased in accuracy by 1 month from July to December and decreased by the same amount in comprehension. However, although all these children obtained an accuracy level above the minimum of 6 years seventeen children obtained a score of between 6 and 7 years. It is possible that this test does not discriminate satisfactorily at the lower end of the scale and therefore the difference in scores may not relate to the total change in reading ability that has occurred over the period.[2]

---

[1] It was found that children given both the Neale and the Daniels and Diack test obtained higher reading ages on the former. This, however, does not affect the progress made over time when judged by the same test.

[2] It is worth noting at this stage the the increase in reading scores made between March and December by the comparison group of children was not great: an increase of 3 months in accuracy from 9 years 5 months to 9 years 8 months and 7 months on the comprehension test from 8 years 9 months to 9 years 4 months.

Analysis of Reading Progress made by the Children at the Centre

Wide individual differences in change in reading score were noticed. The scores ranged from one child whose reading age increased by 2·2 years to two children whose reading age decreased by 5 months on the Daniels and Diack test. Half the children increased their reading age by 6 months or over. An analysis was therefore carried out on the change in scores made by different groups of children to see if it was possible to draw any conclusions concerning the characteristics of the children who appeared to have benefited most and who had benefited least in terms of increase in reading ages from their time at the centre.

The children were divided into two groups. Nineteen children who had made over 6 months progress were defined as children who had made "good" progress and 21 children who had made under 6 months progress as those who had made "little" progress. It was found that the children who had made good progress had had a higher mean reading age at the start of the project (6 years 1 month, Daniels and Diack test) than those who had made poor progress (5 years 7 months). This indicates that once a child has begun to read at a certain level he is likely to make better progress in terms of reading tests than those who have not yet begun. However, the fact that in each group there were some children who had not yet started reading and some with reading ages of over 5 years 6 months indicates that the degree of retardation of the child at the beginning of a remedial programme will not necessarily determine the chances of success of that programme.

It is, however, also important to consider how the reading age at the start of this project relates to the amount of time the child has already spent at the centre and the age of the child. It is possible that a considerable amount of time is necessary before a child has overcome the first barrier of beginning to read and that those who had made little progress during the time of the tests had in fact only been at the centre for a short period. However, little difference was found between the two groups in the number of children who had been at the centre before the project began and the number who had only been there from the start of the project. The important difference between the two groups was therefore their reading age when they were admitted to the centre.

A higher proportion of the children who had made over 6 months progress had obtained scores on the Raven's matrices which placed them in the top two categories (28·6 per cent compared to 9·5 per cent) although the mean vocabulary score at the start of the year of those who made good progress was less than that of those who made little progress (75·8 per cent compared to 78·6 per cent). Both groups showed approximately the same change in vocabulary score throughout the year.

A noticeable difference between the two groups was found to be in the behaviour ratings they were given on the Rutter behaviour scale. On the ratings made by the centre staff 90·5 per cent of the children who had made little progress were given abnormal scores on this scale (71·4 per cent when the class teacher's ratings are used). This compared to 52·4 per cent of those who had made good progress (42·9 per cent class teacher rating). Children with anti-social behaviour sub-scores had made less progress than those with neurotic sub-scores. (Of the children classified by the centre staff as anti-social 63·4 per cent were in the low progress group compared to only 42·8 per cent of those in the neurotic sub-group.) However, the results are such that children of each classification fall into both the good progress and poor progress groups. Therefore although in general an anti-social score on the Rutter behaviour scale was related to poor progress in reading there were examples of children in this category who had made progress of up to 1 year 7 months.[1]

As the children at the centre attended their own schools for 6 half-days a week and attended the centre for only 4 half-days it was thought that it would be useful to compare the children's progress in terms of the schools which they atttended. The number from each school however was small (between one and ten children) which makes comparison very difficult, but it was found that the progress made varied between a mean of 2 months and a mean of 11 months. Finally it was also found that the British children made better progress than the West Indian children—the former made up 57·1 per cent of the progress group whereas they formed only 47·6 per cent of the total population.

Summary of Reading Results

In summary therefore the 40 children tested on the Daniels and Diack reading test in both February and December showed a mean increase in reading age of 7 months in the 10 months between the two testing sessions. The range of change in scores on this test was from an increase of 2 years 2 months to a decrease of 5 months.

Half the children tested twice showed an increase of over 6 months. This group of children contained a higher proportion of children than would be expected with the following characteristics:

 (i) a reading age at the beginning of the project of over 5 years 6 months;
 (ii) with scores above the median on Raven's matrices;
 (iii) with "normal" behaviour ratings on the Rutter behaviour scale;
 (iv) with neurotic rather than anti-social behaviour ratings;
 (v) of British ethnic origin.

However, children with each of the above characteristics were also found in the group who had made under six months progress and children without these characteristics were found in the higher progress group.

Comments on the Reading Results

The mean increase in reading age for the whole group is small in terms of the fact that in December 1969 their mean reading age was still only 6 years

---

[1] A strong relationship between poor reading attainment and anti-social disorder was also found by Yule and Rutter in their study on the Isle of Wight. They also found little association between reading attainment and neurosis. W. Yule and M. Rutter, *Educational Aspects of Childhood Maladjustment: Some Epidemiological Findings*, a contribution to a symposium on "Recent Research on Maladjustment". British Psychological Society, Educational Section, Annual Conference, September 1967.

2 months and on average 3 years 9 months behind their chronological age. However, several facts should be borne in mind when considering these results.

The first is that although the project lasted for virtually one academic year, there was on average only 10 months between the first and the last testing period. It is unlikely that the children who have had the most difficulty in reading in the past will suddenly make such progress that they will advance at a rate far faster not only than their previous rate of progress but also than the rate of progress made by children of their own age who have advanced normally until this time. It is therefore possible that the period of 10 months over which this project was conducted was too short a period for the effects of the centre to be noticeable in the reading ages of the children. Six children had not begun to read at all at the start of the project and a further 12 had reading ages of only 5 years 2 months. Lack of advancement in terms of the reading ages of these children may therefore not reflect the true picture concerning the progress of these children. Several months of work may be needed with them before they begin to show improvement in terms of their reading ages.

In the second place these children had all been selected because they were considered by the head teachers of the schools from which they came to be the children most in need of individual attention. It is therefore also probably unrealistic to expect that even in a different school setting the children would make rapid progress in a very short time.

The Social and Cultural Effectiveness of the Centre

Although the social and cultural effects of the centre are difficult to measure in objective terms an attempt was made through interviews with head teachers and others concerned with the centre to obtain such an assessment. All the head teachers were asked if they could see any difference in the way in which the children behaved in their own school and also in their general level of maturity. The answers received were vague and differed considerably between the nine head teachers.

One head teacher said he thought the children "blossomed out" while at the centre and this improvement was particularly reflected in their written work. Another said that although he could not say how they developed, he knew they liked going. However, a third head teacher remarked that he thought that only one of the four children from his school who were at the centre during the course of the study had developed considerably in the year he was there. This particular child was a recent immigrant who had had difficulty settling into the school on arrival in this country. However, this head teacher also said of this child that it was difficult to attribute his development to any particular cause as he also had a good class teacher and appeared to have gone through a normal maturational stage. Two other head teachers were unconditionally in favour of the centre and felt that all the children benefited from their attendance there. The children on whom the head teachers most frequently reported that the centre had had most effect were those who had been very withdrawn in their behaviour. These children frequently remained withdrawn in comparison with the rest of their classes but were often reported to show a greater willingness to participate in class activities.

Disagreement was expressed among the head teachers as to whether or not the children's behaviour in their own schools deteriorated as a result of attendance at the centre. Some thought that half-day education did lead to poor behaviour partly because the children had difficulty in identifying with their own classes as they were not in them the whole time and partly because the children were encouraged to express themselves at the centre. However, others said that these children were the worse behaved anyway.

One head teacher also thought that there were dangers in selecting a group of children with special problems from a school and sending them to mix with another group of children all of whom had been selected because they too had problems. He also felt that some children were unable to cope with the "dual day" and could not settle at two schools at once. On the children's attitude to the centre he felt that there was a stigma attached to attendance although one of the four children he sent enjoyed attending. This head teacher thought that provision should be made within the schools to help the children with these types of problems but that it should begin at an earlier stage (infants level) and be carried out by specially trained teachers.

Finally a point that was made by several head teachers which does not relate to the effectiveness of the centre in dealing with the children sent to it but rather to its effectiveness in dealing with problems in the area was that the centre was only touching on these problems. Several head teachers felt that over half the children in each class were in need of more individual attention and that it was therefore difficult to select those which were priority cases. The description of the comparison children showed that these children had a very poor vocabulary level and a higher than expected proportion of them had behaviour problems. Although at the time of the project there was no waiting list for the centre and the head teachers could therefore have put forward more children for the centre it is probable that they did not do so because they were unwilling to spend the time selecting children for the centre when they felt it was not really coping with the problems in their schools and that they were deterred by the administrative problems of having to arrange special programmes for small groups of children.

The evaluation of the social and cultural effectiveness of the centre therefore cannot be conclusive as there are no objective measures of social development. The interview with the head teachers revealed a variety of opinions on the centre and also indicated that the head teachers perceived several different problems in sending children to the centre.

The Value of the Observation Function of the Centre

Although the centre was not specifically set up as a centre for the observation of children who were showing educational or emotional problems but for whom the best form of treatment was as yet undecided it has, however, come to be used as a centre with such a function.

Several of the admission forms completed by the psychologists recommended that the child should be referred to the centre for a "trial period for observation". However, once referred to the centre, the task of observing the child and consulting the educational psychologist should any change of referral be considered necessary, was left to the teachers. During the course of this study one child was recommended for a boarding school for the maladjusted and one was accepted for a special school, when it became apparent at a medical at the centre that his poor behaviour was due to brain damage. Two children were recommended for tutorial classes and two were put forward for child guidance but their parents then refused appointments. One child was placed in an E.S.N. school, and one was recommended for specialist treatment at the centre for spastic children. Therefore six of the children who were attending the centre at the beginning of this project had either been placed in special schools or were on the waiting list for specialist help when this project ended. Two others had been recommended for but had not received specialist treatment.

IV   Summary of Main Points

(i) The reasons for selecting children for the centre varied between schools and between the educational psychologists. As a result those connected with the centre had differing expectations of how the children should be affected by their attendance.

(ii) Nearly three-quarters of the children at the centre were boys and over half were of West Indian origin. At the beginning of the study the children's mean reading age was 3 years 6 months behind their mean chronological age (mean reading age 5 years 7 months, mean chronological age 9 years 1 month). The children's mean vocabulary level was 79·4, considerably below the national mean of 100. The children were not disproportionately placed in the lower part of the Raven's matrices but a considerably higher proportion than expected obtained abnormal scores on the Rutter behaviour scale.

(iii) The children showed little increase in score on the vocabulary test although their vocabulary level in relation to their age did not decrease (79·4 to 80·3).

(iv) The increase in reading age made on the Daniels and Diack test was 7 months in the 10 months between the two testing sessions.

(v) The range of change in reading age was from an increase of 2 years 2 months to a decrease of 5 months.

(vi) Nineteen children showed an increase in reading age of over 6 months in the 10 months of the survey.

(vii) Six children were referred for other forms of special education.

(viii) Eighteen children showed an increase in reading age of less than 6 months in the time of the study and were not referred for special education. Eight of these children had been discharged before December 1969. One was discharged because he was thought to have made considerable improvement in his social adjustment and one child left because his family left the area. Of the remaining six, four were discharged because they were about to enter the fourth year of the junior school and two because it was considered that a prolonged stay at the centre would not benefit them. Both the latter children were those who had been recommended for treatment at a Child Guidance Clinic but for whom the treatment had been refused by their parents. The remaining 10 children were still attending the centre in December 1969.

(ix) The head teachers varied in their attitudes towards the centre. Some had reservations about selecting children for special education outside their own school and thought that when changes occurred in the children it was difficult to determine the cause of these changes. Others thought that the children benefited socially and educationally from their time at the centre. Several of them said, however, that the centre was only touching on the problem in the area and that a large number of the children in their schools were in need of individual attention.

This description and study of the half-day centre has suggested several points concerning special education which have wider implications than for this centre alone.

The Types of Special Education Needed

The difficulties of selection described above show that it may not be realistic to assume that children with problems fall into easily defined groups. Each child may have a variety of problems so that he cannot readily be described as either E.S.N. or maladjusted or retarded in reading. The centre described has been used for the following four main functions since it was opened:

(i) To provide additional reading tuition to those who are retarded in reading.

(ii) To give more attention to the children who are emotionally disturbed and to relieve some class teachers of their worst trouble makers for 4 half-days a week.

(iii) To observe and diagnose the problems of children for whom no satisfactory diagnosis has yet been made.

(iv) To teach English to immigrant children.

Providing special education for children in terms of one particular difficulty may therefore be unrealistic. However, the provision of centres for children with a variety of problems may place a heavy burden on the teachers involved and the need for continued diagnostic assessment of children for whom it is unclear which is the most appropriate form of treatment, places heavy demands on the educational psychological service.

In an article by A. C. Nicholls[1] the following statement is made:

"If we can at least identify our problems, then we may have some chance to give effective help."

---

[1] A. C. Nicholls, "Special education", *Child Education*, August 1968, Volume 46, Number 10.

Identification of the problem is, however, obviously one of the greatest difficulties of remedial education. Nicholls suggests that three levels of failure can be identified:

(i) Children with a moderate degree of difficulty resulting from a poor social environment, who need more help than normal but who principally need good teaching—particularly of reading—i.e., the coaching side of remedial education which can be dealt with in schools.

(ii) Children whose failure is due to emotional difficulties and to some degree of maladjustment: this aspect is best dealt with by a "teacher-therapist" or perhaps more properly by an educational psychologist, and here the need for co-operation can really be seen.

(iii) Children with marked difficulties who will need the greatest degree of help of the most skilled nature and whose assessment needs to be carefully undertaken by a number of specialists in different fields.

The problems, however, arise in deciding into which category each child falls and diagnosing a remedial programme for each child. An immediate remedial programme may be necessary but no immediate diagnosis may be possible. The training of remedial teachers therefore needs to be more specialised than is frequently the case at present so that they can assist in planning a remedial programme as well as being able to assist the psychologist in providing continued informed observation of the children involved.

The Possible Forms of Remedial Education

The study of the centre has also touched upon the advantages and disadvantages of remedial education being placed within the normal school environment or in special centres and whether that help should be given full-time or part-time. The advantages of provision within the schools is that if it is on a half-time basis, closer liaison can be maintained between the remedial teacher and the class teacher, the child does not have to miss out on normal school activities such as football which may have a positive motivational function, the child does not have to travel between two schools, he may not feel so much stigma at being selected for special education and the administrative problems for the head teachers are reduced. Advantages of education outside the school are that it may spread scarce resources between schools especially in terms of specialised teaching and psychological help and for children who have difficulties in adjusting to the size of the "normal" school and class it may provide them with an environment small enough for them to adjust to. The major disadvantage of half-day special education either within a school or outside the school is that the child has to adjust to two types of classroom situations. This adjustment may not be too great if both are run on traditional or progressive lines but may cause difficulties for the child if one is run in the former and one in the latter way.

An alternative way of looking at whether children in need of special help should remain in their own schools or classes or be placed in some form of special education outside the school is in terms of the effect on the other children in the "normal" school class-room. This aspect of the effects of any form of special education has not been considered in the study but it is possible that the children left in the schools may benefit from the removal from their classes of those children who create disturbances and take a disproportionate amount of the teacher's attention.

The Provision of Records on Children

The study of the centre revealed that in certain cases information (of a non-confidential nature) had been obtained on a child and had not been passed onto those to whom it would be useful, e.g., the centre staff did not know that one child had previously received psychiatric treatment until they recommended he should receive special help such as child guidance. This information (which was already known to his head teacher) was then made available to them. The child had therefore been at the centre for a year before any further progress was made in providing treatment for him. A second instance occurred when a child moved during the year and his new headmistress had no knowledge that he had previously been attending the centre as well as his own school and therefore none of the information or recommendations of the educational psychologist were made available to her. The question of the provision of records on children is related to the education of all children and not just those who are receiving remedial education. It is, however, particularly important, as far as the limits of confidentiality will apply, that teachers of children with educational problems should know what work has been done with those children in the past.

The Optimum Age for Remedial Education

Although the question of the optimum age for remedial education has not been discussed in this study, as the majority of children were drawn from the second and third year of the junior school, this too needs to be considered further and in particular attention should be given to the attempts now being made to find predictive measures of educational and emotional problems, so that children who are likely to need help can be given special attention at the earliest possible stage.

The Optimum Period of Attendance at a Remedial Centre

The results obtained on the reading and vocabulary tests do not give any indication of an optimum period of attendance at the remedial centre. The centre staff felt most children needed at least a term to settle before they began to make progress and many children did not show signs of the progress they had made until after about a year. It was often not until this time that they reached a stage of being ready to learn to read. They therefore suggested that children needed at least four terms at the centre and it was often not until after two or three terms that it became apparent whether a child would or would not learn to read or whether he needed other help. However, the difference in time needed by each child is apparent in the following two children. One child was admitted to the centre in February 1969 with a Neale accuracy reading score of 7 years 11 months and a comprehension score of 7 years 3 months. In December his accuracy score had risen to 9 years 4 months and his comprehension score to 8 years 2 months. He was of slightly below-average intelligence on the Raven's Coloured Progressive Matrices. Another child who had been at the centre for four terms when the study began had a reading age of 5·8 years on the Daniels and Diack test at the start of the project, she was discharged 6 months later in July and in December had a reading age of 7·3 on the same test. This child had therefore made little measurable progress to begin with but had then made sudden rapid progress.

A second factor relating to the optimum period of attendance is from the point of view of the length of time for which a child should attend two schools. One head teacher interviewed in the study did not consider it desirable for a child to attend two schools for too long a period. However, it is also possible that for children with the greatest educational problem a length of time such as two years (second and third year of junior school life) is too short to help the children approach the standards normally expected of children of their age.

Research Problems in Remedial Education

A major problem in the evaluation of remedial education is the lack of situations with which that being studied can be compared and the difficulties involved in setting up control groups especially where a particular centre or class is already in operation. Children in remedial classes have diverse problems and therefore comparing them with the other children in other situations is very difficult as the matching of large numbers of children would be a lengthy and uncertain process.

A second problem experienced in this study was the difficulty of defining in objective, measurable terms the aims of the particular organisation. The possible lack of common agreement as to the aims of the organisation may also increase this problem.

Finally, if a centre or school is already in operation and admits children at any time throughout the year then there is a problem of collecting a sample of children for the study and taking into account the differences in the length of time they have attended the centre when the results are analysed. These limitations on the research situation should be borne in mind when considering the results given in the text.

Part Four

The Nursery School Language Work
Jim Stevenson

The Nursery School Language Work

The nursery class teachers in the London E.P.A. Project schools did not wish to take part in the National Programme's pre-school experiment.[1] They were in sympathy with its aims in as far as these concerned the language development of pre-school children in educational priority areas, but they found it impossible to be associated with the methods being tried out.

The national experiment was designed to test the effect on the language development of children in educational priority areas of a sequential programme of teaching, designed specifically to advance it. And the teaching devices to be used were those contained in a kit put together in the United States: the Peabody Language Development Kit (P.L.D.K.). This kit was designed to meet a set of problems that many considered to be different from those faced by the E.P.A. Project. In the early 1960s the United States promoted a range of programmes to assist the disadvantaged pre-school child. There was no shortage of funds for this but scarcities of existing provision and qualified personnel. The P.L.D.K. provides well for these circumstances; for 20 minutes a day the pre-school organiser can follow a precise sequence of training exercises with her children; these exercises are internally consistent and for each the material builds upon knowledge gained from previous sessions. Therefore, during a period of expansion the minimally trained or untrained teacher could rely on a programme of proven educational merit around which her day could be organised.

The situation in the United Kingdom was seen by the London E.P.A. nursery teachers to be dramatically different from this. There was, admittedly, an excess of demand over the supply of pre-school provision, but in the nursery sector there were well-established traditions of training and practice.[2,3] In particular, these traditions emphasised the utility of free play and child-initiated activity, which were directly confronted by the experimental use of teaching devices like the P.L.D.K. The London teachers, therefore, having decided against participation in the national experiment, began to explore ways of developing their own nursery practice to provide more emphasis on the language development of their children.

The Development of Programme

The concept behind the initial activities produced by the teachers was that by removing children from the nursery class in small groups (of four or five children), and by using normal nursery equipment in a small separate room within the school, more intensive attention would be given to the expansion

---

[1] See Volume II of the E.P.A. series: *Statistics and Surveys*.
[2] T. Blackstone, *A fair start—the provision of pre-school education*, Allen Lane, 1971.
[3] J. Kent and P. Kent, *Nursery Schools for all*, Ward Lock Educational, 1970.

of language accompanying normal play activities. Originally just one adult (a nursery assistant) was to have this contact with the children.

During discussions concerning the arrangements for the evaluation of this, the teachers thought the constraints that were necessary for research were making the programme too remote from normal nursery practice.[1] For instance, it was thought necessary to select a group of children at random to experience this special treatment, together with another group to act as controls. Even then the withdrawn experimental groups which an individual attended would need to be changed constantly so that all the experimental children would have as far as possible the same experience. It was also thought necessary to document extensively the activities that were to take place during these small group sessions, and as an aid to documentation, it was advised that each session be broken up into roughly the same categories. For example:

    10 minutes—Free play
    10 minutes—Story telling or reading a poem
    10 minutes—Discussion of the story or related subjects
    15 minutes—Creative work
    15 minutes—Game playing, music or tape-recording of verbal activities
    —
    60 minutes

At this stage the expressed and agreed aim of the programme was to "facilitate the language development of pre-school children by the intensification of good nursery practice". But the teachers felt that what was being created failed to meet this aim in three ways.

1. There was insufficient involvement of the ordinary class teacher in either the production or execution of the programme.
2. Although the activities in the programme were not outside good nursery practice, they were in too artificial a setting to be of general applicability, because they took place in a separate room and were constrained by the structure given for each hourly session.
3. The intention to plan the use of the material and the time allocated to each activity meant that the programme was not sufficiently dependent on the spontaneity of the child.

There was a further development at this stage; the leader of the playgroup being financed by the London Project expressed a willingness to co-ordinate the activities in the playgroup with those at the nursery school which had initiated the work. One important difference between the playgroup and the nursery school was that the latter received a far greater supply of adults in the classrooms, and so it was necessary for any additional work in the playgroup to be undertaken by extra staff. In this respect arrangements were made for four students from a neighbouring College of Education to attend the playgroup in groups of two. Each pair of students attended the playgroup for half a year during the college term. Therefore, between them the students were present in the playgroup for four half-day sessions per week for a period slightly less than a school year.

---

[1] See D. E. M. Gardner and J. E. Cass, *The Role of the Teacher in the Infant and Nursery School*, Pergamon, 1965.

It was necessary to formulate a structure for the pre-school work that would support the language development activities during the school year 1970–71. It was decided that these activities had to concern the class teacher[1] in her classroom, or in any other normally available environment. These activities should be on a one-to-one basis between teacher and child, and had to include as much as possible of the available nursery activities and equipment. It was resolved that the purchase of materials not already available in the nursery class be minimised. The co-ordination of the activities was to take place at weekly meetings between the Project staff and all the teachers involved in the programme.

The objectives of the programme were as follows:

1. To accelerate the language development of the subject children.
2. To document which of the nursery school activities seemed to facilitate the establishment of one-to-one contacts with the children for language work.
3. To record the types and frequency of verbal exchanges present during the normal nursery day.

The means of achieving the first of these objectives was to change the verbal behaviour of the teachers, i.e., the way in which the teacher talks to the children. There was a tacit assumption that if the teachers would converse more frequently to the children, for long periods of one-to-one contact, the children's language development would be accelerated. This change in the teachers' verbal behaviour should really be the first objective of the programme, although it was never specifically mentioned as such during the discussions.

In many ways then, this programme should not be seen as an attempt to implement pre-specified games or activities that would assist language development. Rather, it was a pilot effort to see whether, within the framework of normal nursery school life, the teachers could, on an *ad hoc* basis, redirect some of their time to provide the children with greater frequency and intensity of interaction with an adult speech model.

The Evaluation Design

The nursery school was organised into six classes, each containing twenty-five to thirty children. Three of these classes were selected to take part in the programme, and the remaining three were to act as controls. From each class a list was prepared of children likely to remain in the school during the year 1970–71, thus eliminating any older children likely to transfer to infant school at Christmas or Easter. In each class ten children were randomly selected from this list either to be experimental children (from Classes A, B and C) or to be controls (from Classes D, E and F), and for the experimental classes a further ten children were randomly selected to act as within class controls. Such children are referred to as the C.1 groups in the text and tables below,

---

[1] Unless otherwise specified, "teacher" refers to the nursery teacher, nursery assistant trainee nursery assistant or student (in the case of the playgroup).

as opposed to the C.2 children from control classes D, E and F. The play-group had twenty-five children attending each of its regular morning and afternoon sessions. The morning session was selected as the experimental period and the students from the College of Education attended at this time. The afternoon playgroup acted as a control. As with the nursery schools, ten experimental, C.1 and C.2 children were selected at random from a list of those likely to remain for three school terms.

Each of the 120 children thus selected were given the Reynell Develop-mental Language Scales (R.D.L.S.) and the pre-school version of the English Picture Vocabulary Test (E.P.V.T.) in September 1970, with the intention of retesting them in July 1971.

However, since the removal rate from the sample was so high, children leaving during the second half of the spring term and during the summer term were post-tested as they left.

This meant that information was obtained concerning the change in the children's expressive language and verbal comprehension (from the R.D.L.S.), and their listening comprehension (from the E.P.V.T.). Thus a measure of the success in achieving the first objective of the programme was obtained (see previous section). This was supplemented by a weekly report on each child's progress produced by its teacher.

To obtain information on which of the nursery activities was best suited to the programme (objective 2), the teachers were asked to keep two sorts of record. One was on display in the classroom and recorded the daily contacts between the teacher and the experimental children, giving information as to the activity concerned and its duration. The second was completed weekly by the teacher, and consisted of comments on each of twenty-one activities which were found most frequently in the nursery classroom.

It was decided that the only feasible way to collect information pertinent to the third objective (the recording of verbal activities during the normal teaching day), was to introduce an observer into the nursery classroom to record the verbal interactions. This, incidentally, allowed us to assess the the tacit objective mentioned above, of changing the verbal behaviour of the teachers.

Thus the formation for the year's activities was as follows:

1. The experimental, C.1 and C.2 children were tested during September 1970.
2. The teachers, assistants and students from the experimental classes attended weekly and subsequently fortnightly meetings with the research worker. These meetings were used to discuss problems and discoveries which the teachers had made during the previous week, to modify the recording procedures, and to discuss, in more general terms, language development in young children. These meetings were jointly chaired by the Project staff and the headmistress of the nursery school, and the content was largely determined by the teachers.
3. During the first part of the spring term 1971, an additional research worker obtained information concerning verbal interactions in the classroom.
4. From the second half of the spring term until the end of the summer term, post-tests were given to any child that left either the nursery school or the playgroup.

Results

1. *The Children's Language Development*

The data presented here show how the children's performance on measures of language development changed in the course of the year. Since this programme was considered to be only a pilot exercise, the importance of the changes in the children's score on these tests should not be over-emphasised. As a result of high drop-out rates, the number of children who were tested at pre- and post-test was very small. This, coupled with the exploratory nature of the work over the first one and a half school terms, means that the number of children receiving prolonged experimental treatment from the programme is very small indeed. These child test results are therefore presented for completeness sake, and are not intended to show the extent to which the type of activities developed in the programme can influence children's language development.

Table 1

The Mean Ages of the Children at Pre- and Post-Test in Months

	Number of children*	Mean age at pre-test	Mean age at post-test
Experimental			
Classes A	8	46·9	54·9
B	10	47·6	56·3
C	9	46·7	54·1
Playgroup AM	7	47·7	55·9
Control 1			
Classes A	3	49·6	57·3
B	7	50·1	58·4
C	5	39·6	48·6
Playgroup AM	3	49·7	58·7
Control 2			
Classes D	6	45·0	53·3
E	4	37·7	46·7
F	5	46·4	54·4

* By the end of the year the high turnover had reduced completely the playgroup C.2 group.

The change in scores between pre- and post-test was calculated for each child, and the average of this change in scores was calculated for each of the groups in the experimental design. Each score given is a standard score, which means that the actual score of each child is compared to the scores of other children from a national sample of its own age. The standard score then expresses how far above or below the average for its age the child is performing. For the R.D.L.S. the national average is 0·00 and for the E.P.V.T. it is 100, and 66 per cent of children score between −1·00 and +1·00 for the R.D.L.S., and 85 and 115 for the E.P.V.T. Anyone scoring below −1·00 (R.D.L.S.) or 85 (E.P.V.T.) is in the bottom 15 per cent of children on that test.

All the groups of children scored below the national average on the pretests except for control group 1, Class C, which had average scores on the expressive language and verbal comprehension parts of the Reynell Test of +0·54 and +0·50 respectively and control group 2, Class F, which had an average E.P.V.T. score of 102·00. The largest gain for the experimental group is in expressive language, see Table 2. However, when compared to the control

Table 2

The Mean Change in Standard Scores for the Various Groups on the English Picture Vocabulary Test and the Two Scales of the Reynell Developmental Language Scales

	Number of children	Mean change in expressive standard score	Mean change in verbal comprehension standard score	Mean change in E.P.V.T. standard score
Experimental				
Class A	8	+1·01	+0·55	+5·25
B	10	+0·67	+0·01	+1·60
C	9	+0·36	+0·65	−0·11
Playgroup AM	7	+0·91	+0·51	−0·14
Total	34	+0·71	+0·41	+3·7
Control 1				
Class A	3	+0·70	−0·70	+11·00
B	7	+0·83	+0·29	+5·86
C	5	−0·18	−0·20	+4·40
Playgroup AM	3	+0·50	+0·17	+0·33
Total	18	+0·47	−0·04	+5·40
Control 2				
Class D	6	+1·43	−0·03	+4·67
E	4	+0·23	+0·85	+5·75
F	5	+1·14	+0·02	−0·60
Total	15	+1·01	+0·23	+3·20

groups, the largest relative gain is for the verbal comprehension scores. In only two cases has an experimental group lost against the national norms in the course of the year, and both of these are very small losses in E.P.V.T. standard score. Similarly, the control groups show consistent gains against national norms, but without a control group not attending a pre-school institution it is impossible to ascribe these gains with any certainty to the effects of attendance at pre-school.

To summarise, these results appear not to show any effect that is solely due to the programme, except perhaps for some additional gains by the experimental children in verbal comprehension. However, all the groups of children have gained in the course of the year; this fact strongly suggests a beneficial effect of pre-school attendance but without extra controls this is not certain.

2. *Activities Found by the Teachers to be Most Useful for Language Interaction*

There are various problems in deciding which of the nursery class activities are most useful in language development work. Table 3 sets out the rank order

Table 3

Rank Order of Recorded Time Spent on Various Activities During Verbal Contact for Each Experimental Class in the Nursery

	Class A	Class B	Class C	Mean rank
Home corner	13	8	13	11·6
Large blocks	9	12	12	11·0
Sand	16	7	11	11·6
Water	10	17	15	14·0
Painting	5	16	10	10·3
Modelling	12	11	14	12·5
Collage	4	9	6	6·3
Woodwork	19	20·5	18	19·2
Book corner	6	5	8	6·3
Music corner	17	13	17	15·6
Singing	15	15	21	17·0
Bathing dolls	11	19	20	16·6
Cooking	18	10	2	10·0
Meal times	8	4	5	5·6
After-rest	20·5	20·5	16	19·0
Mid-session group time	20·5	18	19	19·2
Table toys	14	1	7	7·3
Dolls house	7	14	9	10·0
Outside visit	1	3	1	1·6
Conversation—Miscellaneous	3	2	3	2·6
Games and puzzles	2	6	4	4·0

of time spent by the nursery teachers with the children on various activities. The results from the playgroup have not been included since the apparatus and space available were different.

As can be seen from this table, there is great variation in the order of activities across classes. This is a reflection of both the teacher's interest in a particular activity and also, because of small sample sizes, the interests of individual children. Interestingly, the activities that come out as absorbing most time are diverse and each have characteristics of value to language work.

Outside visits certainly used up most of the teacher's time partly because each visit, even to the local shops or the neighbouring College of Education, took a minimum of 30 minutes. But their advantages were twofold. Firstly, the teachers took only one or two children at a time, and this reduced interference with the development of a dialogue. And secondly, fresh subject matter in a new context for the teacher/child relationship allowed for the exploration of vocabulary and question/answer sessions.

Conversation and miscellaneous is a category of interactions that are usually short in duration and not related to a particular activity. They contrast strongly with outside visits in content, but are found as the second most time-consuming one-to-one interaction. The assumption behind this section is that the length of time spent on an activity is an indicator of its usefulness in language development work. For most activities this is true, since most are teacher-initiated; and given that the teacher received constant feedback concerning the success of the activities in other groups, she could select those activities of agreed worth, but this does not hold for the conversation and miscellaneous activities, since these are largely child-initiated. However, the teachers did report this to be a beneficial starting point for one-to-one interactions because in general the functional aspect of language was predominant; the child was using language as a tool to achieve an immediate goal.

Another example of contrasting activities that come high in Table 3 are those of meal-times and games and puzzles. The former is a gregarious activity with frequent interruptions; but it does allow sustained conversation, since the child is forced to remain stationary during the meal. Games and puzzles, on the other hand, were essentially solitary activities where quiet uninterrupted conversation could take place but which ended quite rapidly, since the child's attention was not constrained.

Two major types of activity that do not appear in Table 3 are outdoor games and imaginative play. The physical nature of the former precluded satisfactory verbal exchanges and the latter was avoided because it was agreed that teacher intervention was undesirable.

The results presented in Table 3 were obtained from the teacher class record form. This form and the others mentioned below were completed by the teachers to document their work and so to ensure equal coverage for all children on all activities. The resulting documentation was also very useful in the weekly discussion groups, where ideas were exchanged on how to encourage different types of children to enter into verbal interactions concerning various activities.

There follow three completed examples of the record forms used by the teachers. It should be noted that the form on which comments were made concerning the utility of the various nursery school activities for language development work is not included. The teachers soon decided that the comments that could be made on a weekly basis did not change, and this form became redundant.

It can be seen that the recorded time spent with each child varied considerably from week to week. It was in general somewhere between 15 and 20 minutes, but the occasional outside visits increased the time for that week to about 75 minutes. Again, it should be emphasised that the times recorded do not constitute the total amount of one-to-one interactions that took place, but only that which was of sufficient duration or with sufficient purpose to merit recording.

3. The Classroom Observations

The purpose of the classroom observations was to obtain information on the impact of the programme on the language use of the children and on whether the experimental teachers' behaviour in the classroom was different from that of the control teachers.

It was necessary to obtain data on all 120 children for whom language test data was available and to do so within a 12-week period. This data gathering took place during the first part of the Spring Term 1971. The first 4 weeks were spent familiarising the children and teachers to the presence of the observer, and one week was spent revising the observation schedule (for details see Appendix I).

It was decided to use a time sampling technique like that of Medley[1] but

---

[1] D. M. Medley, C. Schluck and M. Ames, *A Manual for PROSE recorders*, Education Testing Service, New Jersey, 1968.

Child's Name	Monday	Tuesday	Wednesday	Thursday	Friday	General Remarks to other teachers
A	Water 3 mins D.H.	Game 5 mins D.H.			Painting 2 mins D.H.	10 mins
B	Drawing 2 mins D.H.	Game 5 mins D.H.			Painting 2 mins D.H.	9 mins
C	Game 3 mins D.H.		Visit to Cutty Sark Anne 90 mins			93 mins
D	Game 3 mins D.H.	Book 4 mins D.H.	Book 2 mins D.H.	Outdoors 2 mins D.H. Wet Sand 5 mins D.H.	A	16 mins
E	Game 3 mins D.H.	Book 4 mins D.H.		Outdoors 2 mins D.H. Wet Sand 5 mins D.H.		14 mins
F	Conversation 2 mins D.H. About Weekend		Conversation 3 mins D.H.	Outdoors 2 mins D.H.		7 mins
G	Game 2 mins D.H.		Visit to Cutty Sark Anne 60 mins			62 mins
H	Cutting Out 5 mins D.H.		Drawing 4 mins D.H.		A	9 mins
I	Cutting Out 5 mins D.H.		Visits to Cutty Sark Anne 90 mins		Doll's House 2 mins D.H.	97 mins

Child's Record Form

Week	Home corner	Large blocks	Sand	Water	Painting	Modelling	Collage	Woodwork	Book corner	Music corner	Singing
1	Absent all week										
2	4 mins				Drawing 4 mins				5 mins		
3							3 mins				
4	3 mins		2 mins		Drawing 2 mins 5 mins						
5					Drawing 3 mins 3 mins						
6	4 mins										
7							Junk construction 3 mins		4 mins		
8				3 mins	2 mins						
9					Drawing 4 mins 2 mins						
10							4 mins				
11											
12											

Child's Record Form—continued

Week	Bathing dolls	Cooking	Meal times	After rest period	Mid-session group time	Table toys	Dolls house	Shop	Others specify
1									
2							5 mins		Puppets 2 mins
3		5 mins							Making Puppets 8 mins
4									Conversation re. clothes 5 mins
5						5 mins			
6						3 mins			
7									
8						5 mins			
9						5 mins			
10						5 mins 6 mins			
11									
12									

Weekly Child Progress Sheet

Name: Margaret Meads   Summer Term

Week 1 8 mins Absent once. Very shy, but not unwilling.	*Week 7* 8 mins Time for sessions limited due to Exhibition
Week 2 22 mins Tried to get in a lot of sessions to try to overcome her shyness with adults. She is not so shy with the other children.	*Week 8* 97 mins One long session—visit to Cutty Sark. Talked, but not volubly.
Week 3 10 mins Absent once. *Week 4* 14 mins Absent once. Still shy during sessions, but comes to tell you things that need attention occasionally.	*Week 9* *Week 10* Margaret is still rather quiet and shy, but takes it all in. She does now, on occasion, come up and offer some remark, which she certainly would not have done earlier in the year.
Week 5 12 mins Does not always join in group conversations—but listens very carefully.	*Week 11*
Week 6 Absent once. Has not yet overcome her shyness.	*Week 12*

extending the time interval from 25 to 60 seconds. In other words, every 60 seconds the child was observed and its behaviour at that moment recorded. For each child this was repeated five times, so that one individual record took 5 minutes to gather. The observer then transferred her attention to another child and spent a few minutes familiarising herself with the child's activities and mood, before taking its record of behaviour.

The experimental design was the same as that used for the language testing. Each of the twelve groups of ten children in the design were observed during a half-day period; each child was observed on two 5-minute occasions during each period and a total of approximately 90 minutes of observation was obtained for each child by the end of the 7-week observation sequence. A system of rotation of observation time was employed so that each of the twelve groups and each child within a group was observed at different times during the day; this was done to randomise the effects on the results of the weather, the proximity to the end of the day, etc.

In general, it would have been preferable to observe the experimental children and their teachers before the programme started, to establish each experimental class's base-line score on the schedule, and then to note changes from this base-line during the programme by a second set of observations. Ho.'ever pupil mobility and the timing of the programme prohibited this approach and an assumption had to be made that idiosyncratic features of individual classrooms and teachers would be randomised across the experimental and control groups. The provision of within-class control children was another attempt to compensate for this weakness of the design.

In the tables presented below the following abrreviations are used:

E.N.T.	experimental nursery teacher
E.N.A.	experimental nursery assistant
E.T.N.A.	experimental trainee nursery assistant
C.N.T.	control nursery teacher
C.N.A.	control nursery assistant
C.T.N.A.	control trainee nursery assistant

The Nursery Class Observation Schedule (N.C.O.S.) provided a wealth of information concerning the children's activities in the nursery classroom (see Appendix I). However, only data pertinent to the evaluation of the programme, particularly that concerning the teachers' interactions with the children, will be reported.

The number of occasions that the children were observed and a teacher was available to interact with them was approximately only one-third of the total observations (see Table 4). However, it was possible to distinguish a difference between the experimental and control classes in the availability of the teachers to the children. The experimental teachers were available more often than the control teachers, and in the nursery school the experimental teachers were present significantly more often than both the experimental nursery assistants and experimental trainee nursery assistants. However, the experimental nursery assistants, who attended the fortnightly discussion sessions, recorded less availability than the experimental trainee nursery assistants (see Table 4).

This above finding is supported by Tables 5 and 6, where the experimental nursery assistants, unlike the experimental trainee assistants, had significantly

Table 4

The Frequency with which the Teachers were Available to the Children

	E.N.T.	E.N.A.	E.T.N.A.	C.N.T.	C.N.A.	C.T.N.A.	Total
Nursery	537	162	173	152	106	95	1,340
Playgroup	3	170	116	3	35	79	393

The total number of observations in the nursery school = 3,189.
The total number of observations in the playgroup = 497.

In the nursery
E.N.T.s were available to the children more often than E.N.A.s ($\chi^2 = 28.9$, d.f. = 1, $p < 0.001$).
E.N.T.s were available to the children more often than E.T.N.A.s ($\chi^2 = 18.3$, d.f. = 1, $p < 0.001$).

In the playgroup
E.N.A. was available to the children more often than the E.T.N.A. ($\chi^2 = 13.7$, d.f. = 1, $p < 0.001$).

Table 5

The Frequency of Specific One-to-One Interactions

	E.N.T.	E.N.A.	E.T.N.A.	C.N.T.	C.N.A.	C.T.N.A.
Nursery						
Verbal	159	60	60	51	30	27
Non-verbal	39	33	20	13	17	14
Playgroup						
Verbal	2	27	31	2	11	19
Non-verbal	0	4	6	0	3	1

The only significant comparison of the frequency of specific one-to-one interactions was:
  The E.N.T.s have significantly more specific one-to-one verbal interactions than the
  E.N.A.s ($\chi^2 = 7\cdot83$, d.f. $= 1$, $0\cdot01 > p > 0\cdot001$).
All the following comparisons produced non-significant χ^2 (i.e., $p > 0\cdot05$):
  Overall experimental teachers vs. overall control teachers.
  Nursery experimental teachers vs. nursery control teachers.
  Playgroup experimental teachers vs. playgroup control teachers.
  E.N.T. vs. E.T.N.A.s, E.T.N.A.s vs. E.N.A.s, C.N.T.s vs. C.N.A.s, C.N.T.s vs.
  C.T.N.A.s, C.N.A.s vs. C.T.N.A.s, E.N.T.s vs. C.N.T.s, E.N.A.s vs. C.N.A.s,
  E.T.N.A.s vs. C.T.N.A.s.

Table 6

The Frequency of General Verbal Interactions

	E.N.T.	E.N.A.	E.T.N.A.	C.N.T.	C.N.A.	C.T.N.A.
Nursery						
Verbal	400	77	107	110	41	54
Non-verbal	49	38	22	15	8	15
Playgroup						
Verbal	3	132	81	3	27	66
Non-verbal	0	6	10	0	4	1

The following significant χ^2 comparisons are obtained (for the nursery groups):
  The E.N.T.s have significantly more general verbal interactions than E.N.A.s
    ($\chi^2 = 31\cdot2$, d.f. $= 1$, $p < 0\cdot001$).
  The E.N.T.s have significantly more general verbal interactions than E.T.N.A.s
    ($\chi^2 = 3\cdot52$, d.f. $= 1$, $0\cdot05 > p > 0\cdot02$).
  The E.T.N.A.s have significantly more general verbal interactions than E.N.A.s
    ($\chi^2 = 8\cdot70$, d.f. $= 1$, $0\cdot01 > p > 0\cdot001$).
  The C.N.T.s have significantly more general verbal interactions than C.N.A.s
    ($\chi^2 = 8\cdot93$, d.f. $= 1$, $0\cdot01 > p > 0\cdot001$).
  The C.N.T.s have significantly more general verbal interactions than C.N.T.A.s
    ($\chi^2 = 3\cdot56$, d.f. $= 1$, $0\cdot05 > p > 0\cdot02$).
The following comparisons are not significant with respect to the frequency of general
  verbal interactions (i.e., $p > 0\cdot05$):
  All experimental teachers vs. all control teachers.
  Nursery experimental teachers vs. nursery control teachers.
  Playgroup experimental teachers vs. playgroup control teachers.
  E.N.A.s vs. E.T.N.A.s, C.N.A.s vs. C.T.N.A.s, E.N.T.s vs. C.N.T.s, E.N.A.s vs.
  C.N.A.s, E.T.N.A.s vs, C.T.N.A.s.

less verbal specific interactions with the children and gave significantly less verbal information than the experimental nursery teachers. The experimental nursery assistants were also the only group for whom the frequency of information and direction-giving was equal—in all other cases the staff were giving information more frequently than they gave directions. It would seem, therefore, that in the experimental classes the nursery assistants were taking on more of the administrative duties in order to release the experimental nursery teachers for the development of contacts with the children.

However, although the experimental nursery teachers were available to the children more often than any other, they were not recorded significantly more often in one-to-one verbal interactions than either the experimental trainee assistants or the control nursery teachers. Also, although both the experimental and control nursery teachers recorded more verbal behaviour than either the assistants or trainee assistants in their classrooms, there was no difference between the teachers in the type of one-to-one verbal interactions (see Tables 7 and 8).

Table 7

The Frequency of General Verbal Interactions that can be Categorised as Procedural or Informational

	E.N.T.	E.N.A.	E.T.N.A.	C.N.T.	C.N.A.	C.T.N.A.
Nursery						
Procedural	101	27	28	37	19	19
Informational	198	30	52	31	13	23
Playgroup						
Procedural	0	21	20	1	3	7
Informational	2	21	40	1	10	23

The following significant χ^2 are obtained:
  The experimental adults overall have significantly more informational related verbal behaviour than the control adults ($\chi^2 = 4\cdot30$, d.f. $= 1$, $0\cdot05 > p > 0\cdot02$).
  The experimental adults in the nursery have significantly more informational related verbal behaviour than the control adults in the nursery ($\chi^2 = 5\cdot30$, d.f. $= 1$, $0\cdot05 > p > 0\cdot02$).
  The E.N.T.s in the nursery have significantly more informational related verbal behaviour than the E.N.A.s in the nursery ($\chi^2 = 3\cdot86$, d.f. $= 1$, $0\cdot05 > p > 0\cdot02$).
The following comparisons were not significant with respect to the amount of informational content in the verbal behaviour of the groups (i.e., $p > 0\cdot05$):
  In the playgroup
  Experimental adults vs. control adults.
  In the nursery
  E.N.T.s vs. E.T.N.A.s, E.N.A.s vs. E.T.N.A.s, C.N.T.s vs. C.N.A.s, C.N.T.s vs. C.T.N.A.s, C.N.A.s vs. C.T.N.A.s, E.N.T.s vs. C.N.T.s, E.N.A.s vs. C.N.A.s, E.T.N.A.s vs. C.T.N.A.s.

And further, although these differences in teacher behaviour are in the predicted direction, they are not reflected in the children's verbal behaviour. From Table 9, for instance, it can be seen that the self-initiated verbal interactions of the experimental children were a smaller proportion of their overall interactions than were those of the control children. And so, although the experimental children were involved in verbal behaviour more often than the control children, they initiated proportionately less of these interactions.

Table 8

The Frequency of One-to-One Verbal Interactions that can be Categorised as either Procedural or Informational

	E.N.T.	E.N.A.	E.T.N.A.	C.N.T.	C.N.A.	C.T.N.A.
Nursery						
Procedural	73	22	21	28	10	10
Informational	57	27	24	18	10	8
Playgroup						
Procedural	0	12	13	10	3	6
Informational	1	7	6	0	5	7

None of the comparisons showed any significant differences between groups in the relative frequencies of procedural and informational related one-to-one verbal interactions.

Table 9

The Frequency of Verbal Interactions where the Child is either the Initiator or Respondent

	Treatment group		
	Experimental children	Control 1 children	Control 2 children
Nursery			
Initiating	138	95	123
Responding	33	25	15
Playgroup			
Initiating	35	24	35
Responding	14	6	15

The following significant χ^2 are obtained:
There is an overall difference between experimental, C.1 and C.2 children in the amount of initiation of verbal behaviour ($\chi^2 = 8.68$, d.f. $= 2$, $0.02 > p > 0.01$).
The overall experimental children initiated less verbal behaviour than the C.2 children ($\chi^2 = 7.1$, d.f. $= 1$, $0.01 > p > 0.001$).
The overall C.2 initiated more verbal behaviour than the C.1 children ($\chi^2 = 5.40$, d.f. $= 1$, $0.05 > p > 0.02$).
In the nursery there is a significant difference between the experimental C.1 and C.2 children in the amount of initiated verbal behaviour ($\chi^2 = 5.69$, d.f. $= 2$, $0.05 > p > 0.02$).
In the nursery the C.2 children initiated more verbal behaviour than the experimental children ($\chi^2 = 4.12$, d.f. $= 1$, $0.05 > p > 0.02$).
In the nursery the C.2 children initiated more verbal behaviour than the C.1 children ($\chi^2 = 4.90$, d.f. $= 1$, $0.05 > p > 0.02$).
The following comparisons did not produce significant χ^2 (i.e., $p > 0.05$):
Overall experimental group vs. overall C.1 group.
Nursery experimental group vs. nursery C.1 group.
Playgroup experimental vs. playgroup C.1 vs. playgroup C.2 group.
Playgroup experimental children vs. nursery experimental children.
Playgroup C.1 children vs. nursery C.1 children.
Playgroup C.2 children vs. nursery C.2 children.

Conclusions

The programme has been shown by the results discussed above to be somewhat equivocal in its effects. Gains were made on all tests by all groups of children, regardless of the treatment received. This seems to indicate a beneficial effect of a pre-school experience on the language development of socially disadvantaged children; but without an extra control group which did not attend a pre-school institution this effect is not really demonstrated. However, no particular gains due to the programme are evidenced by the test score data.

A diverse pattern emerged from the assessment of which nursery activities were most useful for language development work. It did appear that the most successful activities were those connected with outside visits; where the teacher had only a very small group of children to deal with and where the unfamiliar context of the teacher/child interaction provided an extra stimulus for language work.

It has been shown that the programme did result in changes in the teachers' behaviour in the classroom. The teachers seemed to have arranged the organisation of the classroom so that the assistants took on more of the managerial duties. In this way the teachers themselves were more available for interaction with the children. But the nature of the interaction entered into by the teachers in the experimental classes did not differ from those of the control nursery teachers.

Appendix I

The Construction of the Nursery Class Observation Schedule (N.C.O.S.)

It was not possible to use any sophisticated recording apparatus in the classrooms (e.g., tape recorder or videotape), so it was necessary to develop a means of recording the children's behaviour using just pencil and paper. Various observation schedules have been developed before to make such records, however, none as far as was known, had been published for English nursery classes. The work of McGrew[1] had not been published at this time.

Accordingly, it was necessary to refer to American work in this field. Two schedules seem most appropriate for our purposes—the Personal Record of School Experiences (P.R.O.S.E.) and the Observational Schedule and Record Form 5 Verbal (O.S.C.A.R. 5V).[2,3,4] The former was a record of an individual child's behaviour and O.S.C.A.R. 5V focused on the overt verbal behaviour of the teacher.

In synthesising these two schedules and making modifications to meet the particular requirements of the present study, the result was the observation schedule, which is described below. It will be seen that the schedule records twenty-six items of behaviour, each with several possible categories. The intention is to document the behavioural context of individual children, covering both the child himself, peers and teachers. The items can be broken down in the following manner:

Items 1–3
The nature of the interaction that the child was having during the observation period.

Items 4–10
The verbal and non-verbal behaviour of the adult, if present, taking part in the interaction.

Items 11–16 and 21
The verbal and non-verbal behaviour of the subject child (S).

Items 17–20
The verbal and non-verbal behaviour of any peer (if there is one) with whom S is having an interaction.

Items 22–26
The context (time, activity, location, etc.) within which the child (S) was observed.

There now follows a detailed account of each of the categories within these items and lastly a specimen of the observation schedule itself. In general, each of the categories are mutually exclusive within any item.

---

[1] W. C. McGrew, *An ethological study of children's behaviour*, London Academic Press, 1972.

[2] D. M. Medley and H. E. Mitzel, "A technique for measuring classroom behaviour", *Journal of Educational Psychology*, 49:86–92, 1958.

[3] D. M. Medley, C. Schluck and M. Ames, *A manual for PROSE recorders*, E.T.S., N.J., 1968.

[4] D. M. Medley, *OSCAR goes to nursery school: a new technique for recording pupil behaviour*, E.T.S., N.J., 1969.

The categories used to describe the child and its interactions were as follows:

Item 1

If S was involved in a specific one-to-one interaction, it was recorded whether S initiated the interaction or was responding to the initiative of another.

Initiator (INIT)[1]—marked if S was the initiator
Respondent (RESP)—marked if S was the respondent
Left blank if no specific one-to-one interaction was taking place.

Item 2

If either category in item 1 was present, it was recorded with whom the interaction was taking place.

Nursery Teacher (NT)	The teacher in charge of the nursery classroom
Nursery Assistant (NA)	A qualified assistant in the nursery classroom
Trainee Nursery Assistant (TNA)	An unqualified assistant in the nursery classroom
Playgroup Leader (PL)	The leader in charge of the playgroup
Playgroup Assistant (PA)	A qualified assistant in the playgroup
Student Teacher (ST)	Trainee nursery teachers who spent some time in the nursery classroom as part of their course requirements. N.B.—In the playgroup these acted as experimental teachers
Observer (OBS)	The person recording the behaviour
Other (OTH)	Any other adult
Peer Male (P(M))	Any other boy of same age
Peer Female (P(F))	Any other girl of same age

Item 3

This describes the social grouping that the child was in at the time the behaviour was recorded. N.B.—Since a one-to-one interaction is possible within a group, this item was recorded in conjunction with item 2. The specific categories are the same as item 2 with the addition of:

Self (SELF)	Marked if the child was alone
Group (GRP)	More than one peer present

Item 4

This item describes the verbal behaviour, concerned with non-teaching procedures, of any adult interacting with the child.

---

[1] The capital letters in parentheses are those used to denote the categories on the observation schedule itself.

Permission (PERM)	Allows S to do something previously requested, e.g., "Yes, you may go outside"
Directions (DIRECT)	Imperatives without affect, e.g., "Wash your hands"
Caution (CAUTN)	Expresses concern for S when engaged in a behaviour that could be harmful, e.g., "Be careful or you will fall off the swing"
Control Indirect (CONT(IND))	Getting S to comply with adult wishes through the use of positive affect, e.g., "Good, everybody. Let's sit quietly"
Control Direct (CONT(DI))	Getting S to comply with adult wishes using negative affect, e.g., "Stop playing with the water you naughty boy"
Co-operative seeking (COOP(SKNG))	Seeking the help of S when working towards a goal, e.g., "Will you help me lay this table?"
Information seeking (INF(SKNG))	Seeking information concerned with procedural matters, e.g., "Where did you put those cups?"

Item 5

The categories describe verbal activities of adults that could be broadly called teaching.

Information sharing that is activity related (INF SH(AR))	e.g., "This ball is red"
Information sharing that is not activity related (INF SH(NAR))	e.g., "Teeth should be cleaned after meals"
Explanations that are activity related (EXP(AR))	e.g., "This ball bounces because it's made of rubber"
Explanations that are not activity related (EXP(NAR))	e.g., "We clean our teeth to stop tooth decay"
Requesting information or explanations that are activity related (RQST(AR))	e.g., "What colour is this ball?"
Requesting information or explanations that are not activity related (RQST(NAR))	e.g., "Why do we clean our teeth?"

Item 6

The categories in this item indicate either verbal or non-verbal expressions of affect and more neutral acceptance or rejection of S's actions.

	Verbal	*Non-verbal*
Affection (AFFECT)—Spontaneous positive affect	"You are a nice boy"	Cuddling, smiling
Appeasement (APPEAS)—Giving comfort when the cause for distress is not obvious	"Don't cry. It will be all right"	Hugging, cuddling

Comforting (COMFORT)— Giving comfort after obviously distressing incident	"Where are you hurt?"	Rubbing, stroking
Supporting (SUPPORT)— Praising S, with enthusiasm	"That's very good, how clever"	Smiling, nodding
Approving (APPROV)— Indicating in a neutral way that S is correct	"That's right"	Nodding
Acknowledging (ACKNOW)— Indicating that S's activity has been noted but with no further feedback	"Yes", "Ah ha"	Raising hand, raising eyebrow
Rebuking (REBUK)— Criticising, showing displeasure	"That's very bad"	Frowning, pushing away
Rejecting (REJECT)— Indicating that what S is doing is not acceptable, without showing negative affect	"That's not right"	Putting aside object handed to her
Ignoring (IGNOR)— No response to S's initiative		

Item 7

Unlike items 4 and 5, which were concerned with classroom management and teaching respectively, this item describes other possible adult roles in the classroom. Again these roles can be expressed verbally or non-verbally.

	Verbal	*Non-verbal*
Assisting (ASST)— The adult helps S when requested	"That piece goes here"	Helps S to button coat
Taking over role (TOR)— The adult does activity that S has been doing or might want to do	Sings a song for child	Shows S how monkeys walk
Acting as a Peer (PEER)— The adult acts like a child, either in a group or with just one S without being a leader	"Please Mummy can I have some milk?"	Plays in the Wendy corner
Leading (LEAD)— Adult and S doing the same activity under the teacher's direction	Saying a nursery rhyme	Marching, dancing

Verbal (VERBL)—If either items 6 or 7 were verbal this category was marked.

Item 8

This describes the ongoing context of adult behaviour within which the specific behaviour recorded took place.

Listening/watching (LW)	The adult is inactive but paying attention to S's behaviour
Supervising (SUPER)	The adult moves around among the S's who are engaged in activities

Available for help (AVL HLP)   The adult is not paying attention to S's
                                  but is available for help

Housekeeping (HSK)   The adult is engaged in chores that pre-
                                  clude interaction with the children

Item 9

This item records the person to whom the adults behaviour is directed.

Self (SELF)   The S under observation

Other (OTHER)   Either a peer of S or another adult

Others (OTHERS)   More than one peer or adult

Group (GRP)   The total group of children in the class-
                    room, e.g., to tell a story

Item 10

This refers to both the type of physical contact and the social distance between the adult and S.

Positive contact (CON(POS))   Cuddling or sitting on adult's knee

Negative contact (CON(NEG))   Adult pushes S away

Distance close (DIST(CLSE))   S is closer to adult than peers

Distance medium (DIST(MED))   S is in the middle of a group

Distance distant (DIST(DIST))   S is at the extremity of a group

Item 11

This records the verbal behaviour of S under observation. This item particularly takes into account the context within which the behaviour occurs, in order to obtain a diversity of categories, i.e., the same behaviour can be recorded in a number of contexts.

Aggressive (AGGRESS)	Name calling or cursing	"You're rotten"
Manipulating (MANIP)	S attempts to direct or control the behaviour of others	"Come and play with me"
Resisting (RESISTING)	S openly fights back against an attack or resists a request or command	"No, I won't"
Disrupting (DISRUPT)	S intervenes into another's ongoing activity	"That's a silly game"
Attention seeking (ATTNSK)	S attempts to get the attention of a peer or adult without behaving inappropriately	"Look at my house"
Leading (LEADING)	S is the leader of a group, who are following S's directions	"I will be the father and you can be a baby"

Sharing (SHARING)	S gives something voluntarily or upon request	"Here is some dough"
Helping (HELPING)	S helps voluntarily or when requested	"I'll do up your coat"
Co-operating (COOPERAT)	S is working towards a common goal with peer or adult	"That piece goes on top"
Integrating (INTEG)	S is involved in mutual give and take relationship	Singing in a group
Affection (AFFECT)	S gives spontaneous expression of warmth directed towards peers or adults	"I think you are nice"
Requesting (REQUEST)	S seeks help or information	"What is that?"
Informing (INFORM)	S shares ideas or interests	"We have a dog"
Explanation (EXPLAIN)	S gives more detailed information or explanations	"We can't go out yet, it's still raining"
Absorbed (ABSORBED)	S pays close attention to the on going activity— may produce egocentric speech	"I'm a fireman going up the ladder"
Compliant (COMPLIANT)	S submits to the requests of others	"Yes, I'll take it to the nature table"
Internal stimulation (INTERNST)	S pays no attention to others	Murmurs or sings to himself

Item 12

This item records the non-verbal equivalents of the behaviour categorised in item 11. The definitions are the same, except for the addition of six categories and the exclusion of manipulating, informing, requesting, explaining and leading.

Aggressive (AGGRESS)	Kicking, hitting
Resisting (RESISTING)	Hitting back against other's attack
Disrupting (DISRUPT)	Knocks over other's tower of bricks
Attention seeking (ATTNSK)	Tugging at clothes or waving hand
Sharing (SHARING)	Giving others materials
Helping (HELPING)	Doing up buttons, carrying this for teacher
Co-operating (COOPERAT)	Pulling another in the cart
Integrating (INTEGRAT)	Taking part in pretend games in Wendy corner
Affection (AFFECT)	Smiling, cuddling
Absorbed (ABSORBED)	Close involvement with activity
Compliant (COMPLIANT)	Washes hands upon request

Internal stimulation (INTERNST)	Rocks back and forth on floor
Distracted (DISTRCTD)	Whilst appearing to be doing an activity is in fact paying attention to other things
Indecisive wandering (INDESW)	Moves around the room without paying particular attention to anything
Ignoring (IGNOR)	Does not respond to another's initiative
Observes passively (OBSPASS)	Whilst not engaged in any activity just sits and watches inattentively what others are doing
Avoidance (AVOID)	Moves away from an unpleasant situation
Listening/watching (LW)	Pays close attention to the activity of another

Item 13
This refers to the nature of the contact that the subject has with the material with which he is in contact.

Fantasy (FANTASY)	S is engaged in acting out some role or situation
Work (WORK)	S is involved in some socially useful activity such as wiping down a table
Convergent (CONVGNT)	S is engaged in activity with a definite goal e.g., a jigsaw puzzle
Divergent (DIVGNT)	S is engaged in an activity where he sets the goal, e.g., building with Lego
Repetition (REPET)	S is engaged in a repetitious unstructured behaviour, e.g., swinging on a door
Exploratory (EXPLOR)	S is investigating an object, situation or materials, e.g., the inside of a clock

Item 14
This item refers to clearly expressed emotions shown by the S under observation.

| Positive affect (POS(AF)) | S is laughing or smiling |
| Negative affect (NEG(AF)) | S is crying or frowning |

Item 15
This item uses the same categories as in item 10, but to describe the physical contact and social distance between S and any peer if they are engaged in a specific interaction.

Item 16
This item records the level of physical activity of the S and whether this is accompanied by a change in location.

Change location, high activity (LHA)	Change in location with vigorous movement of arms and legs, e.g., running
Change location, moderate activity (LMA)	Change in location with more restrained limb movement, e.g., walking
High activity (HA)	No location change and vigorous movement, e.g., jumping

Moderate activity (MA)   No location change with moderate movement, e.g., reading in a group

Low activity (LA)   Only slight bodily movement, e.g., sitting passively

Items 17–20

These items have the same categories as items 11–14, but refer to the behaviour of the peer with whom the subject child is having a specific interaction.

Item 21

(This item and those up to 26 were recorded on the reverse side of the observation schedule.) The categories recorded in this item refer to infrequently occurring behaviour that accompany specific interactions between peers. They are used to describe the behaviour of the subject child, and are rather heterogeneous.

Comforting other child (COMFORT OTH)   The child shows concern with another child's distress

Yawning (YAWNING)   The child yawns

Crying (CRYING)   The child is crying

Accident (ACCIDENT)   The child falls, knocks himself or in general injures himself

Teasing (TEASING)   The child taunts and verbally provokes another

Disobedient (DISOBEY)   The child refuses to comply with the wishes of another

Temper (TEMPER)   The child demonstrates anger usually after frustration of its wishes

Rejected by Group (REJDBY GRP) The child approaches a group of peers but is not allowed access to their activity

Imitating (IMITATING)   The child copies the activity of a peer

Item 22

Here is noted the location of the subject child during the period of observation

Main room (MAIN ROOM)   The central classroom of the child, where most of the indoor activities take place

Bathroom (BATHROOM)   The area of the toilets and the washbasins

Music Room (MUSIC ROOM)   A room shared by all classes in the nursery school used for separate group activities

Club Room (CLUB ROOM)   Another shared room, particularly suited for small group activities, including the television set

Cloak Room (CLOAKROOM)   The area where coats are hung

Annexe (ANNEXE)   In the playgroup this room was used for painting, clay and woodwork

Outside (OUTSIDE)   The outdoor areas in the nursery school

Other (OTHER)   Activities more remote from the building, particularly visits to the shops

Item 23

The categories are common everyday occurrences that are more regular than those activities itemized in 25 and 26.

Toilet (TOILET)
Washing (WASHING)   These activities take place mainly in the bathroom area and are self-explanatory
Dressing (DRESSING)

Eating (EATING)   The full-time children have a midday meal and the playgroup children have something to eat mid-session
Drinking (DRINKING)

Resting (RESTING)   The sleep taken by some full-time nursery children

Item 24

The occasions during the day when definite group behaviours take place are recorded in this item.

Before Meal   The period between 11.30 and 12.00 in the
(BEFORE MEAL)   nursery classroom when all the children are grouped under their teacher's supervision for a story and then for washing, etc., in preparation for meal time

Meal time   The period between 12.00 and 12.30 when the
(MEAL TIME)   nursery children eat their lunch under adult supervision

Mid-Session Break   The period of about 30 minutes in the play-
(MID M/A)   group when the children are grouped under adult supervision for a snack, story and special games

Rest (REST)   The period between 12.30 and 1.30 when most full-time nursery children are resting or asleep

After rest (AFTER REST)   A less well-defined period during which the children are being dressed, drinking milk, etc.

Item 25

These categories refer to types of group behaviour that can accompany any of the specific activities listed in item 26.

Building (BUILDING)   Construction can take place using building blocks, small bricks, etc.

Singing (SINGING)   These activities can take place in conjunction
Dancing (DANCING)   with many of the specific activities

Colours (COLOURS)
Shapes (SHAPES)   The development of these skills can be achieved
Numbers/Letters   using puzzles, dough, etc.
(NOS/LTS)

Item 26
These main activities that take place in the nursery classroom and the play-group are listed here. Some activities are exclusive to the nursery (*) and some to the playgroup (†). Other activities take place indoors for the playgroup and out of doors for the nursery school (‡). Most of these activities are self-explanatory.

Water (WATER)
Dough (DOUGH)
Painting (PTNG)
Crayons (CRAYONS)
Collage (COLLG)
Dolls House (DOLL HSE)
Garage (GARAGE)—A small model garage for toy cars
* Puppet Theatre (PUPPTH)
Book Corner (BOOK CNR)
Home Corner (HOME CNR)
Shop (SHOP)
† Hospital (HOSPITAL)
Hairdressers (HAIRDS)
Jigsaw (JIGSAW)
Construction Games (CONST GMS)—Lego, Stickle brix, etc.
Table Toys (TABLE T)—Small model people, cars, etc.
Musical Instruments (MUSIC INST.)
* Tape Recorder (TAPE RECOR)
* Records (RECORDS)
Television (T.V.)
Puppets (PUPPET)
Dressing Up (DRESSUP)—Old clothes were kept in a special corner for this
Telephone (TELPH)
* Pets (PETS)
* Plants (PLANTS)
* Large Blocks (LARGE BLKS)—Large wooden blocks that could be arranged for different activities
Chore Equipment (CHORE EQ.)—Brooms, brushes, etc.
* Gypsy House (GYPSY HSE)
* Boat (BOAT)
* Swing (SWING)
‡ Slide (SLIDE)
‡ See Saw (SEE SAW)
* Barrel Tunnel (BARREL TUN)
* Climbing Frame (CLIMB FR)
* Play House (PLAY HSE)
‡ Boxes (BOXES)
‡ Tyres (TYRES)
‡ Prams (PRAMS)
‡ Wheel Toys (WHEELT)—Bikes, scooters, etc.
† Woodwork (WOODWORK)

Part Five

The Junior School Language Work
J. H. Barnes

The Junior School Language Work

The work reported here had begun in the local E.P.A. schools before the arrival of the London Project and was continued after the Project had been disbanded. For a two year period (from 1969 to 1971) the Project added extra ingredients: resources, evaluation and different ways of seeing the various problems. The work had two principal components, one of purpose and the other of method. The intention was to gear the curriculum of E.P.A. junior schools more closely to the perceived spoken language needs of E.P.A. children. The most significant aspect of the method was that the teachers who were to implement the curriculum were involved in the process of developing it: both diagnosing situations that needed and could sustain intervention by teachers, and creating teaching materials to facilitate this.

From the point of view of the E.P.A. Project a partnership with those already involved in the language work was attractive. To begin with, there was a general climate of educational opinion at the end of the 1960s in favour of attempts to modify the linguistic behaviour of children living in educational priority areas. There was much discussion of "linguistic deprivation"; there was literature on the subject, most of which at that time came from the United States. In principle there were a range of linguistic theories which could be used to inform whatever activities were developed. And work on a junior school language curriculum was paralleled by the national E.P.A. research effort, where an attempt was being made to test the effects of structured learning situations on the linguistic behaviour of E.P.A. children in nursery classes and playgroups.[1]

Collaboration also seemed sensible for practical reasons. It meant that there could be co-ordinated rather than competing curriculum development work in the Project schools. It meant, for the Project, that some of the groundwork had already been done; to use the terminology of the specialists on how to promote innovation—the situation was already "unfrozen".[2] It meant further, that the activity would be backed by the authority of the ILEA Inspectorate. There need be no search for credibility on this occasion; it was built into the terms of the contract.

But there were costs as well as benefits to the Project. Involvement meant that the considerations of the E.P.A. Project were only a number, among many other points of view being accommodated. The programme was, for instance, only seen as a field trial by the Project research workers. For most of the other people involved it was part of a routine in-service training and curriculum development activity—admittedly perhaps a prestigious one, but little more. This placed the work close to the reality of how curriculum development might normally take place in E.P.A. junior schools; but effectively it ruled out any hope of a pristine research evaluation of it.

From the point of view of the local teachers and their advisers, the benefits

---

[1] See Volume 2 of the E.P.A. series: *Statistics and Surveys.*
[2] See Lippitt, Watson and Bendix, *The Dynamics of Planned Change*, Harcourt, Brace and World Inc.

which came from the Project's involvement outweighed any costs. The partnership allowed the scale of the language programme work to increase. More teachers worked on it. More resources were available. Activities could be more systematically planned and conducted. More things became possible. But for the teachers also there were costs. Considerable investments of their time were demanded. In order to implement the programme a fairly radical overhaul of their teaching day was needed. Above all, the Project was a field trial with instructions to report, at the end of a finite period, on the more general viability of those activities which it had promoted. The teachers' development work was constantly being assessed and analysed and, in the second year, the effect of all the activity on the linguistic behaviour of the children was evaluated. For the local teachers, perhaps the most surprising and disturbing consequence of the Project's involvement was that their expressed satisfaction or dissatisfaction with a particular activity was taken by the research workers as information, and not as a sufficient condition for its viability.

The Substance of the Programme

During the first year of the Project's sponsorship, the language programme contents were largely an expansion and a more systematic application of previous work. The first ingredient was an exhortation to the participating teachers to be more aware of the children's need to verbalise about their experience. The teachers were told, for instance, "The primary aspect of the programme was, therefore, a recognition of . . . the greater need for the class teacher to be aware of the aims of a language programme and to take all possible steps . . . to encourage group and class discussion, to saturate the work with readings from literature both in poetry and prose story, to encourage drama and choral speech and to give opportunities for wider experience with the essential conversations about that experience".[1] To this purpose a small library of books was bought by the E.P.A. Project; an anthology of useful poems was brought together and made available, and regular meetings were held to discuss the practice of a greater oral emphasis in the curriculum.

In addition to this fairly general and wide ranging counsel to allow the children more opportunity to express themselves verbally, more specific talking activities and conversation pieces were recommended. There were basically three kinds:

(i) In the first place *the talking book* was suggested as a class activity. This involved the recreation of a simple story with phonic elaborations. Individual children took the parts of characters or noises in the story. Thus one story was about three robbers; each robber was introduced by the story teller; and he then introduced and described himself. During the course of the story there were great winds, doors were smashed down with axes, and pepper was thrown into people's faces. Individual children were given the responsibility for the phonic creation of these incidents, and the children's phonic "happen-

---

[1] Taken from an information sheet given to the teachers attending the initial meetings during 1969.

ing" was tape-recorded. The exercise was designed to stimulate the children's interest in and awareness of language. In addition, as repetition of the story and of each part to be played in it was needed before a completed version could be produced and tape-recorded, the actors acquired familiarity with the roles given them and with set piece speeches that went with the parts. For example, one of the robbers might have been called Azuk the merchant, who was fat, sleazy and asthmatic and who, although he had a great deal of money, became a robber at night . . . etc. Thus it was hoped, familiarity with role playing techniques, and with complex linguistic structures, would be acquired as a by-product of the exercise.

(ii) Secondly, specific *conversation pieces* were recommended. Some of these were small group activities. For instance, "blacked-out books" were used. These were simple story books with pictures, but with the text of the story blacked out; and a group of children were asked to create their own story from the sequence of pictures. Others were for pairs of children. For example, telephones were installed in each classroom and children used these to pass messages and instructions to each other. And there was a constructional toy activity. For this children were placed on either side of a screen, and one child instructed another on how to draw a particular shape or how to build a Lego model. A common feature of practically all the conversation pieces was that they needed spoken language for the successful performance of a task; and they provided an end-product which checked that performance.

(iii) Lastly, *language drills* were created. The format for these was as follows. The teacher's voice on a tape recorder asked a question. A voice answered the question in a sentence containing, perhaps, a subordinate clause. The question was asked again. The answer was repeated, this time with the class joining in. The question was repeated. There was a blank space on the tape for the children's repetition of the answer as a class. This last sequence was repeated several times. An example of the drills, which used material from the three robbers talking book, was:

Question: "Why did the third robber have a huge red axe?"
Answer: "He had a huge red axe because he wanted to smash the carriage wheels."

Both the talking activities and the more general oral emphasis were supplemented for the teachers by fortnightly discussion groups with the E.P.A. Project Team and the local District Inspector. Initially an invitation to take part was open to all teachers in the E.P.A. Project junior schools. In practice this was refined down to focus on the teachers of second year junior classes; but the invitation remained open to all in principle. The talking activities were offered as suggestions to teachers who expressed an interest. They were to be integrated into the normal teaching day; and they could be adopted, amended or rejected in the light of experience of their use and of how well they combined with the rest of the curriculum. It was recommended, however, that at least three separate hourly sessions each week should be spent on them if they were to be effective.

The research workers were observers of this activity during its first year (1969 to 1970), and they conducted a series of interviews with the participating teachers during the 1970 summer term. As a result, an interim report was written which helped to change the course of development for the second year. While noting the achievements of the programme to date—for instance that it had helped teachers to be more confident in approaching this aspect of their work—three areas of weakness were identified.

In the first place the language work programme was a solution without rational justification, and many of the teachers were not aware why they were implementing it. The programme had been offered to the teachers at the beginning of the school year as a solution to the language problems of the E.P.A. child. There had been no attempt to justify this claim; teachers had simply been told that, if they helped the children to perform at certain activities at a given frequency, they could expect the children's language to improve. In consequence there were no means available to the teachers for deciding how successful each activity had been: except perhaps that it was successful if it took place. A further consequence was that there were no means of generating activities in addition to those recommended. Lastly, with no way of knowing the relative importance of what they were doing, the recommended frequency for the talking activities was being ignored by the teachers as the activities ran into competition from other subjects in the curriculum.

Secondly, the means of achieving the language programme had become ends in themselves. The structured conversation pieces were seen by the teachers as the language programme, rather than as supplements to an oral curriculum. Further, there was no teacher perception of the different requirements that different language activities placed on the children. It had been universally agreed that the drilling was unacceptable, for instance; but the reasons given for this were that it seemed pointless and boring, and it caused discipline problems. Its contribution, or lack of it, to a pattern of change in the children's linguistic behaviour did not appear to be a criterion.[1]

Finally, by the end of the summer term 1970 it was impossible to identify a coherent theme in the classroom practice of those teachers who attended the language programme meetings which conformed to the original ideas for the programme. Some teachers were simply going through the motions of taking part, attending meetings but not changing their classroom practice. Others, who were indeed trying to create a new sort of curriculum, were finding it increasingly necessary to work away from the finite, recommended talking activities, to innovate and, in effect, to create their own programme. But with no rationale for what they were doing, and no understanding of the linguistic requirements of the various new teaching situations they were devising, teachers who attempted this increasingly disregarded the original intentions. In particular, contrary to the principles of an oral curriculum, the "talking activities" were being used as introductions to written work, which was considered more important than spoken language.[2]

---

[1] This is neither to defend nor to attack language drills in junior schools. It is to observe that the reasons for their rejection in this work had nothing to do with their perceived effect on the children's language behaviour.

[2] Once again this is neither to defend nor attack the use of conversation pieces as preludes to written work. It is simply to state that this is not what they had been designed for; and it was against the spirit of the original intention of an oral curriculum.

The interim report suggested three ways in which the work could be changed for the school year 1970–71, all of which were accepted in principle.

It was suggested that more consideration be given to the objectives and purposes of the programme. In particular, it was suggested that the teachers should know why, as well as what they were being asked to do. In a sense the structured activities of the first year had been "teacher free". They had been constructed before the teachers were introduced to them; and participants in the 1969–70 programme were simply asked to ensure that they took place. The hope was that the tasks themselves would in some way raise the subject children's level of linguistic skill. At the least a consequence of this was that the tasks became isolated from all the other things that were going on in the classroom; and it is probably more realistic to say that they became irrelevant to the normal curriculum. Clearly therefore, if spoken language work was to be integrated into the curriculum, the class teachers themselves must know what they were doing, must be committed to this end and must be given the freedom, as well as the knowledge, to generate their own programme of work. It was suggested and agreed, therefore, that the language programme should move from a pre-specified package of activities to an open and evolving work programme. The emphasis was to be on teacher commitment, knowledge and skill, rather than on circumventing the need for these.

In this respect it was suggested that the conversation pieces of the previous year should not be identified in terms of what they required the teacher to do. It was suggested that they should, instead, be categorised in terms of what they required from the children, and that they should be seen as language producing situations for them. For instance, most of the conversation pieces of the 1969–70 programme demanded what came to be called instructional language for their successful performance. In other words, for various tasks to be accomplished, information was passed from one child to another; and each task resulted in an end-product which verified how successfully information had been transmitted and received. During the summer of 1970 there seemed to be effectively only one other functional category of language. This was called descriptive language initially; but potentially it covered a range of different sorts of language producing situations. A dramatically simplified classification of the previous year's work was produced. And it was suggested, and again agreed, that this should provide the starting point for teacher discussion during the coming year.[1]

Lastly it was recommended that the in-service training aspect of the scheme be more carefully administered. Certainly the teacher discussion group should be continued: to begin with, working on the classification of language producing situations from the previous year, and then creating new practices by developing, and eventually rejecting, the initial classification. But these meetings provided no guarantee that anything happened in individual classrooms. It was suggested, and again agreed in principle, that the local District Inspector and the Project Director should visit individual teachers in their own classrooms regularly and frequently—to observe and to assist the development of the language work in specific contexts.

---

[1] See Appendix 1 for an account of the classification that was produced at this time.

For the second year of the E.P.A. Project's sponsorship (the school year 1970–71), all the teachers of second year junior children in the local Project schools were invited to take part. One school and four teachers from the other six schools decided not to do so. Nine teachers did participate, five of whom had been involved during the previous year.[1]

The regular discussion groups met as before—sometimes weekly and sometimes fortnightly. During the autumn term discussion centred around the classification of the previous year's language producing situations. The classification served as a heuristic device. In the first place it revealed some of the demands that various language producing situations imposed on the children; and subsequently it enabled the teachers to create new types of situation. Once the teachers began to understand what was required they re-formulated issues in their own terms; and during the year successive features of the classification device were dropped from consideration as their over-simplifications ceased to appeal to the teachers.

After this introductory period, discussion in the teachers' meetings was of two further topics. In the first place individuals were encouraged to observe the children they taught, to describe their linguistic behaviour and to diagnose weaknesses. As a result of this, attempts were made to create small remedial work programmes—the discussion groups providing starting points, problem solving arenas and places to exchange ideas and assess the quality of the work programmes.

Throughout the period the teacher descriptions of the children's linguistic behaviour remained at the everyday, common sense level. Some children were said not to speak "grammatically", others were "shy", "inhibited" and "didn't want to talk." A common observation was that the children did not ordinarily "use" language to perform tasks. Differences between West Indian children and non-immigrant children were noted, as were the difficulties many children had reporting orally to people who had not themselves experienced the events in question. Attempts were made to relate these diverse accounts to formulated theories of linguistic behaviour and so to increase their explanatory power. The formulations which most often seemed relevant were those of Bernstein.[2] But Halliday's models of language were presented as a further means of classifying language activities[3]; reference was made to Chomsky's descriptions of language competence[4] and to phonetic accounts of dialectic differences. Thus the range of theoretical formulations brought to bear on the teacher observations ranged from phonology to socio-linguistics. But the observations of the teachers remained persistently at the pragmatic level.

The second discussion topic at the teacher meetings was seen by them to be more interesting, and contributions were more imaginative and more positive. Kaleidoscopic combinations of work programmes were produced. The conversation pieces of the previous year were used, and developed, in

---

[1] When the impact of the work on the subject children was evaluated there were no significant differences between the results obtained by teachers in their first and second year of the programme.

[2] See B. Bernstein, *Class Codes and Control*, Routledge and Kegan Paul, 1971.

[3] See M. Halliday, "Relevant Models of Language", *Education Review*, Volume 22, Number 1, November 1969, page 26.

[4] See N. Chomsky, *Syntactic Structures*, 1957, and *Aspects of the Theory of Syntax*, 1965, M.I.T. Press.

the context of the classification of language producing situations. Events were identified, which occurred normally in the classroom and which provided opportunities to set up new situations for the children. For instance, a monitor system was devised, with frequent changes of monitor and the previous one being responsible for telling the new one what was required. In addition, teachers worked to produce "packages" involving ideas and materials for small schemes of work which concentrated on an aspect of language or on language producing situations. Many of these were more flexible versions of the original conversation pieces, being designed to improve performance at transmitting and receiving instructions. But they also involved work on concept formation: on position (draw a square above a circle), on size (draw a large square, etc.), on sequence (after these draw . . . and before you can, etc.). Some of the packages demanded a short term memory facility from the children (here is a list of instructions . . .). Many of them retained the "what went wrong" check point at their completion; but this was expanded to include not only a finished product which confronted the children with the consequences of their communicative skills, but also a discussion with the teacher about it. Other work focused on the meanings of words, and on conditions and consequences. For instance, the children were asked to identify, to discuss and to reproduce the behaviour associated with emotions (fear, anger, remorse); there were sequences which attempted to clarify the way in which certain events or situations (the boy read his comic in bed) were only possible when prior conditions had been fulfilled (the light was on); and there was work on the reason why (the ice-cream melted, or ducks have webbed feet).[1]

There were times when the range of things being attempted seemed almost bewildering. But for the purpose of an assessment of it all, a series of under-lying themes and tendencies can be identified. In their practice, many of the schemes of work were concerned with a language for control. The teachers rarely made this explicit; but they seemed to want the children to receive and to act on information more effectively, and to dispatch instructions and knowledge more accurately. Obviously this bias was to some extent a carry-over from the previous year's work; but it continued, and became stronger when the teachers diagnosed and created their own working arrangements. Secondly, and perhaps less positively, some other characteristics of the previous programme remained latent but significant. There was always a tendency to see situations more in terms of what was required from the teacher than of what was needed from the children. Spoken language was persistently seen as a prelude to written work rather than as a legitimate means of communication in itself. And more generally, there was always competition from other parts of an already crowded curriculum.[2]

---

[1] Clearly there are senses in which all these activities are a part of what constitutes "normal good teaching practice." Their distinctive feature here was that successful practices were shared with other teachers from different schools; that work which was attempted in individual classrooms was scrutinised by teaching colleagues and by people who were not themselves teachers; and overriding this, there was persistent encourage-ment to all the teachers to get the children to talk to them, and to each other, in a purposeful way.

[2] There was an ambiguity in this which was never openly exposed or resolved. Clearly language is a vehicle for communication. But given the commitment to teach it, language must also be seen as a subject on the curriculum. It was thus both a means and an end. As a means it did not compete with other curriculum contents; as an end it certainly did.

Visits and assistance to individual teachers in their classrooms were neither regular nor frequent. Neither the Project Director nor the local District Inspector—the two experienced educational practitioners among the organisers—were able to meet the demands of the schedule. Quite simply, they were both too busy. Instead, individual classrooms were visited by one or other of them on demand from the teacher in question, and perhaps once a month in any case. This was probably sufficient to ensure that something happened, but not enough to provide regular and individual, detailed guidance. It is difficult to be sure how this affected the overall development and implementation of the work. What happened as a result is probably closer to the reality of what "normally" happens[1]; but probably also the quality of work could have been improved had the regular visiting been sustained. One certain consequence is that tensions experienced by individual teachers, over the need to reconcile demands from the language work with those from the rest of the curriculum, would have been eased. In its crudest sense this tension was simply a matter of how to cover the existing curriculum and to undertake new work in the time available. But it was also a question of different practices leading in different directions. It was noticeable, for instance, how people who needed to meet many different demands on their time used one teaching activity for a number of different purposes: which were not always compatible. A relatively trivial example provides the clearest illustration of this. One of the teachers developed a scheme to show children how to transmit clear and precise instructions using a technique based on the teaching of standardised writing. Letters of the alphabet were broken down into a set of characters, each of which was referred to by a descriptive phrase—short, medium or long vertical line, curve, diagonal from left to right, etc. To produce the written characters precisely "coded messages" were passed from speaker to listener. For the purpose of teaching writing skills, it was important that the recipient knew in advance which letter he was trying to reproduce. For the purposes of the language programme, it was important that the child relied only on the "coded message" to reproduce the letter. The teacher only recognised this dilemma fully after he had spent time developing the scheme, and he then decided that standardised writing was more important than spoken language. The teacher learned by experience. The incident provides for us an illustration of perhaps a more general dilemma: that multiple teaching objectives are not always in harmony with each other. The difficulty was discussed and resolved at a teachers' meeting. But the specific point remains: it could have been resolved in the individual teacher's classroom if his activities had been more closely monitored.

The contribution of the research workers during this second year was significant; but also at this time an important mistake was made. During the first year the research workers had been observers of, rather than participants in, the on-going programme. By the second year, however, they had become involved in its development and implementation. And they ex-

---

[1] What teacher, whether he is working on a special project or not, receives visits and individualised advice from an educational adviser more often than once a month?

perienced the role conflicts inherent in both participation and observation: conflicts which were made more acute by the nature of their participation. An integral element to the plan for the 1970–71 programme had been that the organisers should provide detailed and individualised classroom advice and help to the participants. Although this part of the plan fell through, the researchers were themselves seen to be members of the organising team. Should they visit classrooms in order to observe how successfully teachers were implementing their work programmes, or in order to advise on improvements? In principle, given courage, experience and confidence, both were possible; in practice the problems seemed insuperable. And there was a further level of conflict: between the demands of a possible classroom advisory role for the researchers, and the group dynamics of the teacher discussion meetings. Prior to each teachers' meeting an agenda was agreed by the organising team: at which time the researchers were positive and constructive. During the meetings themselves, however, they adopted questioning roles. All the other participants were educational practitioners: each understanding the presumptions and reference points of the others. The researchers deliberately refused to become part of this community of understanding. The validity, or relevance, or significance, or consequences, sometimes even the truth and always the unspoken premises of teacher observations were questioned. In principle again, even this role change—from being a creative classroom adviser to being an irritant at the meetings of like minds—might have been achieved. But it was not attempted.[1] Classroom visits by the researchers were—like those of the rest of the organising team—neither regular nor systematic. And there was no collection of reliable data on the implementation of the work.

The Purpose of the Programme

The substantive content of the work was developed from existing teacher practices through an in-service training programme which offered new information, ideas and advice to its members. Seen as a training programme, its purpose was fulfilled simply because it took place. Teachers joined it; were subject to the ideas currently being propagated; put those ideas into some form of practice and discussed their experience with others taking part; they could then leave the programme, and even the schools they were in, carrying the ideas and practices with them. In this sense the activity was a device for disseminating the innovation of more spoken language work in E.P.A. junior schools. But it begs the question of whether what was happening had any effect.

It had a clear and observable effect on the teachers. They became more confident. They saw themselves to be more knowledgeable and to have more skills. And this confidence was not confined to the language work in a narrow sense. There was a danger in the immediate post-Plowden period that teachers who were working in E.P.A. schools would feel sorry for themselves because of it. Incremental extra resources going to some of those

---

[1] There was a further point. Before the 1970–71 year began, the decision not to undertake participant observation of the Environmental Studies Scheme (see Part 6) had been made. On reflection this certainly also coloured the decision not to do so over the language work.

schools helped to create a feeling that something was happening. In the E.P.A. Project, a large volume of resources going on particular activities (like the Environmental Studies Scheme)[1] created a feeling that a lot was happening. The effect of in-service training in the language programme helped the teachers to believe that a lot was possible. But this begs the question of what was happening to the children. Everybody knew, and agreed with what should be happening to them: their linguistic behaviour should improve. But it was not immediately clear what this actually meant. For the practitioners, further refinement was unnecessary; general objectives were needed, but the real work was to create a content for the programme. For the researchers, the general objectives needed to be more precise before the effectiveness of the content could be assessed. But their attempts to achieve this were of little interest to the majority; indeed they were seen to be unhelpful as they detracted from the major purpose of deciding what to do and how to do it.

The initial rounds of the engagement illustrate the point. All through the language work considerable reference was made to the theories of Bernstein[2] about the linguistic behaviour of working class children. Bernstein's argument is that the speech of some working class, as opposed to some middle class children is determined by their conceptual approach to communication. Socially disadvantaged children tacitly seem to assume an understanding as to the reference of their speech. And, therefore, social psychologists talk of their speech as being context bound, and linguists observe the large number of pronouns they use. The theory itself does not tell teachers what they should do when teaching children whose speech is "context bound" however—even if there were recognised and reliable ways of isolating such children from a more general population. Therefore, as early as 1969 a set of operational objectives was created from the theory and all the teachers agreed to them. These were:

(1) To improve the children's fluency and efficiency of using language in the performance of tasks.
(2) To increase the children's vocabulary.
(3) To give them the opportunity of using more complex linguistic structures.

But when they were broken down into their constituent parts, these covered virtually all aspects of a child's linguistic behaviour.[3] At a later stage the concept of "language enrichment" began to be used, and sanctioned, as an umbrella term to cover the intentions of the work.[4] This concept is, of

---

[1] See Part 6.

[2] See Bernstein, *op. cit.*

[3] A possible exception was phonics, and that was partly covered by the interpretation given to "fluency".

[4] At this stage the situation was thus: the language programme had specific objectives which had been generated with reference to Bernstein's sociocultural theory of linguistic behaviour. At a more general level it was being designed to "enrich" the language of the subject children, even though the author of the theory was, at that time, arguing that the subjects of his research did not need to have their language "enriched". In his essay "Compensatory Education" in Rubinstein and Stoneman, eds., *Education for Democracy*, for instance, Bernstein argues that the equation that has been made between the concepts "restricted code" (or "context bound speech") and "linguistic deprivation" is erroneous. For him the speech of low working class children may be context specific, but it is also very rich.

course, even less specific than the original operational intentions; and so a consequence of the attempt to make them more specific had been to make the stated objectives of the work more general! Discussions of the content and of the objectives continued to take place more or less in parallel. It could easily be agreed that there were hoped for improvements in the subject children's spoken language. But more than this seemed to evade any formulations; and in the end everybody settled for an assessment of the effect of the work on the children's spoken language in some gross sense.

The Effect on the Children

The research task, therefore, was to assess the effect of the language work on the behaviour of the subject children over their second junior school year. But three factors constrained how this might be done. In the first place, the teachers and the classes taking part were self selecting. Nine teachers were to construct language activities for their children; and *de facto* these were the experimental group. Secondly, although there was a common frame of reference for the activities, their purpose remained open to different interpretations; and attempts to refine the objectives of the work were failing. Lastly, as it happened, we were not to know in any systematic or detailed way how each of the teachers organised their teaching day and how successfully the language work programmes were implemented. We have to assume that the teachers were doing what they said they were doing.[1]

Naturally there was a time dimension to all this. A design for the evaluation was constructed during the summer term prior to the 1970–71 school year. At that stage, although it was clear that there would be a *de facto* experimental group, the possibility still existed that more precise statements of objectives would be achieved. But the realisation grew that any evaluation must match, in some way, what *would in any case* happen: and that having carefully prescribed objectives, which nobody actually believed in or was prepared to abide by but which everybody was happy to sanction formally, would not help in this respect. A fairly loose statement of intentions seemed the most realistic option, therefore: given the assumption that classroom assistance by the Project Director and District Inspector, and then classroom observation by the researchers, would both become a reality. Since they did not, we need to be cautious over what can be inferred from the evaluation that was conducted. From the first constraint it must be accepted that the teachers were probably more highly motivated than the average E.P.A. teacher. From the second it is unclear exactly how the motivation was directed during the 1970–71 school year; and from the error of judgement which led to the third, there was no check on the actual process of implementing the language work programmes. What must be said, therefore, is that the evaluation is, and can

---

[1] And the teachers said, throughout the 1970–71 period, that the work was proceeding successfully. There were sufficient checks during this time to ensure that language work was taking place. And the point must be made that the very fact of their continuing with the work was a sign that the teachers saw it to be successful. They could hardly have continued with it had they not thought so.

only be, an overall appraisal: of the effect, over a broad range of linguistic abilities, on E.P.A. children; of in-service teacher training activity, which was directed towards creating greater emphasis in the curriculum on oral work.

Within the constraints as they existed, three major decisions needed to be made: what comparisons to make, what tests to use and how to analyse the data.

Since a group of teachers of second year children in the E.P.A. Project schools had decided against taking part in the language work, a *de facto* within-school control group existed in addition to the experimental classes. There were obvious limitations to any comparisons made between two such self-selecting groups; but the advantages were also substantial. For instance, although it would be impossible to say whether the within-school control teachers were not motivated to develop a spoken language curriculum or were simply not motivated, we would know what happened over a school year to the linguistic development of children taught by such teachers.[1] At the same time, therefore, a further control group of children was needed, which would provide information on the behaviour of children taught by a "normal" range of E.P.A. teachers. The District Inspector of a neighbouring I.L.E.A. Division was consulted and he suggested a group of schools which were in a neighbourhood similar to that of the E.P.A. Project; these were asked, and agreed to assist.[2] The comparisons made in the evaluation, therefore, are between the self-selecting experimental, the within-school control and other E.P.A. school groups: over the period of one school year.

Since the language work was to be a catholic affair, broad measures of linguistic abilities were needed to assess its impact. And since the work was to concentrate on spoken language, written methods of assessment were ruled out. And the choice of testing instruments was curtailed by the combination of these factors. Language tests were available for younger children[3]; and the verbal components of intelligence tests were available for children of the right age group. Yet the strongest contender as a complete and sophisticated test of linguistic abilities seemed to be the Illinois Test of Psycho-Linguistic Abilities (the I.T.P.A.)[4]; and this was chosen as the major test with which to evaluate the language work. It contained no direct measure of vocabulary, however; and the English Picture Vocabulary Test (the E.P.V.T.), a measure of passive vocabulary, was chosen to supplement the I.T.P.A.

The I.T.P.A. was to be administered individually—taking approximately 50 minutes for each administration. It could not, therefore, be given to all the children in the evaluation; and so it was decided not to obtain I.T.P.A. scores for the within-school control group, and to sample by school within the

---

[1] The within-school control group was used in the evaluation. See Appendix 2.

[2] This between-school control group in fact had fewer immigrant children in it—see Appendix 2. But we control for any effect of this in the data analysis—see Appendix 3. and the text below.

[3] See, for instance, the Reynell Language Development Scales which were used to evaluate the scheme reported in Part 4.

[4] See Appendix 2 for a more detailed account of the tests used. A major weakness of the I.T.P.A. was that it had no norms for English children of the right age; the E.P.A. children could not therefore be compared to an "outside" or "normal" English group.

experimental and other-school controls.[1] The E.P.V.T. was a group test and was given to all classes of second year children.

The last decision of the three—on how to analyse the data—was made on the advice of the National Foundation for Educational Research.[2] We were to have data on the children's performance at the beginning and at the end of one school year, and two statistical techniques were used on these data. A two-way analysis of variance (A.N.O.V.A.) was used to see whether the scores for any groups were significantly different either at pre-or post-test; and an analysis of covariance was used to test for the significance of different changes in score over the period.

The "psycholinguistic profile"[3]

In addition to their use to measure changes in score over the school year, the I.T.P.A. results were used to obtain a diagnostic profile of the language behaviour of E.P.A. children.

Figure 1 shows the "psycholinguistic profile" of the experimental and the other-school control groups as they were measured on the I.T.P.A. pre-test. It must be borne in mind that the only available norms on the test for children of this age were American. Consequently, although these profiles have been created in such a way that comparisons can be made between defined groups of children, and between sub-tests for any one group, nothing can be said about the profile for E.P.A. as opposed to "normal" English children.

The profile of a "normal" American child would appear as a horizontal straight line in Figure 1. At the same time American research findings indicate that mentally retarded children, children with speech disorders and children for whom reading difficulty can be predicted are likely to have lower scores on the automatic level items of the I.T.P.A. than on the representational items.[4] In other words, they are likely to have difficulty integrating experience in such activities as—"visual and auditory closure, speed of perception, ability to reproduce a sequence seen or heard, rote learning . . ."[5] And they are relatively less likely to have difficulties dealing with symbols or images which carry the meaning of, or represent, an object.

The overall profile for English E.P.A. children is below, and distinctly different from, the average American profile. But it is also different from the profile that could be expected from retarded American children. Relative to their representational level of functioning, these English E.P.A. children's performance at the automatic level is not retarded. Indeed the memory items are amongst the highest achieved in the profile. Although we might concede

---

[1] If a school had one class, then the I.T.P.A. was given to that class. If it had several classes of second year juniors, then one was selected at random. On reflection, the decision not to test the within-school controls on the I.T.P.A. was the second major mistake made in the evaluation.

[2] Miss Wendy Fader of the N.F.E.R.'s statistical services department advised in this respect and arranged for the necessary computing.

[3] See Appendix 2 for a discussion of the I.T.P.A. and the "psycholinguistic profile".

[4] For summaries of these see S. A. Kirk and D. Kirk, *Psycholinguistic Learning Disabilities: Diagnosis and Remediation*, University of Illinois Press.

[5] See the *Manual for Administering the I.T.P.A.*

Figure 1: "Psycholinguistic profiles" of the experimental and control groups: using pre-test scores

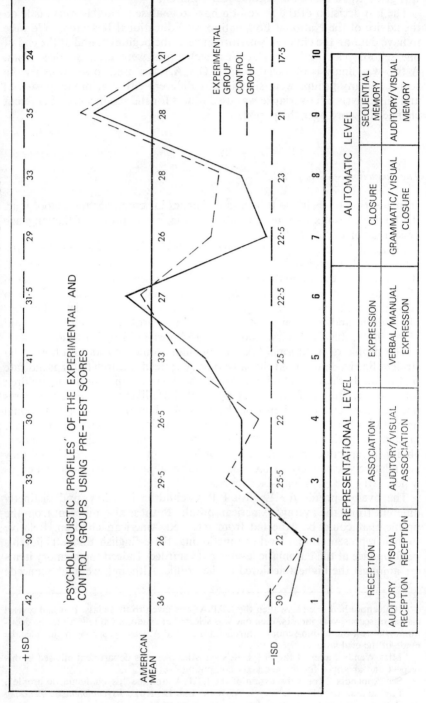

that their total profile is depressed; nobody could argue from this evidence that E.P.A. children are likely to be backward through an inability to remember or to integrate their experience.

Further, the two expression items on the test show relatively high performances for the E.P.A. children. It would seem—again relative to other areas of their psycholinguistic functioning—that E.P.A. children have little difficulty expressing themselves using either verbal or manual symbols.

The auditory and visual decoding items (reception) show the most depressed scores on the "psycholinguistic profile". And so the evidence points to the most severe psycholinguistic handicap suffered by these children being their inability to comprehend symbolic stimuli. In short, and relative to their other areas of functioning, they cannot understand what is being said, or indicated to them.

The profiles for the experimental and for the other-school control group differ in only one respect. The Grammatic Closure scores of the experimental group are significantly worse than those of the control group.[1] This is explained by the extremely low scores on this item of the higher number of immigrant children in the experimental group.[2]

Figure 2 shows the "psycholinguistic profiles" of boys and of girls in the experimental and control groups. It can be seen that they all have similar profiles. Girls seem to have lower scores on the reception and association items but the differences are not statistically significant; and on the expression, closure and memory items there are no observable differences.

On the other hand Figure 3, which shows the profiles of the experimental children grouped with respect to their immigrant status, reveals significant differences between the three groups on half of the items: on auditory reception, auditory association, verbal expression, grammatic closure and visual closure.[3]

Of all the sub-tests which were concerned with the auditory-vocal channel, only auditory memory reveals no significant differences between the groups; and all groups achieved their highest score for the profile on this item.

Since the "other immigrant" group is a relatively heterogeneous residual category, it is sensible to look directly at the profiles for the two groups defined with respect to positive criteria. Non-immigrants have a "higher" profile than the West Indian immigrants on all items; their automatic level of performance is relatively superior to their representational level; but in only two cases—manual expression and auditory memory—does their average score exceed the American norm. The profile for West Indian immigrants follows the overall pattern of that for the non-immigrants but is significantly lower in auditory-vocal areas.[4]

The results for the individual children they taught were shown to all the teachers whose classes were tested. The results were presented in such a way

---

[1] See Tables 1 and 2 in Appendix 3 and Table 1 in the text below.

[2] There were no significant differences at pre-test between the scores of the experimental and control non-immigrants.

[3] See Appendix 2 for the definition of the three groups. See Tables 13 to 19 in Appendix 3 and the text below for the results of the data analysis.

[4] The grammatic closure item is a significant exception to this; the West Indian immigrant's average score on this item falls to a very low level. Since this reflects the considerable culture bias integral to the notion of correct grammatic structures, the result is not surprising.

Figure 2: "Psycholinguistic profiles" of experimental and control boys and girls

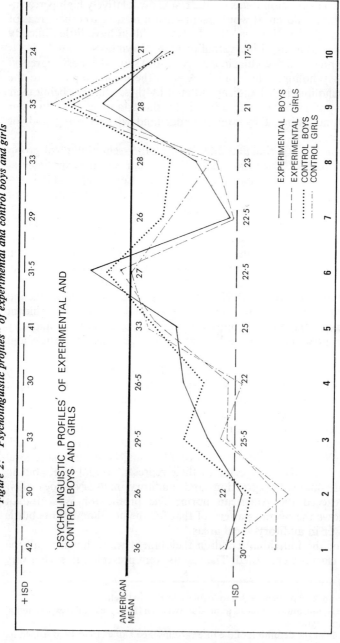

Figure 3: " Psycholinguistic profiles" of children of different immigrant status

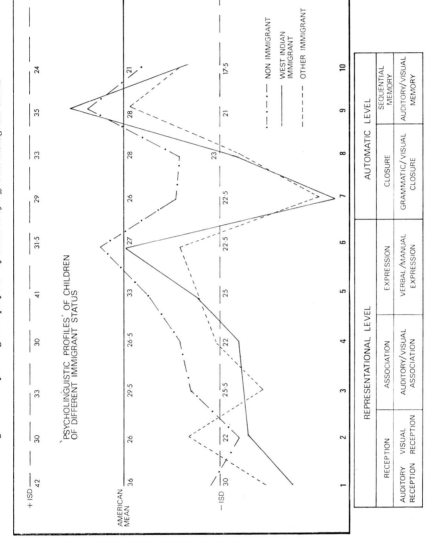

that intra class comparisons could be made, as could comparisons between the class in question and the overall scores. But no attempt was made to interpret the profiles during the 1970–71 period. There are nevertheless interesting comparisons to be made between the teacher and the I.T.P.A. diagnosis of E.P.A. children's linguistic behaviour. The teachers' emphasis on the need for work to promote higher levels of receptive skills is confirmed by the "psycholinguistic profiles". Their diagnosis, that immigrant children (and particularly West Indian immigrants in these schools) are a group with significant and different learning and language problems, is also confirmed by the I.T.P.A. profile. But the teachers did not develop this; and there was no work on separate "immigrant language activities". The observation that the overall level of language competence of E.P.A. children is low also appears to be correct; but, contrary to the teacher observations, the children appear not to have difficulty expressing themselves.[1]

The analysis of changes in score over the year[2]

Comparing the experimental with the control groups

There were significant differences between the experimental and control group scores on the grammatic closure item of the I.T.P.A. (see Tables 1 and 2 below). But this result is a function of the low experimental immigrant children's scores on this sub-test.[3]

There were significantly different change scores between the experimental and control groups on two I.T.P.A. items—on visual reception and manual expression. In both cases the control group's gain in raw score was greater than that of the experimental group (see Tables 1 and 2 below). But these results cannot be related to the overall planned or observed contents of the language work.

At the least then, we must conclude that the language programme activities did not make a discernible impact on the linguistic behaviour of the total group of subject children.[4]

The comparisons on the E.P.V.T. are complicated because there are both within-school and other-school control groups. There were no significant differences between the groups on the pre-test, but the change scores and the

---

[1] The research was concerned with the relative behaviour of *groups* of children; although the average scores differed there was nearly as much variation in score within groups as there was within the total population. The teachers, on the other hand, were used to dealing with a situation where they talked about individual children.

[2] It needs to be made clear at this point that there were no significant differences in the respective ages of any of the groups. And further therefore, that the analysis was performed to assess differences in the variation in measured raw scores. In order to illustrate differences between groups in a way which is easy to understand, differences in average score are often used; but the decisions about which results are significant were made with reference to the variance and co-variance analysis—see Appendix 2.

[3] See Table 5 below and Tables 13 to 19 in Appendix 3.

[4] Tables 5 to 12 in Appendix 3 show the measured scores for experimental and control boys and girls on the I.T.P.A. and the E.P.V.T. The results are complicated in the case of the E.P.V.T. because of the significantly better performance of boys on the test; but overall the language work made relatively no greater difference to the measured performance of either of the two sexes.

Table 1

Average raw scores at pre- and post-test, and difference in score, for the experimental and control groups on the I.T.P.A.

	Experimental group			Control group		
	Pre-test mean $N = 134$	Post-test mean	Differ-ence in mean	Pre-test mean $N = 113$	Post-test mean	Differ-ence in mean
Auditory reception	29·13	32·78	3·65	30·27	32·97	2·70
	8·37	8·21		9·17	8·57	
Visual reception	21·06	23·76	2·70	20·74	24·88	4·14
	4·86	4·78		5·62	5·81	
Auditory association	26·25	28·53	2·28	26·65	28·88	2·23
	4·56	6·30		6·23	5·30	
Visual association	23·08	24·81	1·73	22·51	24·55	2·04
	5·05	5·21		5·02	5·04	
Verbal expression	30·14	34·04	3·90	30·89	34·48	3·59
	7·26	7·97		8·74	7·57	
Manual expression	28·02	27·80	−0·22	27·41	28·65	1·24
	4·90	4·61		5·60	5·12	
Grammatic closure	22·68	24·88	2·20	24·52	26·69	2·17
	5·98	5·50		6·27	5·24	
Visual closure	24·34	30·59	6·25	25·19	31·08	5·89
	5·29	6·43		5·93	7·02	
Auditory memory	31·07	34·49	3·42	32·77	35·27	2·50
	8·15	9·16		9·37	8·97	
Visual memory	19·69	22·99	3·30	19·86	23·88	4·02
	4·05	5·66		3·69	5·27	

Table 2

Analysis of variance and covariance on the I.T.P.A. scores for the experimental and control groups

	A.N.O.V.A. on pre-test scores: F value	A.N.O.V.A. on post-test scores: F value	Difference in change scores: F value
Auditory reception	1·0424 (ns)	0·03338 (ns)	0·1082 (ns)
Visual reception	0·2253 (ns)	2·9057 (ns)	5·7505 ($0.025 > p > 0.001$)
Auditory association	0·3249 (ns)	0·2138 (ns)	0.0160 (ns)
Visual association	0·7806 (ns)	0·1624 (ns)	0·0055 (ns)
Verbal expression	0·5453 (ns)	0·1893 (ns)	0·0129 (ns)
Manual expression	0·8348 (ns)	1·8892 (ns)	5·2571 ($0.025 > p > 0.01$)
Grammatic closure	5·5711 ($0.025 > p > 0.01$)	6·9353 ($0.01 > p > 0.005$)	1·4034 (ns)
Visual closure	1·3926 (ns)	0·7096 (ns)	0·0088 (ns)
Auditory memory	2·3325 (ns)	0·4445 (ns)	0·8382 (ns)
Visual memory	0·1201 (ns)	1·6221 (ns)	1·5794 (ns)

Table 3

Average pre- and post-test scores on the E.P.V.T. for the experimental and two control groups

	Pre-test score		Post-test score		Difference in mean score
	Mean	Standard deviation	Mean	Standard deviation	
Experimental group, $N = 191$	93·5	13·5	93·5	14·0	0
Control group (1), $N = 116$	91·4	12·9	90·3	12·6	−1·1
Control group (2), $N = 161$	93·3	13·2	95·2	13·5	+1·9

Table 4

Analysis comparing change scores

Pre-test: F value	Post-test: F value	Difference in change score: F value
(ns)	$(0·01 > p > 0·005)$	$(0·05 > p > 0·025)$

post-test scores were significantly different (see Table 3 above). The average score of all three groups was below the national mean of 100 at the pre-test. The average score of the control schools, from outside the Project area, improved by two standard points over the period. The score of the experimental classes remained virtually constant; and the score of the control classes deteriorated by one standard point.

The conclusion from this must be then that the motivated teachers taking part in the language work did not succeed in raising their children's level of passive vocabulary, although the performance of the control schools did improve slightly in this respect. But the teachers in the E.P.A. Project schools, who were less interested in language work, taught children who on average lost ground over that year relative to the experimental children, control schools and national norms.

Comparing the scores of the non-immigrant and immigrant groups

There were no significant differences at pre-test, at post-test or over the change scores on the I.T.P.A., between experimental and control non-immigrant groups[1]; and their respective patterns are remarkably similar. On the E.P.V.T. the scores reflect those found for all children. The experimental non-immigrant group's average standard score remains constant, the control classes lose by about a standard point and the control schools gain: this time by more than two standard points (see Table 6 on page 122 for a summary). But in the case of these comparisons the numbers prevent the differences being statistically significant.

The small numbers of control immigrant children make it necessary to compare immigrant groups only within the experimental schools.[2] On the

---

[1] See the "psycholinguistic profiles" above and Tables 13 and 16 in Appendix 3.
[2] See Appendix 2 for the relative sizes of the various experimental and control groups.

Table 5

Change in Mean Raw Scores on the I.T.P.A. Between Pre- and Post-Test for Experimental and Control Children Grouped with Respect to Their Immigrant Status

	Non-immigrant		West Indian immigrant		Other immigrant	
	Experimental $N = 101$	Control $N = 104$	Experimental $N = 27$	Control $N = 3$	Experimental $N = 6$	Control $N = 6$
Auditory reception	+3·3	+2·7	+4·9	+7·7	+3·0	−0·5
Visual reception	+3·0	+4·0	+2·0	+7·7	+0·5	+4·2
Auditory association	+2·5	+2·2	+1·1	+0·7	+3·0	+4·5
Visual association	+1·6	+2·0	+2·3	+3·7	+1·3	+2·2
Verbal expression*	+4·5	+3·3	+2·0	+6·7	+2·3	+7·7
Manual expression	−0·4	+0·9	−0·3	+6·7	+3·0	+5·8
Grammatic closure*	+2·5	+2·1	+1·5	+0·7	+1·3	+4·0
Visual closure	+5·7	+5·9	+5·7	+8·0	+8·8	+4·5
Auditory memory	+3·6	+2·4	+3·3	+4·0	+3·7	+3·3
Visual memory	+3·2	+4·1	+3·3	+4·3	+5·0	+2·0

* Statistically significant change scores within the experimental group.

I.T.P.A., pre-test differences are, with one exception, maintained at post-test.[1] There are two statistically significant changes in score—on grammatic closure and verbal expression. In both cases the average improvements for the experimental non-immigrant group are twice those of the two immigrant groups (see Table 5 above for a summary). On the E.P.V.T. there were significantly different pre- and post-test scores between experimental groups differing with respect to their immigrant status; but the size of the differences did not change over time.[2]

In summary then: the experimental non-immigrants did not improve relative to the control non-immigrants, and differences between experimental immigrant groups increased over the year. A possible interpretation of this pattern of results is that the language work capitalised on some of the differential strengths in linguistic performance between groups—different with respect to their immigrant status—but unfortunately only to widen existing differences. And one conclusion must be that a consequence of the work was to assist in the deterioration of the already weak performance of immigrant children on grammatic closure and verbal expression.

[1] See Tables 13 and 14 in Appendix 3.
[2] See Tables 20 and 21 in Appendix 3.

Table 6

Mean Pre-Test Standard Score and Change in Mean Score on the E.P.V.T. for Experimental and Control Children Grouped with Respect to Their Immigrant Status.

	Non-immigrant			West Indian immigrant			Other immigrant		
	Experimental $N = 149$	Control 1 $N = 70$	Control 2 $N = 146$	Experimental $N = 34$	Control 1 $N = 40$	Control 2 $N = 7$	Experimental $N = 8$	Control 1 $N = 6$	Control 2 $N = 8$
Pre-test mean score	95·3	93·4	93·3	87·7	89·3	94·0	86·1	81·5	83·5
Standard deviation	13·3	13·6	13·0	12·4	10·4	19·4	12·3	14·7	5·8
Change in mean score	0·0	-0·9	+2·3	-0·6	-2·5	+4·7	+0·5	-1·2	+1·5

Comparing the scores of low, medium and high scoring groups[1]

By definition there were no differences between low, medium and high scoring groups at pre-test; and there were, in fact, very few significant differences between them at post-test (see Table 7 below). The language

Table 7

Differences in Post-Test Mean Raw Score, and Results of Variance Analysis on I.T.P.A. Post-Test Scores, for Experimental and Control Children Who Were Defined as Low, Medium and High Scorers on the Pre-Test

	Low scorers E–C		Medium scorers E–C		High scorers E–C	
Auditory reception	1·32	(ns)	0·05	(ns)	0·81	(ns)
Visual reception	−0·42	(ns)	−1·35	$0.05 > p > 0.025$	−3·06	$0·05 > p > 0·025$
Auditory association	1·22	(ns)	−1·04	(ns)	1·81	(ns)
Visual association	−0·72	(ns)	0·33	(ns)	−1·43	(ns)
Verbal expression	−2·14	(ns)	−0·15	(ns)	1·03	(ns)
Manual expression	0·06	(ns)	−0·80	(ns)	−2·73	$0·025 > p > 0·01$
Grammatic closure	0·51	(ns)	−1·41	$0·025 > p > 0·01$	0·44	(ns)
Visual closure	−1·61	(ns)	−0·40	(ns)	−0·59	(ns)
Auditory memory	0·48	(ns)	0·67	(ns)	0·06	(ns)
Visual memory	0·68	(ns)	−1·71	$0·025 > p > 0·01$	−1·06	(ns)

programme does not seem to have had many significant differential effects on the overall performance of high, medium or low performing children.[2]

One pattern is distinctive, however, and it offers an explanation of the finding that there were different change scores between the total experimental and control groups on the visual reception and manual expression items of the I.T.P.A. On both sub-tests the differences between initially low scoring groups are minimal; they are larger for the initially medium scorers (being statistically significant over visual reception); and are larger still, and significant, for the high scorers. There appears then to be a trend of increasing disparity on these items, which isolates the finding for the total experimental and control groups.[3] The higher scoring experimental groups failed to improve as much as the high scoring control groups; and low performing children in both groups were relatively unaffected by what happened to them over the year.

Comparing the scores of classes and schools

The pattern of changes on the I.T.P.A. and E.P.V.T. between the experimental classes is extremely complex. It is difficult to regard the observed

[1] See Appendix 2 for the way in which the groups were defined.
[2] Interpretation of the E.P.V.T. comparisons is confounded by the initial over representation of boys in the high scoring group.
[3] See page 118 and Tables 1 and 2 in the text.

Table 8

Differences in Mean Raw Scores for the Experimental Schools on the I.T.P.A., and the Results of Variance Analysis on Pre-Test, Post-Test and Change Scores

	School						Pre-test A.N.O.V.A.	Post-test A.N.O.V.A.	Covariance analysis on change scores
	00	01	02	03	04	05			
Auditory reception	4·15	0·23	5·04	2·28	4·19	2·84	(ns)	(ns)	(ns)
Visual reception	2·48	2·69	2·48	1·17	3·08	3·88	(ns)	(ns)	(ns)
Auditory association	2·18	1·31	1·96	4·95	2·00	1·56	(ns)	(ns)	(ns)
Visual association	2·15	0·92	2·44	−0·45	3·84	0·36	(ns)	(ns)	$0·05 > p > 0·025$
Verbal expression	5·30	2·54	9·16	4·83	1·15	−0·04	(ns)	$p < 0·001$	$p < 0·001$
Manual expression	1·97	−4·31	−1·04	−1·34	1·38	0·56	$0·05 > p > 0·025$	(ns)	$0·05 > p > 0·025$
Grammatic closure	3·22	0·77	2·68	0·72	2·66	1·96	$0·05 > p > 0·025$	$0·025 > p > 0·01$	$0·05 > p > 0·025$
Visual closure	6·22	4·54	8·32	5·33	6·77	4·98	(ns)	$0·005 > p > 0·001$	$0·01 > p > 0·005$
Auditory memory	4·68	1·07	2·60	1·22	3·69	5·40	(ns)	(ns)	(ns)
Visual memory	5·48	3·69	4·76	0·50	3·53	1·08	(ns)	$p < 0·001$	$p < 0·001$

Table 9

Differences in Mean Standard Scores for the Experimental Schools on the E.P.V.T.

	School						Pre-test A.N.O.V.A.	Post-test A.N.O.V.A.	Covariance analysis on change scores
	00	01	02	03	04	05			
Pre-test mean	99·4	90·5	95·8	90·1	95·1	94·4			
SD	14·6	12·1	15·2	12·0	14·0	12·1			
Change in standard score	−2·5	−6·4	+2·9	−0·8	−1·3	+1·5	(ns)	$0·025 > p > 0·01$	(ns)

124

differences as subject entirely to chance. But at the same time they appear to have no overall or coherent direction, and they cannot be related to known characteristics of groups of children or to class teachers. With the data available they appear almost idiosyncratic. All we can say, therefore, is that different experimental classes improved by different amounts on different sub-tests, and that this may reflect strengths and weaknesses in the work of different teachers. But that, at the planning stage of the action, these characteristics were not distinguished, and we can say nothing of general significance about them. Further the research evaluation has failed to identify them; and in this sense it has failed to add to our knowledge.

A pattern of results

It would be reasonable to expect one in twenty of the comparisons of score to be statistically different purely by chance. In fact one in five of the comparisons of change-score were significant; and even excluding differences between classes within each of the various treatment groups, one in seven comparisons were significantly different.

These differences might be interpreted in terms of:

a. The organisation of the tests, in particular of the I.T.P.A.
b. The educational content of the language work programmes.
c. Changes in the most depressed areas of the children's psycholinguistic functioning at the pre-test.
d. Changes in the least depressed areas of the children's psycholinguistic functioning at the pre-test.

Seen in these ways the overall pattern becomes a little more clear. In the first place, there was no pattern of change that could be related to the organisation of the tests (for instance, to the channels of communication, psycholinguistic processes or levels of organisation employed in the I.T.P.A.). Of the range of skills measured on the tests, four seem particularly related to the general content of the language work as it evolved: the verbal expression and the auditory reception and association (processing) items on the I.T.P.A., and the passive vocabulary as it was measured on the E.P.V.T. There was no pattern of change on the I.T.P.A. items. But the passive vocabulary of the experimental group remained constant over the period; the internal control group's passive vocabulary deteriorated slightly with reference to national norms, while the external control group's vocabulary improved markedly.

The language work was intended to be both diagnostic and remedial. The psycholinguistic weaknesses revealed by the I.T.P.A. were on reception (for the total E.P.A. group) and grammatic closure (for the experimental immigrant groups). The visual reception score of the control group changed more positively than that of the experimental group, but there was no significant post-test difference between the two. Within the experimental group the grammatic closure (and the verbal expression) performance of the West Indian immigrant children fell further behind that of their non-immigrant peers over the period of the programme. Lastly, looking at how far the work programme capitalised on the relative strengths in the psycholinguistic skills of the subject children, we can identify manual expression and auditory memory as the areas of relatively the greatest skill. The control group's manual expression performance improved more positively than that of the experimental group.

In summary then, we can make two observations about the general pattern. There are some signs of a relatively greater improvement in performance of the control group over the experimental group. But within the experimental group there are fluctuations in the rates of change which are greater than chance, but not attributable to known characteristics of teachers, children or the overall content of the work.

Conclusions and Implications

Two decisions were made in the design of the evaluation which seriously limit any appraisal of the programme. In a specific sense the errors, indeed the evaluation, were irrelevant; and the language work continued after the period of sponsorship by the E.P.A. Project more or less without regard to the test results. Nevertheless there are some considerations of general consequence.

There is no information on the behaviour of the within-school control children measured on the I.T.P.A. The results on the E.P.V.T. (the passive vocabulary test) are interesting in this respect, however. Although the experimental group did not improve relative to national norms over the period and the other-school control group did, the within-school control children lost ground. Clearly one interpretation of this is that the teachers of second year junior children in the E.P.A. Project schools were split, by the proposal for a language programme, into groups with high and low motivation: and that the E.P.V.T. results measured the effect of this on the performance of the children they taught. But there is another explanation. It is that the E.P.A. Project schools and the other-control schools were different: that, for instance, children in the other-control schools had a "natural" tendency to improve over time: that the Project Schools' "natural" tendency was to deteriorate; and that, therefore, the language work was successful in that it stopped any further decline in the children's performance.

It is difficult to prove this second explanation wrong; and more test results within the given design would not necessarily have helped. But I think it should be discounted. Whatever differences there were emerged over the period. To sustain the theory of a "natural" tendency for the average performance of children in the two groups of schools to diverge, it would presumably be necessary to argue that divergent tendencies would continue in the third and fourth year in junior school. The fourth year children in these schools were also used as experimental and control groups for the evaluation of the Environmental Studies Scheme. And at this level, admittedly on different tests, the necessary pattern was not observed: there were no significant differences at pre-test, and differences again emerged over the period of the evaluation.[1]

But there is still a need to interpret the results; and the lack of research

---

[1] See Part 6.

information again limits what can be said. We do not know in any systematic way what actually happened between the teachers and their children. We know in a general sense what the experimental teachers were attempting to do; we know that they saw themselves, and were seen, to be succeeding. We know that the overall trend as measured on the tests was, at best, no change and, at worst, some minimal deterioration above what might reasonably be expected. We also know that there was an enormous variety of results obtained between experimental classes: a variety which we cannot interpret with the information available. But the important point in this respect is as follows. All the teachers were more highly motivated than average. Let us suppose that some of them actually succeeded in improving some aspects of the children's measured language skills (but in unknown ways): then at least we can say that it is possible to do it. Yet the overall trend was towards no change. The research has failed to find the reasons for isolated examples of success; but the in-service training scheme has failed to generalise that success. The consequences are extremely important. Success is possible. But more than motivation is needed to achieve it; and in-service training schemes of the sort used here cannot yet give to the majority what it takes to achieve it. Indeed, from this example of innovation we are unsure what it takes. Consider for a moment what was being attempted. Leaving aside any considerations of a genetic contribution to language skills, the children in this work programme had developed styles of linguistic behaviour over eight years of life. Even allowing maximum school time during the year to be spent on spoken language work, approximately one thousand hours could be devoted to adapting behaviour which was developing over four times that period outside school during the programme year, and had already developed during some forty thousand hours prior to that year. A possible reaction is to say that the task is too difficult. A more positive reaction is to say that, if the task is considered important, then more time and thought should be devoted to it. Even if a radical transformation in behaviour cannot be achieved, at least there is some value to be added to the children's levels of skill by competent school work. At least then, language work should begin earlier in schools and go on longer and be more integrated into a normal curriculum. Some might assert that infant schools are already doing this work. Some E.P.A. schools may intend to, some may succeed; but clearly the dominant pattern is for most to fail when relative standards of assessment are used.[1] We return to the problem of in-service training, of teacher-group support for curriculum innovation, of the nature of a teacher's working day and of how to generalise success—this time with as much attention being devoted to the problems of the teacher as to the problems of the children.

---

[1] See, for instance, the cross-sectional analysis of E.P.V.T. scores for children in all four English E.P.A. Project areas reported in Volume 2 of the series: *Statistics and Surveys*.

APPENDIX 1

THE CLASSIFICATION OF LANGUAGE PROGRAMME ACTIVITIES OF THE FIRST YEAR.

J. H. Barnes and J. Stevenson

The following table that appears on page 129 was produced as a means of classifying the language production situations that can occur in the classroom. Consideration was given to the demands on the speaker not the listener. The classification was by the nature of the stimulus used and the function of the the language to be produced. The classification was offered to participants in the language programme during its second year, the intention was to:

(a) illustrate the types of linguistic and conceptual skill associated with different types of language production situations;

(b) reveal areas of the curriculum which are most open to intervention by the teacher with the aim of improved language performance by the children;

(c) give an indication of the most effective intervention style appropriate to these curriculum areas and linguistic features.

The device is clearly heuristic. Its sole intention was to heighten awareness through the in-service training aspect of the programme.

The rows in the table on page 129 refer to qualities of the stimulus used in the language production situations and the columns classify these situations according to the functions of the language produced.

The terms "real", "symbolic" and "conceptual" denote the level of representation of the stimulus. "Real" stimuli are concrete and exist in the real world; "symbolic" stimuli are ones that represent "real" objects and situations but are not the objects themselves, e.g., a picture of a ball rather than a ball itself; "conceptual" stimuli do not exist in the real world, the child usually has to recall from memory events from the past or an image of familiar objects, or has to construct for himself an imaginary situation.

Each of the features of the stimuli in fact becomes blurred when considering actual teaching situations; they are considered as discrete categories only for purposes of analysis.

At each of these levels of representation, we have distinguished between two categories of stimuli, i.e. "objects" and "situations". The former are essentially "perceivable stimuli", in that information about them is received through the sense modalities. "Situations", on the other hand, we are calling "projected stimuli", i.e. the receiver, in order to understand their important features, must use information beyond the purely visual or auditory stimulation and make projections either about another person's reactions or about the workings of a process which are not perceivable in the sense used above.

It should be noted that the types of stimulus that will be referred to in these illustrations will be essentially those associated with visual perception, but that the same analysis holds for other sense modalities.

The two columns in the table on page 129 are labelled "instructions" and "descriptions"; although we have called these functional categories, they are more realistically defined by the features of the produced language. These distinguishing features are set out on page 130.

Types of Linguistic and Conceptual Tools associated with Various Language Producing Situations

		Instructions	Descriptions
Real	Object	*Cognitive Skills:* Perceptual switching. *Linguistic Tools:* Correct use of prepositions and adverbs.	*Cognitive Skills:* Able to distinguish attributes of a commonplace object. *Linguistic Tools:* Ability to use correctly a large number of adjectives.
	Situation	*Cognitive Skills:* Ability to analyse the most *relevant* feature of a situation. *Linguistic Tools:* Understanding of correct use of imperative.	*Cognitive Skills:* Role switching. *Linguistic Tools:* Use of qualifying adjectival and adverbal phrases and clauses.
Symbolic	Object	*Cognitive Skills:* Perceptual power to recognise and attach labels to symbols. *Linguistic Tools:* Understanding of subject/object distinction.	*Cognitive Skills:* Ability to construct a 3-dimensional world from a 2-dimensional picture. *Linguistic Tools:* Idea of the use of simile.
	Situation	*Cognitive Skills:* Ability to construct causal chains of events. *Linguistic Tools:* Correct use of pronouns (esp. personal).	*Cognitive Skills:* Ability to account for changes of scale in the symbolic world. *Linguistic Tools:* Able to distinguish active and passive verb forms.
Conceptual	Object	*Cognitive Skills:* Ability to recall accurately from memory. *Linguistic Tools:* Ability to generalise linguistic categories from own experience, e.g., in answer to "What is a ship?"	*Cognitive Skills:* Able to ascribe attributes to images. *Linguistic Tools:* Idea of use of metaphors.
	Situation	*Cognitive Skills:* Ability to construct an accurate "inner world" picture. *Linguistic Tools:* Use of verbs and modifying of verbs.	*Cognitive Skills:* Ability to attribute motives, emotions, etc., in the absence of any physical stimulus indicating their presence. *Linguistic Tools:* Correct use of conditional clauses.

For each of the language production situations in the initial table, we have ascribed a "cognitive skill" and "linguistic tool" which seem to be most appropriate to that situation. It must be stressed that the skills we have attributed are not only found in that situation, but are necessary in other situations, and other skills will be required to cope with that situation. For example, an important linguistic tool in the description of "real situations",

Distinguishing Features of "Instructions" and "Descriptions"

"Instructions"	"Descriptions"
No scope for the imaginative use of language, except where metaphor and simile are used for concision.	The child's imagination is allowed freedom to operate.
The truth and accuracy of what is being said is verifiable.	Verification is not necessarily possible.
There is a premium on concision and precision in the use of words, phrases, etc., to aid the listener's ability to comprehend the instructions being given.	Verbosity, although not necessarily encouraged, is *not* considered a sin when the child is describing something.
There is usually a definable end-product, e.g., the speaker wants somebody else to reproduce an action that the speaker has just performed himself.	The result of a process of describing something is indefinite and non-predictable, in that the expectancies of the participants are undefined beyond the acceptance that a communication process is desirable.

whatever the level of representation, is the correct use of a large number of adjectives, but we consider that if a teacher wishes to concentrate on this linguistic tool it is best done when the child is "describing real objects", because of the greater immediacy of the sensation which the adjective is describing. It is probably best here to give an idea of how we envisage this formulation being used in the course of the language programme. Firstly, the teacher must decide which feature of the child's language she wishes to improve. Having made this decision, she must search through the table for the most appropriate situation to produce this aspect of language. She will then be able to construct a situation with the appropriate stimuli and can give the child an idea of the function of the language expected from the situation.

She will find that we have also given a cognitive skill associated with this language producing situation. In a sense, these skills are prerequisite to the child being able to respond in this situation. The diagnosis as to whether these skills are present or not in the children is beyond the scope of this note, but it is worth emphasising that linguistic ability and conceptual ability will affect one another. For example, when the child is in a language-producing situation that requires role switching (i.e., the ability to place oneself in the position of somebody else so that the motivations, feelings, etc., of the person switched to can be communicated), if he is unable to do this the child will produce inappropriate language. However, as this cognitive skill develops, the use of conditional clauses will increase and then subsequently decrease, as the complete role switch is achieved. It should also be mentioned that the gross categories into which the stimuli have been grouped should not disguise the fact that more specific types of stimulus will require different skills. For example, when working at the symbolic level, a single picture and a series of pictures will require different skills in order to produce language descriptive of the situation. A single picture entails that the child is able to project backwards and forwards in time in order to understand and then communicate the causes and consequences of the situation portrayed. A series of pictures, on the other hand, gives the child more clues as to the above features of the situation, but requires that the child is capable of relating the series of symbols together.

Linguistic Aspects of the Curriculum

These language producing situations occur throughout the whole of the curriculum in the primary school. Below we make some generalisations about which language producing situations are most commonly found in each area of the curriculum. Yet again it must be emphasised that any activity involving the use of language will contain elements that fit into many places in our description of language producing situations.

Maths—Essentially instructional language about real and symbolic objects and relationships between objects.

Nature/Science—Instructional language concerned with real situations and objects.

History/R.I.—Descriptive language about symbolic and conceptual situations.

Geography and Environmental Studies—Descriptive language about real objects.

P.E.—Child in an essentially listener situation, but having to understand instructions about real situations, especially the imperative.

Art—In itself a non-linguistic activity but child uses congnitive skills of perceptual switching, manipulating symbolic and conceptual objects and situations.

Craft/Needlework—Instructional language with real objects.

English—This includes many different language-based activities: poetry, creative writing, reading, drama, etc., so that most of the language producing situations occur.

Classroom Administration—(i.e., registration, dinner money, etc.) requires the child to respond to instructions at all levels, mainly the conceptual.

Conversation Pieces

It is possible, however, to construct situations specifically designed to promote the use of certain types of language. Over the last year, in the course of the language programme development, many conversation pieces have been formulated. In the table on page 132 we have allocated each of these activities to one part of our classification of language producing situations. We have also added a few activities not so far introduced into the language programme. This illustrates that our approach to language in the classroom should not be considered as a limited collection of activities, which have been prescribed to remedy the children's linguistic problems, but rather that language-producing situations are occurring throughout the curriculum.

Very many more activities can be constructed as conversation pieces, to augment and illustrate language-producing situations.

Verbal Interaction Points

Up till now we have referred to these language-producing situations without consideration of who is taking part, who is speaking and who is listening.

A Classification of Possible Conversational Pieces

		Instructions	Descriptions
Real	Object	Describing a coloured cube. Lego—building at same time as telling someone else what you have done.	Chinese puzzles. Guessing bag.
	Situation	Get a child to talk about what another child is doing at the same time. How to use a telephone.	Shooting gamesmaster (teacher creates an unusual event in the classroom, which the children observe and later report).
Symbolic	Object	Photographs of objects from unusual angles, stimulus cards. Lego—using a model already constructed.	Description of a Picasso still life.
	Situation	"Tell me about" pictures.	Talking books. Reconstruction of story without words (blacked out books). Make up a story using glove puppets.
Conceptual	Object	What does your front room look like?	What is a man from Mars like?
	Situation	How can I get to the High Street?	Recall of past events.

We are essentially interested in the child as a speaker—but we must bear in mind that, by listening to the teacher's speech model, the child is given an opportunity to assess his own linguistic performance.

The number of different combinations of people who can enter into a conversation in the classroom is large, but we have here restricted ourselves to those most commonly found in the classroom. Those we have excluded tend to be the most administratively inconvenient, however it could be that they would be very much more appropriate on linguistic grounds, e.g., the class listening to the conversation of two teachers or each of the children recording their own version of a story on one tape recorder whilst listening to the story on another.

There seem to us to be four commonly found "verbal interaction points"; we will list the organisational conveniences and language implications of each of these. It should be borne in mind that any of the previously mentioned language-producing situations can act as a "content" for any of these verbal interactions.

Teacher/Class

This is probably the easiest type of interaction for the teacher to deal with. The class is usually seated and relatively quiet, in order to hear the teacher and any reply from one of its members. At any one time the teacher only has to deal with one particular content, and, at least theoretically, has control over the situation. It is often, therefore, a good way of imparting information quickly. However, the children's active language can suffer under these conditions, mainly in that at any one time only one child can be speaking. This fact, coupled with that of the teacher probably talking for half of the time during say a 30 minute session, means that any one child, if each spoke in turn, would have about 30 seconds in which to develop his language abilities.

Teacher/Group
    Under these conditions the objection to the teacher/class interaction on linguistic grounds still holds but is decreased as the size of the group decreases. Unfortunately there are organisational problems with this situation. Namely the supervision of the other children in the class. These can be given a non-verbal task to perform but this increases the detrimental effects of limiting the number of children that speak during a given period. If the remaining children are given a verbal task, then they must do so unsupervised. This not only increases the noise level in the classroom, producing an adverse effect on the teacher/group activity, but also leaves unmonitored and uncontrolled the language produced by the remaining group.

Teacher/Child
    This situation creates the greatest teacher control of the language of a given child. Not only can the teacher ensure that a given task is being used to its full advantage, but she can also introduce new material and correct the speech of the child according to its own needs.
    There is, however, proportionate increase in the problem of "the others" mentioned under teacher/group interaction.

Child/Child
    This is the type of interaction that probably gives the child the greatest amount of dialogue. It also overcomes to a certain extent the organisational problems mentioned above, in that the teacher is not necessarily actively involved with any particular sub-group in the classroom, and is therefore free to regulate the overall classroom situation.
    It does mean, though, that the children are not receiving an adult's speech model, either with which to compare their own or to control the language-producing situation. Also, if this situation is to be distinct from the teacher/child interaction, the teacher must know how and when to intervene in the dialogue between child and child. This is necessary, since in this type of situation the children are likely to reinforce or at least leave uncorrected their own linguistic failings.

APPENDIX 2

THE DESIGN OF THE EVALUATION
AND THE TESTS USED

J. H. Barnes and J. Stevenson

The Design of the Evaluation

All classes in the evaluation were in their second year in the junior school. The children taught by the nine teachers taking part in the regular discussion groups comprised the *de facto* experimental group. The second year junior children taught by the E.P.A. Project teachers who did not attend the discussion groups comprised a *de facto* within school control group (C1). In addition, a between school control group was used (C2): for this the District Inspector of a neighbouring I.L.E.A. Division was asked to suggest a group of schools similar in character to the E.P.A. Project schools.

The evaluation period was the school year 1970–71; and children were tested at the beginning and end of that year.

Two tests were used in the evaluation (see below): one—the E.P.V.T.—was a group test, and the other—the I.T.P.A.—was administered to individual children. The E.P.V.T. was administered to all classes. For the I.T.P.A. we excluded the within school control classes, and sampled by class within experimental and control (C2) schools. If a school had only one class of second year junior children they were tested on the I.T.P.A.; if there was more than one class, then one was selected at random. Table 1 below shows the numbers involved overall.

Table 1

Numbers of Children Involved*

		Experimental	Control 1: within school	Control 2: other school
I.T.P.A.	Pre-test	166	—	128
	Post-test	134	—	113
E.P.V.T.	Pre-test	227	134	198
	Post-test	191	116	161

* All children present in their respective classes were tested in October 1970—at pre-test. All children who had been tested in October 1970—were retested in June 1971—at post-test. Only scores for those children who were present at both pre- and post-test were used in the data analysis.

Table 2 below shows the size of the groups used for the analysis.

Comparisons of test scores—at pre-test, post-test and relative changes in score—were made for the following groups:

(i) All experimental, control (1) and control (2) children.

(ii) Those groups broken down into boy and girl sub-groupings.

(iii) Those groups broken down into sub-groups defined with respect to their immigrant status (according to the Department of Education

134

Table 2

Numbers of Children Involved by Sex and Immigrant Status

	I.T.P.A.		E.P.V.T.		
	Experi-mental	Control 2	Experi-mental	Control 1	Control 2
Total	134	113	191	116	161
Boys	69	54	102	57	74
Girls	65	59	89	59	87
Non-immigrant	101	104	149	70	146
West Indian immigrant	27	3	34	40	7
Other immigrants	6	6	8	6	8

and Science definitions). The groups in this respect were defined as follows:

—all non-immigrant children

—all West Indian immigrant children (which was the only relatively homogeneous immigrant group sufficiently large for analysis)

—a "residual" other immigrant group

(iv) Comparison of school or class scores within the various treatment groups.

A further comparison—of post-test scores—was made between groups of children in the various treatment groups which, on pre-test scores, had been allocated a high, medium or low scoring status. Children were allocated to the low, medium or high scoring groups if their pre-test scores were respectively minus one standard deviation, within one standard deviation or above one standard deviation of the calculated mean for all children on that particular test or sub-test. Such a definition meant that relative change scores could not be used as a basis for comparison, because the pre-test score would then have been used twice—both to define the groups initially and in the calculation of change scores.

The Tests Used

1. The English Picture Vocabulary Test: Level 2 (the E.P.V.T.) was used as a test of passive vocabulary.[1]

2. The Illinois Test of Psycholinguistic Abilities (the I.T.P.A.)[2] was used to test a broad and comprehensive range of linguistic abilities.

The underlying structure of the I.T.P.A. is a model of language derived from a communication model of Osgood. The model uses three basic dimen-

---

[1] See M. A. Brimer and L. Dunn, *Manual for the English Picture Vocabulary Test*, Educational Evaluation Enterprises.

[2] See S. A. Kirk, S. S. McCarthy and W. D. Kirk, *Examiners' Manual: Illinois Test of Psycholinguistic Abilities*, Illinois University, 1968.

sions: which constitute the cognitive abilities necessary for language communication.

1. *Channels of communication*: These constitute pathways of information flow. The I.T.P.A. uses two: auditory-vocal and motor-visual.
2. *Psycholinguistic processes*: The I.T.P.A. measures performance at three different levels of information processing.
    (a) Receptive: The ability necessary to recognise and understand what is being seen or heard.
    (b) Expressive: The capacity to express ideas vocally or by movement.
    (c) Organising: The internal manipulation of things perceived, remembered or constructed that comes between the receptive and expressive processes.
3. *Levels of organisation*: These levels, the I.T.P.A. assesses two, are concerned with the overall way in which a task is achieved. If the task does not require much recall of past experience, or the construction of new ideas and relationships, the subject is said to be functioning at the *automatic level*. If the task does require such mediating processes, then the subject is said to be functioning at the *representational level*.

It is important to bear these three dimensions in mind when inspecting the "psycholinguistic profiles" (see pages 113–118), since *a priori* the clustering of good and bad performance on separate items should be related to them.

The Sub-Tests

Table 3 lists the sub-tests of the I.T.P.A. with a brief account of the area of linguistic functioning assessed. Each of these sub-tests has been classified with reference to the respective communication channel, psycholinguistic process and level of organisation. It will be seen that the psycholinguistic processes have not been isolated at the automatic level of organisation; the test constructors believe this to be impossible and call the automatic sub-tests "whole level" tests.

The "Psycholinguistic" Profile

The profiles presented in the text are a means of representing the data for the separate sub-tests on a uniform scale. The profile is designed as a diagnostic device for individual children; the profiles in the text are for various groups of children. If normative data are available the simplest way to create a group profile is to use the standard scores on each test. But the only standardised data for children of this age are for American children. The main part of the analysis was performed on raw scores, therefore. (The groups were homogeneous with respect to age.)

This procedure is satisfactory as long as only one sub-test at a time is compared. But when we are trying to relate the sub-tests to each other the raw score data are inadequate as they are not equally distributed. And so it is necessary to construct a quantifiable interrelationship between sub-tests.

Table 3
Classification of I.T.P.A. Sub-tests into Dimensions

	Area of linguistic functioning measured	Communication channel	Psycholinguistic process	Level of organisation
1. Auditory reception	The ability of a child to derive meaning from verbally presented material.	Auditory-vocal	Receptive	Representational
2. Visual reception	The ability of a child to derive meaning from visual symbols.	Visual-motor	Receptive	Representational
3. Auditory association	The ability of a child to relate concepts presented orally.	Auditory-vocal	Organizing	Representational
4. Visual association	The ability of a child to relate concepts presented visually.	Visual-motor	Organizing	Representational
5. Verbal expression	The ability of a child to express his own concepts vocally.	Auditory-vocal	Expressive	Representational
6. Manual expression	The ability of a child to express ideas manually.	Visual-motor	Expressive	Representational
7. Grammatic closure	The ability of a child to make use of the redundancies of oral language in acquiring automatic habits for handling syntax and grammatical inflections.	Auditory-vocal	Whole-level	Automatic
8. Visual closure	The ability of a child to identify a common object from an incomplete visual presentation.	Visual-motor	Whole-level	Automatic
9. Auditory memory	The ability of a child to reproduce from memory sequences of digits increasing in length from two to eight.	Auditory-vocal	Whole-level	Automatic
10. Visual memory	The ability of a child to reproduce from memory sequences of non-meaningful figures.	Visual-motor	Whole-level	Automatic

To achieve this the distribution of raw scores on each sub-test in the American sample with equivalent ages (8:4–8:7) were transformed into raw score standard units. Thus a fixed proportion of the sample can be expected to fall within a known range of scores, and therefore scores of the E.P.A. groups on different sub-tests can be equated.

A normal American child should obtain a "flat" profile; and so, if the American and English norms were equivalent for this age group, a normal English profile would also be "flat". If E.P.A. children's performance on this test followed the pattern obtained from other standardised tests, then although it would be below the mid point (below average), there would be no *a priori* grounds to assume their profile to be other than "flat". In fact their profile is both below the mid point and uneven. But we cannot confidently attribute the variation between sub-tests either to inter-cultural differences (between American and English children) or to intra-cultural differences (between normal English and English E.P.A. children). Either of these, or a combination of them, could explain the result.

Intercorrelations among the Ten Sub-tests

Table 4 gives the intercorrelations among the ten sub-tests for the total pre-test group of E.P.A. children (including children whose scores were not taken into account in the evaluation of the language programme as they left their schools before the post-test) and for a sample of normal American children of the same age. It can be seen from the matrix that the relationships between items within the test are of the same order for the two groups.

The statistical techniques used for the data analysis were analysis of variance (on pre- and post-test raw scores) and analysis of covariance (on changes in raw scores)[1].

In all cases a level of significance with $p < 0.05$ was accepted as significant.

---

[1] For the evaluation of this curriculum scheme, and for that reported in Part 6, Miss Wendy Fader of the National Foundation for Educational Research's statistical services department advised on the statistical techniques and arranged for the computing.

Table 4

Intercorrelations Among the Ten I.T.P.A. Sub-tests for a Goup of American Children and for the Total E.P.A. Group

	1	2	3	4	5	6	7	8	9	10
				American Group, $N = 127$						
1. Auditory reception	—	0·38	0·48	0·34	0·30	0·11	0·45	0·31	-0·03	0·02
2. Visual reception	0·33	—	0·46	0·46	0·36	0·23	0·41	0·40	-0·04	0·27
3. Auditory association	0·56	0·35	—	0·42	0·42	0·35	0·50	0·37	0·05	0·08
4. Visual association	0·33	0·35	0·42	—	0·43	0·27	0·50	0·37	0·08	0·17
5. Verbal expression	0·27	0·27	0·37	0·23	—	0·43	0·46	0·44	0·16	-0·06
6. Manual expression	0·28	0·24	0·39	0·29	0·39	—	0·18	0·38	0·01	-0·01
7. Grammatic closure	0·57	0·25	0·64	0·36	0·34	0·53	—	0·40	0·09	0·06
8. Visual closure	0·32	0·32	0·40	0·40	0·30	0·28	0·38	—	0·00	0·10
9. Auditory memory	0·22	0·04	0·29	0·10	0·19	0·10	0·35	0·10	—	-0·06
10. Visual memory	0·27	0·21	0·27	0·23	0·15	0·17	0·30	0·22	0·06	—

E.P.A. English Group, $N = 294$.

APPENDIX 3

THE RESULTS OF THE EVALUATION
J. H. Barnes and J. Stevenson

Table 1

Average Pre- and Post-test Scores on the I.T.P.A. for the Experimental and Control Groups

	Experimental group: $N = 134$			Control group: $N = 113$		
	Pre-test mean and standard deviation	Post-test mean and standard deviation	Difference in mean	Pre-test mean and standard deviation	Post-test mean and standard deviation	Difference in mean
Auditory	29·13	32·78	3·65	30·27	32·97	2·70
reception	8·37	8·21		9·17	8·57	
Visual	21·06	23·76	2·70	20·74	24·88	4·14
reception	4·86	4·78		5·62	5·81	
Auditory	26·25	28·53	2·28	26·65	28·88	2·23
association	4·56	6·30		6·23	5·30	
Visual	23·08	24·81	1·73	22·51	24·55	2·04
association	5·05	5·21		5·02	5·04	
Verbal	30·14	34·04	3·90	30·89	34·48	3·59
expression	7·26	7·97		8·74	7·57	
Manual	28·02	27·80	−0·22	27·41	28·65	1·24
expression	4·90	4·61		5·60	5·12	
Grammatic	22·68	24·88	2·20	24·52	26·69	2·17
closure	5·98	5·50		6·27	5·24	
Visual	24·34	30·59	6·25	25·19	31·08	5·89
closure	5·29	6·43		5·93	7·02	
Auditory	31·07	34·49	3·42	32·77	35·27	2·50
memory	8·15	9·16		9·37	8·97	
Visual	19·69	22·99	3·30	19·86	23·88	4·02
memory	4·05	5·66		3·69	5.27	

Table 2

Analysis comparing changes in score on the I.T.P.A. for the Experimental and Control Groups

	A.N.O.V.A. on pre-test scores: F value	A.N.O.V.A. on post-test scores: F value	Difference in regressions: F value	Pooled regression: F value	Difference in change scores: F value
Auditory	1.0424	0·0338	0·0253	34·0344	0·1082
reception	(ns)	(ns)	(ns)	$(p < 0.001)$	(ns)
Visual	0·2253	2·9057	0·6269	59·1678	5·7504
reception	(ns)	(ns)	(ns)	$(p < 0.001)$	$(0.025 > p > 0.001)$
Auditory	0·3249	0·2138	0·2030	82·5014	0·0160
association	(ns)	(ns)	(ns)	$(p < 0.001)$	(ns)
Visual	0·7806	0·1624	0·2604	48·4152	0·0055
association	(ns)	(ns)	(ns)	$(p < 0.001)$	(ns)
Verbal	0·5453	0·1893	2·5867	33·2094	0·0129
expression	(ns)	(ns)	(ns)	$(p < 0.001)$	(ns)
Manual	0·8348	1·8892	1·8546	58·6828	5·2571
expression	(ns)	(ns)	(ns)	$(p < 0.001)$	$(0.025 > p > 0.01)$
Grammatic	5·5711	6·9353	1·6491	298·0620	1·4034
closure	$(0.025 > p > 0.01)$	$(0.01 > p > 0.005)$	(ns)	$(p < 0.001)$	(ns)
Visual	1·3926	0·7096	0·2014	92·8917	0·0088
closure	(ns)	(ns)	(ns)	$(p < 0.001)$	(ns)
Auditory	2·3325	0·4445	2·4509	217·2164	0·8382
memory	(ns)	(ns)	(ns)	$(p < 0.001)$	(ns)
Visual	0·1201	1·6221	0·0128	36·0686	1·5794
memory	(ns)	(ns)	(ns)	$(p < 0.001)$	(ns)

Table 3

Average pre- and post-test scores on the E.P.V.T. for the experimental and control groups

	Pre-test mean and standard deviation		Post-test mean and standard deviation		Difference in mean
	Raw Score	Standard Score	Raw Score	Standard Score	Standard Scores
Experiment [191]					
Mean	13·13	93·51	16·16	93·45	−0·06
SD	6·50	13·46	7·42	14·01	
Control (1) [116] (within school)					
Mean	12·26	91·37	14·50	90·30	−1·07
SD	6·17	12·85	6·77	12·55	
Control (2) [158] (other school)					
Mean	13·58	93·26	17·19	95·24	+1·98
SD	6·59	13·18	7·25	13·45	

Table 4

Analysis comparing changes in score on the E.P.V.T. for the experimental and control groups

A.N.O.V.A. on pre-test: F value	A.N.O.V.A. on post-test: F value	Difference in regressions: F value	Pooled regressions: F value	Difference in change scores: F value
1·4368	4·6954	0·4288	75·7308	3·2330
(ns)	$(0.01 > p > 0.005)$	(ns)	$(p < 0.001)$	$(0.05 > p > 0.025)$

Table 5

Average pre- and post-test scores on the I.T.P.A. for the experimental and control group boys and girls

	Male						Female					
	Experimental			Control			Experimental			Control		
	Pre-test	Post-test	Difference in mean	Pre-test	Post-test	Difference in mean	Pre-test	Post-test	Difference in mean	Pre-test	Post-test	Difference in mean
Auditory reception												
Mean	30·31	33·82	3·51	29·67	33·57	3·90	27·96	31·73	3·77	30·83	32·42	1·59
SD	8·60	8·15		9·33	8·97		8·03	8·18		9·05	8·23	
Visual reception												
Mean	21·54	24·81	3·27	21·35	25·91	4·56	20·58	22·72	2·14	20·19	23·95	3·76
SD	4·93	4·81		5·61	5·38		4·78	4·55		5·61	5·64	
Auditory association												
Mean	26·69	28·79	2·10	27·33	29·80	2·47	25·82	28·27	2·45	26·02	28·03	2·01
SD	4·89	5·08		7·04	5·30		4·20	7·36		5·36	5·20	
Visual association												
Mean	23·91	25·33	1·42	23·31	25·06	1·75	22·25	24·30	2·05	21·78	24·08	2·30
SD	4·92	5·34		4·98	4·96		5·09	5·07		4·99	5·11	
Verbal expression												
Mean	29·72	34·09	4·37	30·72	35·17	4·45	30·57	34·00	3·43	31·05	33·85	2·80
SD	6·99	8·43		9·61	8·19		7·55	7·55		7·94	6·97	
Manual expression												
Mean	28·58	28·51	-0·07	27·93	29·74	1·81	27·46	27·09	-0·37	26·93	27·64	0·71
SD	4·82	4·68		5·45	4·80		4·96	4·46		5·73	5·25	
Grammatic closure												
Mean	22·79	25·18	2·39	24·61	26·50	1·89	22·57	24·58	2·01	24·40	26·86	2·46
SD	5·89	4·92		6·38	5·34		6·11	6·04		6·23	5·19	
Visual closure												
Mean	24·94	29·96	5·02	26·24	31·76	5·52	23·76	30·76	7·01	24·22	30·46	6·24
SD	4·74	6·12		6·40	6·84		5·76	6·75		5·34	7·18	
Auditory memory												
Mean	29·88	33·40	3·52	32·35	35·28	3·03	32·25	35·58	3·33	33·15	35·25	2·10
SD	8·04	9·21		9·00	8·96		8·15	9·05		9·75	9·05	
Visual memory												
Mean	19·55	22·79	3·24	19·43	22·61	3·18	19·82	23·19	3·37	20·25	25·05	4·80
SD	4·13	4·71		3·81	4·43		4·00	6·50		3·56	5·73	

Table 6

Analysis comparing changes in score on the I.T.P.A.: Experimental boys and experimental girls

	A.N.O.V.A. on pre-test scores: F value	A.N.O.V.A. on post-test scores: F value	Difference in regression: F value	Pooled regression: F value	Differences in change scores: F value
Auditory reception	2·6936 (ns)	2·1919 (ns)	0·0206 (ns)	17·0844 ($p < 0·001$)	0·6533 (ns)
Visual reception	1·2971 (ns)	6·6761 ($0·025 > p > 0·01$)	0·7278 (ns)	24·9874 ($p < 0·001$)	5·3366 ($0·025 > p > 0·01$)
Auditory association	1·2077 (ns)	0·2285 (ns)	0·0098 (ns)	24·3153 ($p < 0·001$)	0·119 (ns)
Visual association	3·6734 (ns)	1·3117 (ns)	0·0151 (ns)	21·0624 ($p < 0·001$)	0·0496 (ns)
Verbal expression	0·4583 (ns)	0·0046 (ns)	0·9911 (ns)	21·8005 ($p < 0·001$)	0·2099 (ns)
Manual expression	1·7576 (ns)	3·2282 (ns)	0·0140 (ns)	19·1124 ($p < 0·001$)	1·7070 (ns)
Grammatic closure	0·0420 (ns)	0·3545 (ns)	6·6142 ($0·025 > p > 0·01$)	160·1186 ($p < 0·001$)	0·6544 (ns)
Visual closure	1·7175 (ns)	0·5238 (ns)	0·4995 (ns)	45·3676 ($p < 0·001$)	4·0261 ($0·05 > p > 0·025$)
Auditory memory	2·8779 (ns)	1·9076 (ns)	0·2679 (ns)	111·2181 ($p < 0·001$)	0·0023 (ns)
Visual memory	0·1461 (ns)	0·1689 (ns)	2·2794 (ns)	21·7973 ($p < 0·001$)	0·0666 (ns)

Table 7

Analysis comparing changes in score on the I.T.P.A.: Control boys and control girls

	A.N.O.V.A. on pre-test scores: F value	A.N.O.V.A. on post-test scores: F value	Difference in regression: F value	Pooled regression: F value	Difference in change scores: F value
Auditory reception	0·4524 (ns)	0·5053 (ns)	0·0023 (ns)	15·9848 ($p < 0·001$)	1·3450 (ns)
Visual reception	1·2159 (ns)	3·5491 (ns)	0·0170 (ns)	30·8844 ($p < 0·001$)	2·2678 (ns)
Auditory association	1·2623 (ns)	3·1782 (ns)	4·7546 ($0·05 > p > 0·025$)	95·5255 ($p < 0·001$)	2·1523 (ns)
Visual association	2·6745 (ns)	1·0460 (ns)	0·0610 (ns)	25·7774 ($p < 0·001$)	0·0133 (ns)
Verbal expression	0·0397 (ns)	0·8545 (ns)	0·0082 (ns)	11·8937 ($p < 0·001$)	1·2162 (ns)
Manual expression	0·8829 (ns)	4·8722 ($0·05 > p > 0·025$)	0·2523 (ns)	38·0281 ($p < 0·001$)	4·2725 ($0·05 > p > 0·025$)
Grammatic closure	0·0229 (ns)	0·1501 (ns)	0·0219 (ns)	143·9816 ($p < 0·001$)	0·8776 (ns)
Visual closure	3·3425 (ns)	0·9693 (ns)	0·4434 (ns)	48·6549 ($p < 0·001$)	0·1309 (ns)
Auditory memory	0·2047 (ns)	0·0000 (ns)	0·1033 (ns)	101·1806 ($p < 0·001$)	0·3998 (ns)
Visual memory	1·4250 (ns)	6·3241 ($0·025 > p > 0·01$)	0·8817 (ns)	14·6612 ($p < 0·001$)	4·7909 ($0·05 > p > 0·025$)

Table 8

Analysis comparing changes in score on the I.T.P.A.: Experimental boys and control boys

	A.N.O.V.A. on pre-test scores: F value	A.N.O.V.A. on post-test scores: F value	Difference in regression: F value	Pooled regression: F value	Difference in change scores: F value
Auditory	0·1566	0·0252	0·0034	17·0907	0·0017
reception	(ns)	(ns)	(ns)	($p < 0.001$)	(ns)
Visual	0·0373	1·4080	0·8141	23·6125	2·2942
reception	(ns)	(ns)	(ns)	($p < 0.001$)	(ns)
Auditory	0·3538	1·1263	1·8235	69·2863	0·8389
association	(ns)	(ns)	(ns)	($p < 0.001$)	(ns)
Visual	0·4338	0·0835	0·0269	20·9594	0·0031
association	(ns)	(ns)	(ns)	($p < 0.001$)	(ns)
Verbal	0·4434	0·5006	2·9933	17·3270	0·2064
expression	(ns)	(ns)	(ns)	($p < 0.001$)	(ns)
Manual	0·4932	2·0309	1·5989	29·0926	4·8781
expression	(ns)	(ns)	(ns)	($p < 0.001$)	($0.05 > p > 0.025$)
Grammatic	2·6539	1·9966	0·1401	111·1130	0·0263
closure	(ns)	(ns)	(ns)	($p < 0.001$)	(ns)
Visual	1·6495	2·3390	0·2591	53·4646	0·7676
closure	(ns)	(ns)	(ns)	($p < 0.001$)	(ns)
Auditory	2·5373	1·2686	2·0304	94·9479	0·0357
memory	(ns)	(ns)	(ns)	($p < 0.001$)	(ns)
Visual	0·0298	0·0456	0·0000	15·5038	0·0225
memory	(ns)	(ns)	(ns)	($p < 0.001$)	(ns)

Table 9

Analysis comparing changes in score on the I.T.P.A.: Experimental girls and control girls

	A.N.O.V.A. on pre-test scores: F value	A.N.O.V.A. on post-test scores: F value	Difference in regression: F value	Pooled regression: F value	Difference in change scores: F value
Auditory	3·5722	0·2234	0·0011	16·0027	0·1828
reception	(ns)	(ns)	(ns)	($p < 0.001$)	(ns)
Visual	0·1826	1·8430	0·0541	33·8376	3·9723
reception	(ns)	(ns)	(ns)	($p < 0.001$)	($0.05 > p > 0.025$)
Auditory	0·0526	0·0414	0·1808	28·9027	0·1619
association	(ns)	(ns)	(ns)	($p < 0.001$)	(ns)
Visual	0·2773	0·0555	0·3137	25·2700	0·0036
association	(ns)	(ns)	(ns)	($p < 0.001$)	(ns)
Verbal	0·1229	0·0141	0·2618	16·1971	0·0954
expression	(ns)	(ns)	(ns)	($p < 0.001$)	(ns)
Manual	0·3089	0·3989	0·4588	27·2341	1·2580
expression	(ns)	(ns)	(ns)	($p < 0.001$)	(ns)
Grammatic	2·8974	5·1081	5·1035	205·4965	2·5240
closure	(ns)	($0.025 > p > 0.01$)	($0.05 > p > 0.025$)	($p < 0.001$)	(ns)
Visual	0·2275	0·0598	0·7299	42·6510	0·5029
closure	(ns)	(ns)	(ns)	($p < 0.001$)	(ns)
Auditory	0·3176	0·0414	0·5135	118·3149	1·2567
memory	(ns)	(ns)	(ns)	($p < 0.001$)	(ns)
Visual	0·4078	2·8577	0·1429	20·2002	2·4595
memory	(ns)	(ns)	(ns)	($p < 0.001$)	(ns)

Table 10

Summary of analysis of change scores for experimental and control boys and girls

	Experimental B:G	Control B:G	Boys E:C	Girls E:C
Representational				
Auditory reception ⎫ Visual reception ⎬	(ns) $(0.025 > p > 0.01)^*$ B > G	(ns) (ns)	(ns) (ns)	(ns) $(0.05 > p > 0.025)$ CG > EG
Auditory association ⎫ Visual association ⎬	(ns) (ns)	(ns) (ns)	(ns) (ns)	(ns) (ns)
Verbal expression ⎫ Manual expression ⎬	(ns) (ns)	(ns) $(0.05 > p > 0.025)^*$ B > G	(ns) $(0.05 > p > 0.025)$ CB > EB	(ns) (ns)
Automatic				
Grammatic closure ⎫ Visual closure ⎬	(ns) $(0.05 > p > 0.025)$ G > B	(ns) (ns)	(ns) (ns)	(ns)* (ns)
Auditory memory ⎫ Visual memory ⎬	(ns) (ns)	(ns) $(0.05 > p > 0.025)^*$ G > B	(ns) (ns)	(ns) (ns)

* Indicates a significant difference at the post-test. There were no significant differences at pre-test.

Table 11

Average pre- and post-test scores in the E.P.V.T. for the experimental and control group boys and girls

| | Boys | | | | | | Girls | | | | | |
| | Pre-test | | Post-test | | Difference | | Pre-test | | Post-test | | Difference | |
	RS	SS	RS	SS	SS		RS	SS	RS	SS	SS	
Experimental												
Mean	14·21	95·75	17·67	96·50	0·75		11·90	90·95	14·43	89·97	−0·98	
SD	7·11	14·26	7·80	14·47			5·52	12·08	6·60	12·68		
Control (1)												
Mean	13·40	93·19	15·68	92·47	−0·73		11·15	89·63	13·36	88·20	−1·43	
SD	7·18	14·48	7·59	13·54			4·81	10·90	5·71	11·24		
Control (2)												
Mean	13·13	94·85	16·16	99·84	4·99		12·26	91·91	14·50	91·31	−0·60	
SD	6·50	13·75	7·42	11·31			6·17	12·60	6·77	13·95		

Table 12

Analysis of variance and covariance on E.P.V.T. scores comparing experimental and control boys and girls

	A.N.O.V.A. on pre-test: F value	A.N.O.V.A. on post-test: F value	Difference in regression: F value	Pooled regression: F value	Difference in change scores: F value
Experimental Boys:Girls	6·1446 ($0·025 > p > 0·01$)	9·4542 ($0·005 > p > 0·001$)	3·4673 (ns)	51·2743 ($p < 0·001$)	3·9168 ($0·05 > p > 0·025$)
Control (1) Boys:Girls	3·9595 (ns)	3·5033 (ns)	0·7867 (ns)	25·2715 ($p < 0·001$)	0·8185 (ns)
Control (2) Boys:Girls	3·1820 (ns)	21·0594 ($p < 0·001$)	0·0133 (ns)	31·1790 ($p < 0·001$)	17·9107 ($p < 0·001$)
Boys:Experiment: Control (1):Control (2)	0·4547 (ns)	5·2300 ($0·01 > p > 0·005$)	1·3458 (ns)	53·8792 ($p < 0·001$)	5·9227 ($0·005 > p > 0·001$)
Girls:Experiment: Control (1):Control (2)	1·4440 (ns)	1·0012 (ns)	0·1350 (ns)	19·3127 ($p < 0·001$)	0·3102 (ns)

Table 13

Average pre- and post-test scores on the I.T.P.A. for the experimental and control groups different with respect to immigrant status.

| | Non-immigrant | | | | | | West Indian | | | | | | Other immigrants | | | | | |
| | Experimental | | | Control | | | Experimental | | | Control | | | Experimental | | | Control | | |
	Pre-test	Post-test	Difference in means	Pre-test	Post-test	Difference in means	Pre-test	Post-test	Difference in means	Pre-test	Post-test	Difference in means	Pre-test	Post-test	Difference in means	Pre-test	Post-test	Difference in means
Auditory reception																		
Mean	30·66	34·00	3·34	30·83	33·57	2·74	23·93	28·85	4·92	27·33	35·00	7·67	26·83	29·83	3·00	22·17	21·67	−0·50
SD	7·90	7·97		8·73	8·25		8·07	7·67		11·93	3·61		8·64	9·50		12·80	8·76	
Visual reception																		
Mean	21·04	24·05	3·01	21·14	25·18	4·04	20·63	22·67	2·04	18·00	25·66	7·66	23·33	23·83	0·50	15·17	19·33	4·16
SD	5·18	4·71		5·58	5·43		3·65	5·26		3·00	0·58		3·78	3·43		4·02	7·20	
Auditory association																		
Mean	26·87	29·41	2·54	27·22	29·37	2·15	24·52	25·63	1·11	26·00	26·67	0·67	23·67	26·67	3·00	17·00	21·50	4·50
SD	4·93	6·78		5·53	4·96		2·28	3·24		3·61	4·16		2·94	4·27		10·73	6·53	
Visual association																		
Mean	23·62	25·22	1·60	22·75	24·73	1·98	21·26	23·59	2·33	20·00	23·67	3·67	22·17	23·50	1·33	19·67	21·83	2·16
SD	5·32	5·30		4·95	5·09		3·71	5·05		2·65	4·73		4·22	3·67		6·50	4·12	
Verbal expression																		
Mean	31·04	35·55	4·51	31·61	34·87	3·26	27·41	29·37	1·96	25·67	32·33	6·66	27·33	29·67	2·34	21·17	28·83	7·66
SD	7·19	8·18		8·48	7·39		7·37	5·24		2·31	6·81		4·46	4·68		9·33	9·83	
Manual expression																		
Mean	28·50	28·11	−0·39	27·79	28·65	0·86	27·07	26·74	−0·33	23·00	29·67	6·67	24·33	27·33	3·00	22·20	28·00	5·80
SD	4·82	4·41		5·42	5·26		5·11	5·28		8·18	2·08		3·56	4·63		5·17	3·54	
Grammatic closure																		
Mean	24·04	26·49	2·45	25·04	27·14	2·10	18·41	19·89	1·48	21·67	22·33	0·66	19·00	20·33	1·33	17·00	21·00	4·00
SD	5·42	4·91		5·96	4·69		6·10	5·61		7·23	8·08		4·15	4·97		7·04	9·01	
Visual closure																		
Mean	25·04	30·71	5·67	25·50	31·41	5·91	22·26	28·93	5·67	23·00	31·00	8·00	22·00	30·83	8·83	20·83	25·33	4·50
SD	5·27	6·47		5·81	6·92		4·69	6·09		0·00	6·56		5·87	7·49		7·99	7·58	
Auditory memory																		
Mean	30·93	34·64	3·61	33·12	35·52	2·40	32·37	34·67	3·30	34·67	38·67	4·00	27·50	31·17	3·67	25·83	29·17	3·34
SD	8·66	9·71		9·45	8·97		6·78	7·85		1·15	5·69		1·87	3·71		7·83	8·70	
Visual memory																		
Mean	20·08	23·30	3·22	20·20	24·34	4·14	18·48	21·74	3·26	15·00	19·33	4·33	18·50	23·50	5·00	16·33	18·33	2·00
SD	4·06	5·81		3·53	5·18		4·06	4·53		6·08	3·78		2·95	7·66		1·21	3·39	

Table 14

Analysis comparing changes in scores on the I.T.P.A. for experimental children grouped with respect to immigrant status

	A.N.O.V.A. on pre-test scores: F value	A.N.O.V.A. on post-test scores: F value	Difference in regression: F value	Pooled regression: F value	Difference in change scores: F value
Auditory reception	7·8797 ($p < 0·001$)	4·8641 ($0·01 > p > 0·005$)	0·5294 (ns)	9·4190 ($p < 0·001$)	1·1858 (ns)
Visual reception	0·7602 (ns)	0·8911 (ns)	1·9598 (ns)	18·6544 ($p < 0·001$)	1·1328 (ns)
Auditory association	4·0154 ($0·025 > p > 0·01$)	4·3243 ($0·025 > p > 0·01$)	0·3136 (ns)	14·1204 ($p < 0·001$)	1·6668 (ns)
Visual association	2·4900 (ns)	1·2404 (ns)	0·3267 (ns)	13·7527 ($p < 0·001$)	0·1925 (ns)
Verbal expression	3·2419 ($0·05 > p > 0·025$)	8·1448 ($p < 0·001$)	0·2392 (ns)	11·5561 ($p < 0·001$)	4·8712 ($0·01 > p > 0·005$)
Manual expression	2·7447 (ns)	0·9716 (ns)	0·8931 (ns)	13·6393 ($p < 0·001$)	0·6186 (ns)
Grammatic closure	12·4889 ($p < 0·001$)	23·3920 ($p < 0·001$)	1·1454 (ns)	86·7988 ($p < 0·001$)	9·5371 ($p < 0·001$)
Visual closure	3·7073 ($0·025 > p > 0·01$)	0·8370 (ns)	0·6882 (ns)	28·2289 ($p < 0·001$)	0·6908 (ns)
Auditory memory	0·9322 (ns)	0·4102 (ns)	0·3794 (ns)	75·3881 ($p < 0·001$)	0·5486 (ns)
Visual memory	1·9501 (ns)	0·8289 (ns)	3·2053 ($0·05 > p > 0·025$)	15·7209 ($p < 0·001$)	0·3240 (ns)

Table 15

Analysis comparing changes in score on the I.T.P.A. for control children grouped with respect to immigrant status

	A.N.O.V.A. on pre-test scores: F value	A.N.O.V.A. on post-test scores: F value	Difference in regression: F value	Pooled regression: F value	Difference in change scores: F value
Auditory reception	2·7763 (ns)	6·0531 ($0·005 > p > 0·001$)	1·5802 (ns)	9·7654 ($p > 0·601$)	3·8668 ($0·05\,\text{>} p > 0·025$)
Visual reception	3·7560 ($0·05 > p > 0·025$)	3·2725 ($0·05 > p > 0·025$)	1·7179 (ns)	20·5735 ($p < 0·001$)	1·2234 (ns)
Auditory association	8·7066 ($p < 0·001$)	7·2400 ($0·005 > p > 0·001$)	0·2310 (ns)	49·8018 ($p < 0·001$)	0·7517 (ns)
Visual association	1·4677 (ns)	0·9839 (ns)	0·2555 (ns)	16·8728 ($p < 0·001$)	0·2333 (ns)
Verbal expression	4·9209 ($0·025 > p > 0·01$)	1·9568 (ns)	1·6181 (ns)	7·6317 ($p < 0·001$)	0·3254 (ns)
Manual expression	3·4847 ($0·05 > p > 0·025$)	0·0975 (ns)	1·8952 (ns)	30·0529 ($p < 0·001$)	2·6262 (ns)
Grammatic closure	5·3661 ($0·01 > p > 0·005$)	5·3491 ($0·01 > p > 0·005$)	4·5723 ($0·025 > p > 0·01$)	85·3777 ($p < 0·001$)	1·2382 (ns)
Visual closure	2·0019 (ns)	2·1729 (ns)	0·004 (ns)	30·3867 ($p < 0·001$)	0·7279 (ns)
Auditory memory	1·8034 (ns)	1·6653 (ns)	0·8129 (ns)	64·7344 ($p < 0·001$)	0·2561 (ns)
Visual memory	6·3371 ($0·005 > p > 0·001$)	5·1861 ($0·01 > p > 0·005$)	0·1990 (ns)	7·4390 ($p < 0·001$)	1·7970 (ns)

Table 16

Analysis comparing change in score on the I.T.P.A. for non-immigrant experimental and control children

	A.N.O.V.A. on pre-test scores: F value	A.N.O.V.A. on post-test scores: F value	Difference in regression: F value	Pooled regression: F value	Difference in change scores: F value
Auditory reception	0·0197 (ns)	0·1460 (ns)	0·0174 (ns)	20·6833 ($p < 0·001$)	0·2312 (ns)
Visual reception	0·0190 (ns)	2·5427 (ns)	0·8292 (ns)	45·3105 ($p < 0·001$)	3·3074 (ns)
Auditory association	0·2278 (ns)	0·0040 (ns)	0·000 (ns)	52·7669 ($p < 0·001$)	0·1760 (ns)
Visual association	1·4845 (ns)	0·4500 (ns)	0·1674 (ns)	42·3003 ($p < 0·001$)	0·0004 (ns)
Verbal expression	0·2648 (ns)	0·4013 (ns)	2·0816 (ns)	21·8536 ($p < 0·001$)	0·8611 (ns)
Manual expression	0·9694 (ns)	0·6437 (ns)	4·0820 ($0·05 > p > 0·025$)	57·2222 ($p < 0·001$)	2·9661 (ns)
Grammatic closure	1·5720 (ns)	0·0543 (ns)	0·1906 (ns)	206·9487 ($p < 0·001$)	0·0021 (ns)
Visual closure	0·3527 (ns)	0·5593 (ns)	0·3026 (ns)	68·6845 ($p < 0·001$)	0·2284 (ns)
Auditory memory	2·9710 (ns)	0·4500 (ns)	2·7395 (ns)	178·7918 ($p < 0·001$)	1·3391 (ns)
Visual memory	0·0534 (ns)	1·8313 (ns)	0·0744 (ns)	22·2803 ($p < 0·001$)	1·9045 (ns)

Table 17

Analysis comparing changes in score on the I.T.P.A. for West Indian immigrant experimental and control children

	A.N.O.V.A. on pre-test scores: F value	A.N.O.V.A. on post-test scores: F value	Difference in regression: F value	Pooled regression: F value	Difference in change scores: F value
Auditory reception	0·4435 (ns)	1·8349 (ns)	3·3167 (ns)	5·5217 ($0.025 > p > 0.01$)	1·4369 (ns)
Visual reception	1·4349 (ns)	0·9441 (ns)	1·2429 (ns)	9·0398 ($0.005 > p > 0.001$)	4·3893 ($0.05 > p > 0.025$)
Auditory association	1·0329 (ns)	0·2648 (ns)	0·0068 (ns)	16·5349 ($p < 0.001$)	0·1218 (ns)
Visual association	0·3229 (ns)	0·0005 (ns)	0·2562 (ns)	1·6035 (ns)	0·0432 (ns)
Verbal expression	0·1609 (ns)	0·8224 (ns)	5·6660 ($0.025 > p > 0.01$)	7·3815 ($0.005 > p > 0.001$)	1·7401 (ns)
Manual expression	1·5456 (ns)	0·8819 (ns)	1·1258 (ns)	3·3046 (ns)	2·3170 (ns)
Grammatic closure	0·7497 (ns)	0·4757 (ns)	0·8491 (ns)	28·5260 ($p < 0.001$)	0·0012 (ns)
Visual closure	0·0723 (ns)	0·3097 (ns)	0·0000 (ns)	11·4227 ($p < 0.001$)	0·2414 (ns)
Auditory memory	0·3329 (ns)	0·7249 (ns)	0·4853 (ns)	19·5102 ($p < 0.001$)	0·3903 (ns)
Visual memory	1·8226 (ns)	0·7797 (ns)	0·0078 (ns)	7·6477 ($0.005 > p > 0.001$)	0·0053 (ns)

Table 18

Analysis comparing changes in score on the I.T.P.A. of other immigrant experimental and control children

	A.N.O.V.A. on pre-test scores: F value	A.N.O.V.A. on post-test scores: F value	Difference in regression: F value	Pooled regression: F value	Difference in change scores: F value
Auditory reception	0·5482 (ns)	2·3985 (ns)	0·0253 (ns)	34·0344 ($p < 0·001$)	0·1082 (ns)
Visual reception	13·1488 ($p < 0·001$)	1·9093 (ns)	1·5437 (ns)	5·8517 ($0·025 > p > 0·01$)	1·2711 (ns)
Auditory association	2·1528 (ns)	2·6271 (ns)	0·0242 (ns)	11·8074 ($0·005 > p > 0·001$)	0·3249 (ns)
Visual association	0·6246 (ns)	0·5470 (ns)	0·8212 (ns)	2·6542 (ns)	0·0986 (ns)
Verbal expression	2·1356 (ns)	0·0351 (ns)	0·1291 (ns)	2·0804 (ns)	0·4284 (ns)
Manual expression	0·6565 (ns)	0·0693 (ns)	1·9864 (ns)	11·7107 ($0·01 > p > 0·005$)	2·8045 (ns)
Grammatic closure	0·3592 (ns)	0·0252 (ns)	0·0051 (ns)	16·4118 ($0·005 > p > 0·001$)	1·9098 (ns)
Visual closure	0·0832 (ns)	1·5972 (ns)	0·4166 (ns)	10·4100 ($0·01 > p > 0·005$)	2·9802 (ns)
Auditory memory	0·2569 (ns)	0·2680 (ns)	3·4337 (ns)	21·0086 ($p < 0·001$)	0·0259 (ns)
Visual memory	2·7706 (ns)	2·2826 (ns)	0·7489 (ns)	24·4100 ($p < 0·001$)	0·0017 (ns)

Table 19

Summary of results of analysis of change scores on the I.T.P.A. groups different with respect to immigrant status

	Experimental NI:WI:OI	Control NI:WI:OI	NI E:C	WI Immigrant E:C	OI E:C
Representational					
Auditory reception	(ns)*†	(0·05 > p > 0·025)† WI > NI > OI	(ns)	(ns)	(ns)
Visual reception	(ns)	(ns)*†	(ns)	(0·05 > p > 0·025) C > E	(ns)*
Auditory association	(ns)*†	(ns)*†	(ns)	(ns)	(ns)
Visual association	(ns)	(ns)	(ns)	(ns)	(ns)
Verbal expression	(0·01 > p > 0·005)*† NI > OI > WI	(ns)*	(ns)	(ns)	(ns)
Manual expression	(ns)	(ns)*	(ns)	(ns)	(ns)
Automatic					
Grammatic closure	(p < 0·001)*† NI > WI > OI	(ns)*†	(ns)	(ns)	(ns)
Visual closure	(ns)*	(ns)	(ns)	(ns)	(ns)
Auditory memory	(ns)	(ns)	(ns)	(ns)	(ns)
Visual memory	(ns)	(ns)*†			(ns)

* Indicates a significant difference on pre-test.
† Indicates a significant difference on post-test.

Table 20

Average pre- and post-test scores on the E.P.V.T. for groups different with respect to immigrant status

		Pre-test		Post-test		Difference in mean standard score
		RS	SS	RS	SS	
Experimental						
Non-imm.	$\bar{X}$	13·97	95·23	17·10	95·26	0·03
$N = 149$	SD	6·66	13·33	7·37	13·55	
W.I. imm.	$\bar{X}$	10·29	87·74	12·79	87·18	−0.56
$N = 34$	SD	5·08	12·44	6·93	14·25	
Other imm.	$\bar{X}$	9·50	86·13	16·16	86·63	0·50
$N = 8$	SD	4·21	12·25	7·42	13·49	
Control 1						
Non-imm.	$\bar{X}$	13·21	93·44	15·56	92·57	−0·87
$N = 70$	SD	6·57	13·55	7·14	12·92	
W.I. imm.	$\bar{X}$	11·20	89·25	13·35	87·83	−2·52
$N = 40$	SD	5·24	10·35	6·05	11·33	
Other imm.	$\bar{X}$	8·17	81·50	9·83	80·33	−1·17
$N = 6$	SD	4·86	14·69	3·49	8·82	
Control 2						
Non-imm.	$\bar{X}$	13·82	93·31	17·40	95·65	2·34
$N = 146$	SD	6·53	13·00	7·26	13·44	
W.I. imm.	$\bar{X}$	14·57	94·00	19·00	98·71	4·71
$N = 7$	SD	9·11	19·41	6·27	10·86	
Other imm.	$\bar{X}$	8·50	83·50	11·75	85·00	1·50
$N = 8$	SD	2·56	5·78	7·25	12·72	

Table 21

Analysis of variance and covariance on E.P.V.T. scores for groups different with respect to immigrant status

	A.N.O.V.A. on pre-test: F value	A.N.O.V.A. on post-test: F value	Difference in regressions: F value	Pooled regressions: F value	Difference in change scores: F value
E. non-imm. W.I. imm. other imm.	6·0365 $(0·05 > p > 0·001)$	5·7475 $(0·005 > p > 0·001)$	2·5748 (ns)	33·1594 $(p < 0·001)$	1·4266 (ns)
C1 non-imm. W.I. imm. other imm.	2·8368 (ns)	2·9528 (ns)	0·4355 (ns)	15·9242 $(p < 0·001)$	0·8518 (ns)
C2 non-imm. W.I. imm. other imm.	2·6028 (ns)	2·5828 (ns)	0·0067 (ns)	20·1066 $(p < 0·001)$	0·7787 (ns)
Non-imm. E:C1:C2	0·3229 (ns)	1·5850 (ns)	0·5421 (ns)	60·3453 $(p < 0·001)$	1·4178 (ns)
W.I. imm. E:C1:C2	1·7193 (ns)	2·7472 (ns)	0·0664 (ns)	7·5120 $(p < 0·001)$	1·3396 (ns)
Other imm. E:C1:C2	0·2312 (ns)	0·5358 (ns)	0·9461 (ns)	0·6307 (ns)	0·4953 (ns)

Table 22

Average scores at post-test on the I.T.P.A. for experimental and control children defined as low, medium and high scorers on the pre-test

| | Experimental | | | | | | | | | Control | | | | | | | | |
| | Low | | | Medium | | | High | | | Low | | | Medium | | | High | | |
	N	Mean	SD	N	Mean	SD	N	Mean	SD	N	Mean	SD	N	Mean	SD	N	Mean	SD
Auditory reception	30	26·03	8·21	85	34·05	7·01	19	37·74	7·10	21	24·71	8·96	65	34·00	7·63	27	36·93	6·13
Visual reception	17	19·53	5·77	98	23·74*	4·13	19	27·63*	3·80	22	19·95	5·37	75	25·09*	4·63	16	30·69*	3·84
Auditory association	15	23·80	4·91	101	28·02	5·97	18	35·33	3·27	19	22·58	5·51	71	29·06	3·99	23	33·52	3·27
Visual association	14	20·07	4·57	94	24·63	4·46	26	28·04	6·01	14	20·79	4·81	84	24·30	4·41	15	29·47	5·10
Verbal expression	19	27·79	5·13	97	34·07	7·64	18	40·50	7·23	14	29·93	6·46	82	34·22	7·23	17	39·47	7·60
Manual expression	16	24·06	3·77	89	27·39	4·25	29	31·10*	4·07	20	24·00	3·23	68	28·19	4·53	24	33·83*	3·31
Grammatic closure	28	17·39	3·93	88	25·99*	3·68	18	31·11	1·57	16	16·88	4·00	70	27·40*	3·33	27	30·67	1·59
Visual closure	20	22·35	4·27	96	30·92	5·16	18	36·28	6·35	21	23·95	4·67	69	31·32	6·26	23	36·87	5·12
Auditory memory	18	24·06	5·85	98	34·10	7·28	18	47·06	6·09	12	23·58	4·12	77	33·43	6·33	24	47·00	4·99
Visual memory	19	20·68	3·38	90	22·27*	4·77	25	27·36	7·65	14	20·00	3·82	87	23·89*	4·73	12	28·42	7·01

* Indicates statistically significant results: control scores are in all such cases greater than those of the experimental group.

Table 23

Average pre- and post-test scores on the I.T.P.A. for experimental schools

School N	00 27			01 13			02 25			03 18			04 26			05 25		
	Pre-test	Post-test	Change in raw score: mean	Pre-test	Post-test	Change in raw score: mean	Pre-test	Post-test	Change in raw score: mean	Pre-test	Post-test	Change in raw score: mean	Pre-test	Post-test	Change in raw score: mean	Pre-test	Post-test	Change in raw score: mean
Auditory reception																		
Mean	29·00	33·15	4·15	28·62	28·85	0·23	30·60	35·63	5·04	27·83	30·11	2·28	28·62	33·81	4·19	29·56	32·40	2·84
SD	8·71	7·76		8·22	5·96		7·40	8·67		10·28	8·07		9·64	8·18		6·44	8·68	
Visual reception																		
Mean	21·26	23·74	2·48	20·00	22·69	2·69	21·76	24·24	2·48	21·89	23·06	1·17	21·23	24·31	3·08	19·92	23·80	3·88
SD	4·93	5·02		3·61	4·11		5·75	5·45		5·79	6·17		4·80	4·26		3·76	3·71	
Auditory association																		
Mean	26·52	28·70	2·18	25·38	26·69	1·31	27·16	29·12	1·96	26·22	31·17	4·95	26·23	28·23	2·00	25·56	27·12	1·56
SD	4·49	5·50		5·16	3·54		4·85	5·59		4·22	11·79		4·76	4·71		4·31	4·33	
Visual association																		
Mean	23·52	25·67	2·15	24·54	25·46	0·92	23·00	25·44	2·44	23·89	23·44	-0·45	22·12	25·96	3·84	22·36	22·72	0·36
SD	5·15	5·28		4·61	4·29		5·42	5·57		5·99	5·44		4·30	4·98		4·97	4·93	
Verbal expression																		
Mean	30·96	36·26	5·30	30·38	32·92	2·54	31·24	40·40	9·16	26·94	31·77	4·83	31·58	32·73	1·15	28·84	28·50	-0·04
SD	7·27	8·33		6·25	7·25		7·79	7·42		5·45	5·25		8·00	7·30		7·24	6·25	
Manual expression																		
Mean	27·70	28·67	1·97	32·31	28·00	-4·31	27·56	26·52	-1·04	27·78	26·44	-1·34	27·77	29·15	1·38	27·04	27·60	0·56
SD	5·14	4·35		3·90	3·79		4·81	4·63		4·12	4·05		5·57	5·10		4·23	4·87	
Grammatic closure																		
Mean	22·11	25·33	3·22	24·08	24·85	0·77	25·20	27·88	2·68	24·28	25·00	0·72	20·42	23·08	2·66	21·24	23·20	1·96
SD	6·08	4·76		6·85	3·74		4·75	4·51		5·54	5·58		6·68	6·60		5·09	5·43	
Visual closure																		
Mean	25·11	31·33	6·22	23·08	27·62	4·54	25·36	33·68	8·32	23·28	28·61	5·33	24·92	31·69	6·77	23·30	27·28	4·98
SD	4·44	6·08		4·11	4·65		5·90	8·53		6·57	5·24		4·40	4·95		5·89	5·48	
Auditory memory																		
Mean	28·56	33·24	4·68	29·31	30·38	1·07	32·52	35·12	2·60	32·06	33·28	1·22	31·04	34·73	3·69	32·56	37·96	5·40
SD	7·34	10·49		9·87	9·36		8·98	9·12		7·84	7·91		6·79	7·45		8·68	9·60	
Visual memory																		
Mean	20·63	26·11	5·48	18·54	22·23	3·69	20·40	25·16	4·76	20·78	21·28	0·50	18·35	21·88	3·53	19·16	20·24	1·08
SD	3·67	7·15		3·45	3·35		4·79	6·55		3·92	3·34		3·70	3·75		4·14	4·85	

Table 24

Average pre- and post-test scores on the I.T.P.A. for control schools

School N	06 30			07 34			08 24			09 25		
	Pre-test	Post-test	Change in raw score: mean	Pre-test	Post-test	Change in raw score: mean	Pre-test	Post-test	Change in raw score: mean	Pre-test	Post-test	Change in raw score: mean
Auditory reception												
Mean	29·23	32·00	1·77	31·50	35·12	3·62	33·13	34·29	1·16	27·12	29·96	2·74
SD	9·08	8·11		7·88	8·51		7·34	8·17		11·55	9·01	
Visual reception												
Mean	19·57	23·83	4·26	21·85	24·94	3·09	20·79	25·46	4·67	20·60	25·52	4·92
SD	5·33	6·09		6·18	5·87		4·83	3·71		5·88	6·15	
Auditory association												
Mean	26·83	29·10	2·27	27·47	29·21	1·74	27·58	29·96	2·38	24·40	27·12	2·72
SD	5·41	4·22		4·59	4·85		5·52	4·80		8·97	7·11	
Visual association												
Mean	21·50	23·83	2·33	22·47	25·15	2·68	24·33	26·00	1·67	22·04	23·20	1·16
SD	4·19	5·05		4·60	4·64		4·35	4·00		6·66	6·14	
Verbal expression												
Mean	30·73	31·23	0·50	30·24	36·29	6·05	32·58	36·88	4·30	30·36	33·60	2·24
SD	8·62	6·76		6·67	6·17		11·15	8·56		9·08	8·08	
Manual expression												
Mean	26·76	28·03	1·27	26·97	28·88	1·91	29·75	29·33	−0·42	26·52	28·40	1·88
SD	5·60	5·05		5·54	4·51		4·33	4·93		6·41	6·27	
Grammatic closure												
Mean	25·23	26·67	1·34	26·00	27·94	1·94	25·46	27·58	2·12	20·76	24·16	3·40
SD	5·45	4·62		5·97	4·67		5·12	3·61		7·36	7·09	
Visual closure												
Mean	24·80	29·20	4·40	25·56	31·38	5·82	25·63	35·00	9·37	24·72	29·16	4·44
SD	5·97	7·30		5·75	6·12		5·44	6·85		6·80	6·74	
Auditory memory												
Mean	36·03	37·20	1·17	30·88	33·32	2·44	33·46	36·83	2·37	30·76	34·08	3·32
SD	9·04	8·77		8·71	9·34		10·55	9·05		8·75	8·36	
Visual memory												
Mean	19·00	23·03	4·03	20·76	24·12	3·36	20·71	25·08	4·37	18·84	23·44	4·60
SD	4·09	4·90		2·92	4·68		3·75	5·75		3·78	6·04	

Table 25

Analysis of variance and covariance on I.T.P.A. scores comparing experimental schools

	A.N.O.V.A. on pre-test scores: F value	A.N.O.V.A. on post-test scores: F value	Difference in regression: F value	Pooled regression: F value	Difference in change scores: F value
Auditory reception	0·2769 (ns)	1·7356 (ns)	0·4931 (ns)	6·1066 ($p < 0.001$)	1·6332 (ns)
Visual reception	0·6136 (ns)	0·3187 (ns)	0·8731 (ns)	9·1551 ($p < 0.001$)	0·5086 (ns)
Auditory association	0·4162 (ns)	1·1681 (ns)	0·6799 (ns)	8·4447 ($p < 0.001$)	1·1580 (ns)
Visual association	0·6329 (ns)	1·6009 (ns)	0·4541 (ns)	8·0784 ($p < 0.001$)	2·2506 (ns)
Verbal expression	1·2608 (ns)	7·7386 ($p < 0.001$)	0·7597 (ns)	7·8653 ($p < 0.001$)	8·1436 ($p < 0.001$)
Manual expression	2·3984 ($0.05 > p > 0.025$)	1·3716 (ns)	0·4620 (ns)	7·8170 ($p < 0.001$)	2·3401 ($p < 0.001$)
Grammatic closure	2·5025 ($0.05 > p > 0.025$)	2·7213 ($0.025 > p > 0.01$)	3·0362 ($0.01 > p > 0.005$)	59·2944 ($p < 0.001$)	2·5189 ($0.05 > p > 0.025$)
Visual closure	0·8387 (ns)	3·9614 ($0.005 > p > 0.001$)	0·4787 (ns)	13·1063 ($p < 0.001$)	3·2495 ($0.05 > p > 0.025$)
Auditory memory	1·0132 (ns)	1·4507 (ns)	0·9340 (ns)	39·1365 ($p < 0.001$)	2·1418 ($0.01 > p > 0.005$)
Visual memory	1·6041 (ns)	4·7101 ($p < 0.001$)	2·0163 (ns)	8·4581 ($p < 0.001$)	4·7303 ($p < 0.001$)

159

Table 26

Analysis of variance and covariance on I.T.P.A. scores comparing control schools

	A.N.O.V.A. on pre-test scores: F value	A.N.O.V.A. on post-test scores: F value	Difference in regression: F value	Pooled regression: F value	Difference in change scores: F value
Auditory reception	2·1575 (ns)	2·1184 (ns)	0·1128 (ns)	6·5384 ($p < 0·001$)	0·9396 (ns)
Visual reception	0·8845 (ns)	0·5416 (ns)	1·0255 (ns)	16·6179 ($p < 0·001$)	0·6061 (ns)
Auditory association	1·4916 (ns)	1·3213 (ns)	1·9179 (ns)	45·4079 ($p < 0·001$)	0·2673 (ns)
Visual association	1·5557 (ns)	1·6490 (ns)	2·2208 (ns)	14·4284 ($p < 0·001$)	0·9389 (ns)
Verbal expression	0·3913 (ns)	3·6435 ($0·025 > p > 0·01$)	1·0359 (ns)	6·9099 ($p < 0·001$)	4·0655 ($0·025 > p > 0·01$)
Manual expression	1·8515 (ns)	0·3188 (ns)	0·2741 (ns)	19·0025 ($p < 0·001$)	0·4981 (ns)
Grammatic closure	4·2796 ($0·01 > p > 0·005$)	2·9694 (ns)	3·7158 ($0·025 > p > 0·01$)	65·0489 ($p < 0·001$)	0·4864 (ns)
Visual closure	0·1785 (ns)	4·1860 ($0·05 > p > 0·025$)	0·8452 (ns)	27·6800 ($p < 0·001$)	6·3768 ($p < 0·001$)
Auditory memory	2·1672 (ns)	1·4026 ($0·01 > p > 0·005$)	2·3461 (ns)	51·5972 ($p < 0·001$)	0·5674 (ns)
Visual memory	2·3665 (ns)	0·7505 (ns)	1·5255 (ns)	8·2238 ($p < 0·001$)	0·2712 (ns)

Table 27

Average pre- and post-test scores on the E.P.V.T. for schools

Schools		N	Pre-test Raw score	Pre-test Standard score	Post-test Raw score	Post-test Standard score	Difference in standard score
Experimental							
00	Mean	28	15·43	99·35	17·18	96·89	−2·46
	SD		7·59	14·60	7·39	13·67	
01	Mean	13	11·46	90·15	11·38	83·76	−6·39
	SD		4·52	12·09	5·71	13·60	
02	Mean	31	14·58	95·77	19·13	98·70	2·93
	SD		7·27	15·15	7·72	13·84	
03	Mean	24	11·17	90·12	14·21	89·29	−0·83
	SD		4·96	11·95	6·69	13·50	
04	Mean	25	14·24	95·08	16·96	93·76	−1·32
	SD		7·38	14·01	9·05	16·65	
05	Mean	70	12·16	91·40	15·70	92·87	1·47
	SD		5·82	12·12	6·70	12·40	
Control 1							
00	Mean	13	17·15	97·53	18·38	95·07	−2·46
	SD		8·22	14·77	9·61	17·37	
02	Mean	31	12·10	92·58	13·03	88·58	−4·00
	SD		5·62	12·92	6·07	12·75	
03	Mean	24	10·25	87·20	14·83	91·79	4·59
	SD		5·03	12·25	4·95	9·70	
04	Mean	48	12·04	91·02	14·23	89·37	−1·65
	SD		5·88	12·15	6·88	12·17	
Control 2							
06	Mean	24	12·12	91·40	15·58	93·09	1·69
	SD		5·43	11·90	7·09	13·90	
07	Mean	32	15·81	97·18	17·78	96·28	−0·09
	SD		7·04	12·58	6·94	12·37	
08	Mean	45	13·51	92·71	18·47	97·00	4·29
	SD		5·87	12·15	7·12	12·83	
09	Mean	60	13·03	93·26	16·55	94·15	0·89
	SD		7·11	14·53	7·53	14·39	

Table 28

Analysis of variance and covariance on E.P.V.T. scores for schools

Schools	A.N.O.V.A. on pre-test: F value	A.N.O.V.A. on post-test: F value	Difference in regression: F value	Pooled regression: F value	Difference in change scores: F value
Experimental	2·1383 (ns)	2·7360 (0·025 > p > 0·01)	1·2144 (ns)	17·3125 p < 0·001	1·8316 (ns)
Control 1	3·8740 (0·05 > p > 0·025)	2·0088 (ns)	2·1139 (ns)	14·4915 (p < 0·001)	1·4177 (ns)
Control 2	1·7909 (ns)	1·0878 (ns)	0·4478 (ns)	16·4960 (p < 0·001)	1·0186 (ns)

Summary of Findings

A. *From the Psycholinguistic Profile*

1. American evidence indicates a marked relationship between depressed scores on the automatic levels of the test and reading difficulty and mental retardation. The English E.P.A. children have group profiles which in most cases are below the American norms for the age group; but relative to their functioning at the representational level their scores on automatic level items are not depressed.

2. The two reception items on the test—visual and auditory reception—are the most depressed for the total E.P.A. groups. This finding holds for sub-groups defined by sex and with respect to immigrant status.

3. West Indian immigrant and other immigrant children also have particularly depressed scores on grammatic closure.

4. Other immigrant children—for most of whom English is a second language—have profiles similar to those of West Indian immigrant children.

5. The West Indian immigrant and other immigrant children have significantly inferior scores to the non-immigrant children on the following I.T.P.A. sub-tests: auditory reception, auditory association, verbal expression; grammatic closure and visual closure.

6. The manual and verbal expression and auditory memory items provide relatively the highest scores for most groups of E.P.A. children.

B. *Using the Illinois Test of Psycholinguistic Abilities to assess the impact of the language programme*

1. There was a significant difference at pre-test on grammatic closure between the experimental and total control group ($0.025 > p > 0.01$). Experimental children were performing less well than control children.

2. On two items the change scores of the total experimental and total control groups were significantly different. On visual reception ($0.025 > p > 0.01$) and on manual expression ($0.025 > p > 0.01$) the control group's scores changed more positively than those of the experimental group. But there seemed to be no conceptual links between these overall different changes in score and the content of the language programme.

3. The following sex and treatment comparisons were made:

   (i)   Within experiment boys:girls. There were no significant differences at pre-test. On visual closure girls changed more positively than boys ($0.05 > p > 0.25$); but there were no significant differences at post test on this item. On visual reception boys changed more positively than girls ($0.025 > p > 0.01$); boys were significantly better than girls at post-test on this item ($0.025 > p > 0.01$). Other than the difference over visual reception, there was no significant difference between experimental boys and girls on the post-test.

   (ii) Within control boys:girls. There were no significant differences at pre-test. On manual expression boys changed more positively than

162

girls ($0.05 > p > 0.025$); and there were significant post-test differences on this item, where boys had a better score than girls ($0.05 > p > 0.025$). On visual memory, girls changed more positively than boys ($0.05 > p > 0.025$) and had a higher post-test score than boys ($0.025 > p > 0.01$). There were no further differences between the groups at post-test.

(iii) Experimental boys:control boys. There were no significant differences between the groups at pre-test. On manual expression, control boys changed more positively than experimental boys ($0.05 > p > 0.025$), although there were no differences between the groups at post-test. There were no other differences between the groups.

(iv) Experimental girls:control girls. There were no significant differences between the groups at pre-test. On the post-test, control girls were performing significantly better than experimental girls on grammatic closure ($0.025 > p > 0.01$), but there was not a significantly different change score between the groups on this sub-test. On only one sub-test was there a significantly different change score: on visual reception, where the control girls changed more positively than the experimental girls.

4. There seemed to be no discernible pattern of differential impact on boys or girls either within the experimental group or compared to the control boys and girls.

5.

(i) There were a number of differences at pre-test between experimental groups different with respect to their immigrant status—see A5 above. The only sub-test on the auditory vocal channel where there was no significant difference at pre-test between these groups was auditory memory, where all groups had relatively high scores.

(ii) All these significant differences at pre-test were maintained at post-test except for visual closure.

(iii) The two significantly different change scores between these groups within the experimental schools served to widen disparities which had existed at pre-test. On verbal expression ($0.01 > p > 0.005$), the non-immigrant group changed most positively and the West Indian immigrant group changed the least. On grammatic closure ($p < 0.001$), the non-immigrant group changed most positively and the other immigrant group changed the least.

6. Within the control group there was a pattern of pre-test differences between groups of children of different immigrant status similar to those in the experimental group, but small numbers tended to create idiosyncracies. The only significantly different change score was on auditory reception ($0.05 > p > 0.025$), where the West Indian immigrants changed most positively and other immigrant children changed the least.

7. Comparing non-immigrant children across treatment groups, there were no significant differences on pre-test, post-test or over change in score.

8. Comparing West Indian immigrant children across treatment groups, there were no significant differences at pre- or post-test and only one—on visual reception ($0.05 > p > 0.025$)—over change scores. On this sub-test the control West Indian immigrants changed more positively than experimental West Indian immigrants.

9. Comparing other immigrant children across treatments, there were no significant differences at post-test or over change score. The only significant

difference at pre-test was over visual reception ($p < 0.001$), where the experimental group scored higher than the control group.

10. Comparing the post-test scores of initially low, medium and high scoring sub-groups the following significant differences were found.

  (i) On visual reception the control medium and high scorers at pre-test had higher post-test scores than the experimental medium and high scorers ($0.05 > p > 0.025$) in both cases).

  (ii) On manual expression the control high scorers at pre-test had higher post-test scores than the experimental high scorers ($0.025 > p > 0.01$).

  (iii) On grammatic closure the control medium scorers at pre-test had higher post-test scores than the experimental medium scorers ($0.025 > p > 0.01$).

  (iv) On visual memory the control medium scorers at pre-test had higher scores than the experimental medium scorers ($0.025 > p > 0.01$).

11. There were no significant differences at post-test between experimental and control groups of children who had been defined as low scorers at the pre-test.

12. There was no coherent pattern of change scores discernible when experimental schools/classes were compared.

C. *Using the English Picture Vocabulary Test to assess the impact on passive vocabulary of the language programme.*

1. The total experimental, within-school control (C1), and other-school control (C2) groups were all below the national mean at the beginning of the year.

2. There were no significant differences in scores between the three groups at the beginning of the year.

3. There were significantly different changes in score between the three groups over the period ($0.05 > p > 0.025$). The three groups had significantly different post-test scores ($0.01 > p > 0.005$).

4. Over the period the mean score of the experimental group hardly changed; the mean score of the within-school control group deteriorated by slightly more than one standard point; and the mean score of the other-school control group improved by almost two standard points.

5. Comparing boys and girls pre-test score, there were statistically significant differences between boys and girls in the experimental group ($0.025 > p > 0.01$) and in the control 2 group ($0.005 > p > 0.001$). In both cases boys' scores were higher than girls'. In the control 1 group there was the same order of measured discrepancy between scores but it was not statistically significant; this was due to the smaller numbers involved in the analysis.

6. There were significant changes in score between the boys in the three groups ($0.005 > p > 0.001$); these differences mirrored the differences found when total treatment groups were compared: the experimental and control 1 boys hardly changed their group score and the control 2 boys improved significantly.

7. There were no significant differences between the scores of girls in the three groups either at pre-test, post-test or in change score.

8. The mean standard scores on the E.P.V.T. pre-test of some of the groups

defined with respect to their immigrant status, were extremely low, i.e., the West Indian immigrant and other immigrant groups are all at least ten standard points below the national mean.

9. There were significant differences at pre-test and post-test between the different immigrant status groups within the experimental schools ($0.005 > p > 0.001$ in both cases). The non immigrant group had a score at least eight standard points above the other two groups at both times.

Part Six

The Environmental Studies Scheme
J. H. Barnes

The Environmental Studies Scheme

The plans for the Environmental Studies Scheme were drawn up during the first year of the London E.P.A. Project. The scheme was tried out during the Project's second year (the school year 1969–70). It was then run again with some minor amendments over the school year 1970–71, during which time its impact on the subject children was evaluated. And when the E.P.A. Project came to an end in 1971, the Inner London Education Authority continued to sponsor the work.

The most striking features of the scheme were its organisational characteristics and their resource implications. Groups of urban E.P.A. children were taken into the country on a regular basis to study and to enjoy a rural environment. A disused rural school, 12 miles from London E.P.A. Project schools, was hired from a county local education authority. This became the environmental studies centre. Some basic equipment was provided; but it was hoped that most of the children's time would be spent away from the centre in the countryside itself. It was decided that the oldest year group of children in the junior school were likely to benefit most from the experience, and that the benefit would be maximised if visits to the country centre were as frequent as possible. And so the plan which emerged was for all the fourth year E.P.A. Project children to go to the country with their own class teachers weekly throughout the school year. All junior schools in the Project area were invited to take part. All did so and, with the exception of one school which withdrew for a period during the first year and then returned, all remained in the scheme until the end.

For the second year of the scheme, the country centre moved to a more rural setting and a centre warden was appointed to advise and to supplement the work of the E.P.A. school teachers.

The educational resources deployed on the scheme were, therefore, substantial. A country centre was provided; transport to and from it was made available; the centre was equipped for environmental studies; and a centre warden worked there full-time. The annual local authority allowance to junior schools for educational visits at the time was less than £0·20 per child; and so the scheme cost eighty times more than would normally be available per capita for school visits. Excluding the cost of teachers' salaries, which were fixed and common items of expenditure, the standard annual per capita allowance to junior schools at the time was approximately £4; and so, in order to run, the scheme needed four times the volume of current resources normally available to a junior school. (See Appendix 1 for details).

The amount of time which the children spent on the scheme was also substantial. A weekly visit throughout the school year meant that one-fifth of their school time during that year—one-twentieth of their time in junior school and one-thirtieth of their time to date in compulsory education—was spent working on environmental studies.

The educational credentials of this type of innovation were impeccable. It conformed to many of the canons of received wisdom about how to promote innovations in schools; and the curriculum principles it adhered to were sanctioned by the most reputable authorities.

Much of what was done in the London E.P.A. Project was based on the belief that innovations must be acceptable to the individual teacher in the classroom. Teachers must be able to understand any proposal; they must want to carry it out; they must be capable and have the extra resources to do so.[1] The Environmental Studies Scheme pushed the logic of this to a further level. The specific form of it originated, in part, from the teachers who were to implement it; and individual teachers were allowed the maximum possible freedom to determine their work programme within general guidelines.

The E.P.A. Project Director began with the intention of developing the environmental studies work he had started previously as the headmaster of a junior school in a Medway town. His initial idea had been to focus a curriculum for the children on the immediate environment of their E.P.A. schools: eroding barriers between traditional school subjects and providing a platform for community studies of various kinds and for the involvement of parents in the schooling process. This original proposal was adapted during the first planning year as a result of discussions with the local E.P.A. teachers and their advisors. The subject of the scheme was changed, from study of a local urban to a contrasting country environment. The local teachers saw E.P.A. children in general as being "inexperienced", as coming from "crowded homes", which "lacked space", and which provided no "cultural incentive".[2] Such perceptions were always qualified. They were seen to apply to only a proportion of the children in an E.P.A. school; but they were generally held and strongly expressed.[3] It was thought that such children needed to have some experience of a different environment: one which would be intrinsically worthwhile; one which would contrast to and might awaken the children's interest in their own.

The plan for the scheme was then an amalgam of relatively disparate ideas: for studies of a country environment, for integrating children's school work through environmental studies, for pursuing the objectives of learning through experience and for experiencing the countryside as a worthwhile end in itself. From this, individual teachers were free to decide what to accept and reject in the light of their own experience, inclinations and the constraints of their normal classroom routines. Teacher discussion groups were held regularly at the Project's London base. These were designed to establish agreement about the nature of the work at the country centre, to exchange ideas about successful practice, and to allow the Project Director to inform participants about the scheme's overall development. During the second year a teacher's manual was produced which contained examples of good practice from the first year, and some further suggestions of the Project Director for schemes of work. But the overall emphasis was on freedom of professional

---

[1] See N. Cross, J. B. Ciacquinta and M. Bernstein, *Implementing Organisational Innovations*, Harper Row, 1971.

[2] See Part 1 for an account of teacher perceptions of "the E.P.A. question".

[3] See for instance Table B17 in Volume II of the E.P.A. Series. Eighty-five per cent of the teachers in the London E.P.A. Project Schools who responded to the March 1969 teacher questionnaire considered the neighbourhood in which they worked was worse than that of friends who were teachers, and fifty-four per cent thought they received less support from parents.

choice over what to do. The Project provided facilities and advice; the teachers took their children to the country centre and taught them in the way they considered most appropriate. The intention was for the scheme to evolve as a rich mixture of current educational thinking and local practitioner experience.

Its curriculum principles contained much of what is considered "best" in British primary education. Environmental studies were thoroughly in the tradition of education "through the soles of the feet"; they corresponded to the "stock clichés of British education . . . that good teaching moves from the concrete to the abstract", and "from the particular to the general".[1] They drew together the Plowden Council's exhortation that "these deprived areas (should have) . . . perfectly normal good primary schools alive with experience from which children of all kinds can benefit",[2] with their recommendations for curriculum flexibility, integration of school subjects, and the use of the children's environment to achieve this: "Another effective way of integrating the curriculum is to relate it through the use of the environment to the boundless curiosity which children have about the world about them."[3] Regular visits to the countryside were also in line with the Plowden Council's recommendations. They saw, for instance, the advantages of taking "the children out of their own environment into a contrasting one, either for a day or for a longer period. This of course applies as much to rural children visiting towns as to urban children visiting the countryside. Such visits, carefully prepared and not just sightseeing, are generally used as the culmination of an interest or interests. They often serve better as starting points— those places are best which make it possible for children to visit and revisit, individually, in groups, or as a class, when new questions arise."[4]

The Question of Objectives

The scheme was an experimental field trial. The primary purpose of setting it up was to enable the long term, and more general viability of such educational programmes to be assessed; and the research workers were employed, at least in part, to generate information for this assessment. Two problems above all others made the evaluation a difficult and tortuous process. In the first place, there was not one scheme but one for each class taking part. In the second place, overtly expressed expectations for the scheme were only indirectly related to what it was hoped would happen; statements of intention were given more to formulations with which all the involved parties could agree than to objectives which would actually guide the behaviour of all.[5]

Any resolution of the first difficulty, short of separate evaluations of what

---

[1] Melville Harris, *Environment Studies*, in the School Council Series, British Primary Schools Today, Macmillan, 1971.

[2] "Children and their Primary Schools: Report of the Central Advisory Council, England," *The Plowden Report*, Volume 1, paragraph 136.

[3] *Ibid.*, paragraph 543.

[4] *Ibid.*, paragraph 545.

[5] There is some general discussion of this matter in *Part 1*. Objectives are multiple, unstable and shift in priority over time. Personnel in a scheme came to terms with them rather than use them as guides to their behaviour. The very opacity of such objectives, and the confusion about what is "really" at issue, make it possible for all parties to agree to them: their ambiguity is functional to their acceptance.

happened for each separate class of children, created a danger that generalisations about the Environmental Studies Scheme would obscure real school to school and class to class differences. Certainly the scheme had administrative features which were the same for all schools; but there were variations even at this level. For instance, one school had the assistance of students from a College of Education for its day at the country centre. Some schools encouraged, and some discouraged parents from visiting the centre with them. Some increased the number of adults with fourth year classes for the environmental studies work, while others left matters entirely to the respective class teachers.

Further, the explicit reliance on the initiative and inclinations of individual teachers meant that, potentially, each class had a unique environmental studies work programme. At a relatively straightforward level, for instance, the amount of time actually devoted to environmental studies varied: from an isolated one day each week in the country to several days each week being devoted to preparation and to follow up work. And this itself varied for any one class over the year.[1]

At the same time, given limited resources, it seemed sensible to attempt an overall appraisal of the scheme before trying to isolate possibly unique factors which might distinguish between relative success in one class as opposed to another. To attempt this latter would have meant tackling the question of what constitutes good teaching in general: something which was clearly beyond the scope of the E.P.A. Project and any evaluation of part of it.

Any doubts there may have been about how to deal with the question of diversity within the scheme were made irrelevant by the request of the Project Director not to observe in detail how it was being implemented by individual teachers. His concern was that any detailed monitoring of the scheme's implementation would threaten the teachers, and tend to disrupt the delicate coalitions of interest he had established.[2] The evaluation needed innovation; the innovation did not need evaluation, and the research acquiesced. We agreed not to attempt any detailed monitoring of the ways in which the scheme was implemented, and not to probe the extent of the variations between individual teachers over what they were doing.

The evaluation was, therefore, designed to produce an account of the overall effect of rural environmental studies on the behaviour of children in urban E.P.A. junior schools: assuming that class to class variations were what could reasonably be expected from any group of E.P.A. schools.[3] It

---

[1] In Appendix 2 the Project Director provides some illustrations of good environmental studies work. These are complemented by accounts from some of the teachers in the Environmental Studies Scheme.

[2] This question also is discussed in a general form in Part 1. The difficulties of actually making the innovation happen tend to be such that they become ends worth achieving in themselves. The overall purpose becomes obscured by the need to make, and to substantiate, a series of small and instrumental gains. Each day is lived as if it were the last.

[3] The teachers were in any case teaching fourth year junior classes; they were, therefore, likely to be more experienced than the average E.P.A. junior school teacher. Further, by the time of the evaluation year a number of them were quite experienced at environmental studies, having worked on the scheme during the previous year. In principle, therefore, the teachers taking part were slightly better prepared for the work than the average teacher. No differences were found in the evaluation between the results obtained by teachers working on the scheme in their first and second year.

was to be suggestive rather than in any sense definitive; and clearly the obvious next step from this—as in any curriculum evaluation—would, in principle, have been to identify situations in which the innovation was more or less effectively implemented. But the test below is an account of the general operation of the whole scheme, without detailed regard for variations within it.

At least once this decision had been made it was clear what could and what could not be attempted. On the other hand, the second major issue—of what the educational expectations of the scheme actually were—created a whole series of recurring problems. Indeed, it was perhaps only after the evaluation year, when the report of the evaluation had been produced, that it finally became clear what the various parties were trying to achieve!

By that time it was obvious that most of the teachers taking part viewed the scheme with enthusiasm and commitment. One of its accomplishments had been to elicit interest and enthusiasm from the teachers concerned, and this had increased over time. The local teachers, the Project Director and a number of the local authority officers on the Project Local Steering Committee were all anxious for it to continue; and considerable energies were devoted to making sure that the local authority continued to support it after the experimental period. Certainly then, a consequence of the scheme was that the teachers became more committed to it; and certainly also an intention of those involved was to ensure that it continued.

A list of formal objectives for the scheme was drawn up by the Project Director during the planning year (1968–69). These were presented to the teachers and to the Local Steering Committee during 1969–70; and all agreed that they were to be the objectives of the scheme. From the way in which it was created and endorsed, it is clear that this is a list of those things over which all the people involved could agree, rather than an exact statement of what the teachers were trying to do with their children at the environmental studies centre, or of their priorities in this respect.

These explicit and formally ratified objectives for the scheme were:

(1) To cause an improvement in pupil attitude and motivation.
(2) To cause an improvement in teacher motivation.
(3) To create an environmental studies curriculum, which relied on real rather than vicarious experience and the sequencing of work over a period of time.
(4) To integrate this curriculum style into the classroom in the participating E.P.A. schools.
(5) To involve parents in the scheme.
(6) For teachers and schools to co-operate with each other in the evolution of the scheme.
(7) To cause an improvement in the capacity of the children to undertake and complete work on their own initiative.

In the light of these the Project Director concluded at the end of the field trial that the scheme had been successful on every count: "There is little doubt (according to teachers, inspectors and administrators) that there was a definite improvement in teachers' and pupils' motivation. In many of the classrooms there was visible evidence of the integration of subjects. There were a considerable number of parents and other adults participating in joint discovery and exploration. Numerous meetings were held between teachers from different schools and our action team, i.e., teachers were consulted from the beginning of the scheme. I have ample evidence of the increased capacity of children to undertake and complete work on their own initiative."[1]

What, it may be asked, does this tell us? Firstly, and most obviously perhaps, in a formal sense there was only a limited concern for the cognitive skills of the subject children. Only the seventh objective seems in any way to be concerned with school performance or study skills. This, although environmental studies had been defined by the Project Director in the teachers' manual as—"a teaching approach utilising activities based on the child's *direct* experience of the environment—*this should lead to a progressive development of study and communicative skills*—there should be a sequential *development of the skills of language both written and oral*—(and)—*an increase in skills normally associated with the classroom.*" (This author's italics.)[2]

Secondly, subsumed behind these declared intentions, there seem to be other hoped-for effects. Relationships are not specified, indeed the purposes themselves remain obscure; but the stated list of priorities can be seen as instrumental to their achievement. For instance, although to have more highly motivated pupils and teachers might, to some extent, be regarded as ends worth achieving in themselves (objectives (1) and (2)), surely something was expected of an environmental studies curriculum beyond having a new sort of curriculum (objective (3))? Teachers and schools were to co-operate in the scheme (objective (6)), and parents were to be involved (objective (5)); but presumably this also was to lead to something in addition to more co-operation and more involvement? Further, presumably this higher order consequence was to be something more than more motivation from pupils and teachers? Even if the pupils were motivated to "undertake and complete work on their own initiative" (objective (7)), was something not expected to result from this? More "work", better "work", a different sort of "work"?

The possible emphasis on instrumental objectives is explained by a third observation: that objectives such as these enable assessment of an educational situation to be made largely in terms of *how well* it is being conducted. Consideration of means is emphasised: estimation of whether or not implementation is conducted in the appropriate way. The quality of the programme is stressed. The ends it is designed to serve are assumed. In such a situation the purposes of the scheme could be implied and understood rather than

---

[1] Letter to the *Times Educational Supplement*, October 1972.

[2] And although the first objective of the whole Project was to find ways of improving the school performance of E.P.A. children. And although, by the time the Environmental Studies Scheme was being implemented, preliminary results of the March 1969 school performance tests were available, and the extent of the educational problem was known to most of those involved. See Volume II of the E.P.A. Series for a comprehensive account of the result of this testing programme.

stated. Everybody, it was assumed, "knew" what the Environmental Studies Scheme was about. As it transpired, I think, the scheme was about three things with an inevitable fourth only in the mid-distance. It was about children enjoying school. It was about providing experiences for children in urban E.P.A. schools which a "good parent" ought to provide. It was about offering children intrinsically worthwhile experiences. And in the distance was a further concern: for the school performance of the youngsters.

The report by the Education Officer to the I.L.E.A. Schools Sub-Committee has synthesised part of this educational philosophy. "The starting point for the action is that the children are deprived. Deprived of what? Of many of the day-to-day experiences of children in more fortunate circumstances: the security of a two parent home, free from anxiety about the necessities of life, the opportunity to play congenially, space in which to behave like a child, widening experience accompanied by developing speech in a literate environment. What may seem an irrelevant example may nevertheless be helpful. The Authority provides opportunities for its children to go to a concert, or a carol festival. No one ever suggests that afterwards we should try to measure some effect or other. The simple point is that the children have had an experience which we believe to be educationally valid. The good happens all the time. The result, if result there be, is literally immeasurable and in any case secondary".[1]

There was thus a community of educational assumptions about what was being attempted. For some teachers the scheme was an extension of normal practice; for others it was a relief from what they were doing in their urban classrooms. Individuals placed their emphasis in different ways; but these were all variations within a common cluster of mutually held beliefs.[2] For the research workers this created two further kinds of problem: initially to understand what, for the practitioner, need not be said and subsequently to ensure that everybody else knew.

In seeking a resolution of the first difficulty, a more general and a more important set of questions are raised. These concern not simply what the Environmental Studies Scheme was designed and implemented to achieve. They concern what it is realistic and appropriate for schools, particularly schools in educational priority areas, to be doing for the children in their care: what they are, and can, and ought to be doing. These questions are raised, in some form, in virtually all the essays in this volume; and, at the general level, they are never resolved. They are, in fact, not questions for resolution by research or by research workers. The purpose of research in this sort of area is to create good questions rather than good answers. Research can show the importance of the issues and the consequences of different kinds of answer; but it should not itself make up the answers. But equally, neither should the professional educators have a monopoly over defining the purpose of schools. Education is too important to be left either to teachers or to research workers.

The purpose of the Environmental Studies Scheme can be found at several different levels of educational thought. In the first place there was the pleasure

---

[1] I.L.E.A. Report to Schools Sub-Committee, 12th October 1972.
[2] See Appendix 2.

principle: that schools have a responsibility to create enjoyment of the here-and-now, irrespective of anything else. Life is hard in the inner city, so the argument goes, and there is not much joy in the lives of E.P.A. children. If these children and their teachers enjoy a day in the country, nothing else need be said: end of evaluation. Except that one-fifth of all the school days for a year were spent there. Perhaps the same pleasure might be given to the children if they went less often, at lower per capita cost? Perhaps the children need not go to the country at all to have that much pleasure? If the purpose of going to school is to have pleasure, why have school? Why not simply have pleasure? Clearly school should be enjoyable; but should it not also be something more?

The pleasure principle was in fact developed further; and in a way that identified more positively some hoped-for outcomes of the Environmental Studies Scheme. It was postulated that, not only should the children enjoy the experience, but their general attitudes to school might improve and they might find school more acceptable as a result. This seemed to be a major and commonly held expectation, and therefore it seemed sensible to conduct evaluation which identified possible changes in the children's attitudes.

A different kind of expectation, and one considerably more difficult to pin down, came from a belief that schools should give to their children those experiences which some parents do not provide. Schools should compensate children whose parents discharge their responsibilities inadequately. In a general sense there are inevitable consequences for schools when, or if, parents fail their children. In this particular case, the belief was that E.P.A. children were deprived of access to the countryside by their urban circumstances. Once again there was little that empirical evaluation could contribute to the discussion at this level. There could be little doubt that the children had not been to the countryside as often, and as frequently, as they were being taken in the Environmental Studies Scheme. It was thought that they should go, and they went: case closed.

The need for such compensation was seen to be clear, in the case of the Environmental Studies Scheme, because of the intrinsic educational validity of the experiences on offer. Experience of the countryside dispelled ignorance about it; the horizons of the children's awareness were expanded; and, as the I.L.E.A. pointed out, "the good happens all the time" (see above). Yet again, viewed in isolation, there is no purpose in evaluating situations which are seen to be intrinsically worthwhile. But at the same time, questions are raised concerning what it is appropriate for activities sponsored by educational institutions to be attempting to do. Accepting that it is a good thing for children to see cows being milked, to know how rhubarb grows, and to have the freedom to run in open fields: are there differences between experiencing these things with "good parents" and experiencing them with good teachers? To put the question another way: suppose all children knew about these things from their parents, would they still be appropriate subjects for school based activities? In theory they could be, because a professional educator is more than simply a good parent. Activities organised by the professional are planned to lead somewhere; interaction between teacher and child in an educational situation is directional. The teacher is attempting to use experiences that the children have to further their development in some way. None of this is necessarily asked of a good parent; a trip to the countryside can be an end in itself. It is no cause for concern if, with the parent, the experience is forgotten immediately after it has happened; but it is, in principle, a cause for concern if educational situations are not used by educators to further the development of children.

This seemed to be a second topic for the empirical evaluation of the Environmental Studies Scheme. In addition to compensating E.P.A. children for having missed intrinsically worthwhile experiences, in addition to how well it was being implemented, the scheme contained assumptions about what schools and teachers and educational experiences are for. And the educational logic of this committed the scheme to advancing the development of children. If it did not attempt to do this, it was not an educational scheme; or, at least, it was not one which it was appropriate for an educational institution to run for any length of time. Had it been simply a small number of isolated trips, a lack of educational purpose and direction could have been assumed. But given the time and resources committed to them, it seemed reasonable to expect the experiences to lead somewhere.

This still left the question of what the "development of children" should be taken to mean. Clearly an appraisal of it by teachers who knew a particular child was important. But in only some senses could it be considered a necessary ingredient, and even then not sufficient. For a comprehensive assessment of it, we need to know not only how well a child is "doing" relative to his previous performance, to his classmates' performance and to some notion of his teacher's expectations of him: we need to know how well he is "doing" relative to other children that are not in his class or in his school. Traditionally we use standardised tests of cognitive skills, school performance, or achievement for this purpose. In many ways the tests are inadequate[1]; but they are what we have available for this purpose. And it seemed reasonable to create some knowledge about the direction of the children's development, as measured by tests of school performance, as a consequence of their experience of environmental studies.

This line of reasoning was not, at any stage, made explicit by the educational practitioners involved. It was developed by the research workers in an attempt to uncover an educational rationale for innovations in environmental studies. It could be wrong. If the general axioms are wrong, then hopefully they will provoke debate which clarifies what innovation in E.P.A. schools should be attempting to do for the children. But it should be recognised that, in this particular case, they were accepted when the proposal to evaluate the scheme was agreed to by the Local Steering Committee, the local teachers and the Project Director.

The proposal was drawn up during 1969-70. It identified two areas where behavioural change might reasonably be expected as a result of the experience of environmental studies: children's attitudes to school and their cognitive skills should improve. It was proposed, therefore, to measure the attitudes and school skills of the children taking part in the 1970-71 scheme at the beginning and at the end of the year. Measured changes were to be compared with changes found in a control group of children, which was to receive no experience of environmental studies. It was suggested that the most appropriate, available measuring instruments were the N.F.E.R. Streaming Study

---

[1] See Christopher Jencks, *Inequality*, Basic Books, for an interesting analysis of what tests of cognitive skills can and do measure.

Children's Attitude Questionnaire and the Bristol Achievement Test (see Appendix 3). The plan was accepted by all those involved.[1]

Some people saw an evaluation to be unrelated to the main exercise. For them, the main decision had been made when it was decided to go ahead with the scheme; what was needed subsequently was to convince others of its viability in practice, and "research knowledge" of its impact on the children was not necessary in this respect. Others saw an evaluation to be only marginally related to the scheme; for them the scheme was a sound one. Should the children's attitudes and performance improve, it would strengthen the case of the environmentalists. Should there be no improvement it would not matter. Others were positively in favour of such an evaluation, seeing it to be ultimately how this and any educational scheme should be assessed.

What Happened to the Children

The effects which it was thought the Environmental Studies Scheme might possibly have on the children taking part in it were as follows:

(i) A direct effect on the children's preferences for various school subjects, on their attitudes to school, their motivation to do well there and an effect on their study skills.[2]

(ii) A "spin off" effect, improving performance in more recognised school performance areas—English and Maths—and in other attitudinal areas.

(iii) An "opportunity-cost" effect, depressing performance in English and Maths as time and attention were devoted to other things.

The basic tables from the data analysis are provided in Appendices 4 and 5. But to understand what follows in the text it should be realised that the techniques of analysis of variance and covariance were used for much of the data analysis. The techniques enable comparisons to be made of the changes in score over time between a group of experimental and of control children; they accommodate variations in score and differences between the groups at the starting point. And so, although much of the reporting in the text below uses average standard scores in order to illustrate the findings, it should be remembered that the statistics on which decisions about significant results were made came from the variance and covariance analysis of raw scores.

1. The children enjoyed their day in the country and, at the end of the programme of visits, ranked it above other school activities.

---

[1] One school decided not to allow its children to be tested. It dropped out of the evaluation but continued to take part in the programme of visits. All other schools taking part in the scheme also took part in its evaluation.

[2] The term study skills has quite a precise meaning in this essay. There was, indeed, a specific test for it in the battery chosen (see Appendix 3). The test of study skills was designed to measure how well children could bring to bear diverse bits of information to resolve various kinds of problems. Knowledge of the logic of measurement, how to read small maps, interpretation of diagrams and data presented in symbolic form and logical ordering of information were required, for instance. The skills required for successful performance on this test seemed to be closely related to the skills which successful environmental studies could be expected to engender.

Table 1

Comparison of the Preferences of the Experimental and Control Children for Different School Subjects

	Subject	Mean rank	Significant difference of mean E–C	Order of preference	Significant difference of mean E–C	Mean rank	Subject	
K	The school in the country	4·28	×	1		3·34	Swimming	J
J	Swimming	4·42		2	⊗	4·55	Outside visits	B
B	Outside visits	5·88	⊗	3		6·05	Games	G
G	Games	5·88		4		6·24	Reading	M
M	Reading	5·97		5		6·70	Model making	C
C	Model making	6·87		6		6·88	Painting	F
D	Maths lesson	7·09		7		7·15	Science experiment	L
F	Painting	7·39		8		7·18	Trip to the park	I
L	Science experiment	7·57		9	×	7·55	School in the country	K
I	Trip to the park	7·81		10		7·99	Maths lesson	D
H	Playtime	8·55		11	⊠	8·35	Local studies	A
A	Local studies	9·33	⊠	12		9·08	Playtime	H
E	Measuring the playground	9·86		13		9·61	Measuring the playground	E

Appendix 4 contains a full account of the attempt to assess both the experimental and the control children's preferences for different school subjects at the end of the environmental studies year. Table 1 over page summarises the contrast between the rank order of preferences of the two groups.

Overall there was a high measure of agreement between children within the two groups as to their relative preferences for different school subjects. Further, the range of preferences was fairly narrow: in the experimental group the activity ranked top has half the score of the bottom ranked activity, and in the control group the top has one third the score of the bottom activity.

The preference ranking of the environmental studies centre by the two groups was significantly different, however: as were the rankings of the two relatively similar activities, "outside visits" and "local studies". Clearly, by the end of their year in the scheme, the E.P.A. Project children preferred the environmental studies innovation to all other school activities. It had, for them, displaced swimming from its most favoured position; and activities similar to it were significantly less highly ranked than they were by the control children.

2. On the other hand, there was no significant pattern of improvement in attitudes to school, or over motivation to do well at school, when the experimental group's measured changes in attitude were compared with those of the control group. Nor was there any pattern of differences when the attitudes of subgroups of children were compared: neither groups of boys and girls, nor immigrant and non-immigrant children, nor groups who began the year with significantly positive and significantly negative attitudes appear to have been affected differentially by contact with the Environmental Studies Scheme.

Table 2 below shows the results for the total experimental and control groups; part B shows that there were no differences between the two groups; part A shows that there were differences within each group examined separately.

Relationships with teacher—Scale G—grew worse for both groups; and children became better adjusted to their peers—Scale I. The experimental group became more anxious over the period and their "other" image of class grew worse—Scales H and E. But to repeat, using the acid test—of whether any of these measured changes for the experimental group were different from those for the control group—the Environmental Studies Scheme cannot be said to have affected the attitudes to school of the children who experienced it.

3. Since the pattern of change scores on the tests of attainment is complex, it is best to examine them comparison by comparison. But broadly the conclusion must be that, in no sense, did the cognitive skills of the children

Table 2

Change Scores on the Attitude Questionnaire for Both the Experimental and Control Groups

A. Summary of the Wilcoxon Test for significance of change scores between pre- and post-tests *within* the two groups			B. Summary of the Komolgorov-Smirnov Test for significance of different change scores *between* experimental and control group	
Attitude scale	Experimental	Control	Attitude scale	Experiment/Control
A. Attitude to school	(ns)	W 0·0434	A. Attitude to school	(ns)
B. Interest in school	(ns)	(ns)	B. Interest in school	(ns)
C. Importance of doing well	B 0·0046	(ns)	C. Importance of doing well	(ns)
D. Attitude to class	(ns)	(ns)	D. Attitude to class	(ns)
E. "Other" image of class	W 0·0006	(ns)	E. "Other" image of class	(ns)
F. Conformity	(ns)	(ns)	F. Conformity	(ns)
G. Relations with teacher	W 0·0010	W 0·0006	G. Relations with teacher	(ns)
H. Anxiety	W 0·0060	(ns)	H. Anxiety	(ns)
I. Social adjustment	B 0·0086	B 0·0244	I. Social adjustment	(ns)
J. Academic self-image	(ns)	(ns)	J. Academic self-image	(ns)

B = Better attitude. W = Worse attitude.

improve as a result of the environmental studies experience and that, in some senses, they deteriorated.

Comparing the experimental with the control group

Both the experimental and control groups had average scores on all three performance tests which were below the national average at the beginning of the year, and which fell further behind over the year. In English the experimental group began the year 10 points of score below the national average and the control group began 7 points of score below; their respective deteriorations over time on this test were marginal. On the Maths test the experimental group began 5 points of score below average and deteriorated by a further 6 points, while the control group began with an average score 6 points below the national average and deteriorated by 5 points. On the Study Skills test both groups began the year around eight and a half points below average and the experimental group deteriorated by nearly 4 more points, while the control group lost less than one more point of score.

These results can be put another way to illustrate the range of scores for the group of children in question. Since 50 per cent of a nationally representative group can be expected to score below 100 on the tests, the

Table 3

Average Pre- and Post-test Performance Scores for the Experimental and Control Groups

Experimental Group

	English (253)		Maths (249)		Study Skills (250)	
	Mean	SD	Mean	SD	Mean	SD
Pre-test						
Standard score	90·08	14·11	95·20	11·41	91·50	11·25
Raw score	20·72	16·47	20·76	13·51	15·83	10·25
Post-test						
Standard score	89·78	12·98	88·82	12·65	87·69	11·53
Raw score	34·06	19·72	28·36	16·37	19·18	10·50
National mean	100	15·00	100	15·00	100	15·00

Control Group

	English (126)		Maths (122)		Study Skills (125)	
	Mean	SD	Mean	SD	Mean	SD
Pre-test						
Standard score	92·63	12·66	93·83	11·12	91·62	14·62
Raw score	23·98	16·32	19·78	13·13	16·92	11·16
Post-test						
Standard score	91·30	13·32	89·13	11·54	91·30	12·27
Raw score	36·34	20·37	28·23	15·00	22·23	11·26

proportion scoring below 100 for any other group can be calculated if the mean and standard deviation of scores are known.[1] Thus, on the English test for instance, 76 per cent of the experimental group scored below the national average at the beginning of the year and 78 per cent at the end, while for the control group the respective proportions were 72 per cent and 74 per cent. And on the Maths test, the experimental group began with 66 per cent of its children scoring below the national average and finished with 81 per cent scoring below it; over the same period, the proportion of children in the control group scoring below the national average on Maths rose from 71 to 82 per cent.

On English and Maths both the experimental and control group lost equivalent amounts of ground relative to their national counterparts. On Study Skills, the experimental group lost ground relative to the control group as well as to the national average. Table 4 below shows this clearly. At the pre-test stage there were no significant differences between the two groups on any of the tests of school performance (first row of Table 4). By the post-test stage there were significant differences on the Study Skills test, however; and

---

[1] Assuming the properties of a normal distribution: see Blalock, *Social Statistics*, McGraw-Hill.

Table 4

Summary of Results of Analysis of Covariance Comparing Experimental and Control Group Scores

	English	Maths	Study Skills
Pre-test			
F value	3·3242 (ns)	0·4356 (ns)	0·8845 (ns)
Post-test			
F value	1·1022 (ns)	0·0054 (ns)	6·7045 $0·01 > p > 0·005$
Difference in regression			
F value	0·7766 (ns)	1·0651 (ns)	0·4584 (ns)
Pooled regressions			
F value	640·8306 $p < 0·001$	423·4071 $p < 0·001$	353·1004 $p < 0·001$
Difference in score			
F value	1·3338 (ns)	0·7522 (ns)	9·6277 $0·005 > p > 0·001$

the differences in Study Skills change score were also significant (last row of Table 4).[1]

The conclusion from this must be that there was no "spin-off" or "opportunity costs" from the Environmental Studies Scheme in as far as they could be measured by relative changes in English and Maths skills. But that there was a *direct* consequence of the experience for the children taking part: their Study Skills deteriorated.

Comparing the scores of non-immigrant and immigrant groups

Twenty-seven per cent of the children who took part in the Environmental Studies Scheme were immigrants (and 20 per cent of the total were West Indian immigrant children). The control schools, on the other hand, had less than half that proportion of immigrant children in them.[2] At the time of the evaluation, there was concern that the proportion of immigrant children in a school had an effect on the performance of the non-immigrant children in it. As it happens, there is now empirical evidence which refutes this;[3] but for the purpose of the environmental studies evaluation it created, in principle, two possibilities: that there was an effect on non-immigrant children from the immigrants in a school: that there was a different effect from the scheme on groups of children who were different with respect to their immigrant status.

---

[1] See, in addition, Tables 1 and 2 in Appendix 5. There was not a significantly different pattern of results from this when the scores of boys and girls in the two groups of schools were compared.
[2] See Appendix 3 for differences between the two groups of schools and Part 5 for how the control schools were chosen.
[3] See Part 7 of this volume.

Table 5

Average Pre-test Standard Scores and Changes in Scores for Groups of Children by Immigrant Status

	English		Maths		Study Skills	
	Pre-Test mean	Change Score	Pre-Test mean	Change Score	Pre-Test mean	Change Score
Experimental: Non-immigrants	91·53	−0·38	96·91	−6·15	93·23	−3·60
Experimental: West Indian immigrants	87·63	−0·33	91·00	−7·20	86·49	−4·70
Experimental: Other immigrants	86·76	−0·90	88·11	−4·44	85·21	−2·74
Control: Non-immigrants	92·60	−1·53	94·36	−5·19	91·78	+0·02
Control: West Indian immigrants	94·00	−1·43	86·86	+1·57	89·86	−2·57
Control: Other immigrants	81·89	−0·11	86·40	−6·40	81·44	−2·66

The first possibility—of the immigrant children in the experimental schools affecting the performance of the non-immigrant children in them, so that their performance differed from that of the control non-immigrants—is relatively easily dispensed with. There were no significant differences in performance, on any of the pre-tests, between the experimental and the control non-immigrant children; thus, over the school years prior to the scheme, no effect from the higher immigrant concentrations in the experimental schools had emerged. Neither were there any significant differences between groups of control and experimental non-immigrant children at the post-test stage;[1] but there were significantly different change scores on the Study Skills test. The experimental non-immigrant group lost ground relative to their control counterparts. This reflects the finding for the total experimental and control groups; that the post-test Study Skills scores were not significantly different is a function of the smaller numbers of children in the analysis, rather than a substantially different magnitude of results.

From this we can conclude that the Study Skills performance of children born in the United Kingdom deteriorated as a result of taking part in the Environmental Studies Scheme, and that this deterioration had nothing to do with the presence of immigrant children on the scheme with them.

At the same time, there were significant differences, on all three of the pre- and post-tests, between groups of experimental children who were different with respect to their immigrant status.[2] As the "other immigrant" group was a fairly heterogeneous category, it is sensible to focus on the performances of the West Indian immigrant group. The most striking point to emerge is the extremely low performance of this group at the end of the Environmental Studies year, by which time the children were ready to transfer to secondary school. The average Maths performance was 16 points below

---

[1] See Tables 4 and 5 in Appendix 5.
[2] See again Tables 4 and 5 in Appendix 5.

the national average at this time, and the average Study Skills score was 18 points below. In other words, the proportions of this group which could be expected to score above the national average by the end of the Scheme on English, Maths and Study Skills were 8 per cent, 5 per cent and 1 per cent respectively.[1] Further, the proportions which could be expected to score above the national average had fallen over the period by 2 per cent, 12 per cent and 5 per cent respectively.[2]

This result can be expressed in another way to illustrate the seriousness of its educational consequences. The West Indian immigrant children's average raw score can be converted into a "performance age"[3]—i.e., the age at which the group with the average raw score in question would achieve the national average score for the test. The notion of a "performance age" is contrived, but it illustrates the point. The initial average chronological age for the group of West Indian immigrant children in question was 10 years and 10 months and they became eight months older over the period. Their "performance age" was 8 years 6 months at both times. They made no absolute progress over the period. Relative to the national average child, they began the year twenty-eight months behind and finished the year thirty-six months behind.

Comparing the performance of initially low, medium and high scoring groups

The possibility existed that the Environmental Studies Scheme would have different effects on the subject children grouped, with respect to their pre-test

Table 6

Post-test Average Scores, and Difference in Score, for Experimental and Control Groups which had Equivalent Pre-test Scores

	English Post-test mean standard score	Maths Post-test mean standard score	Study Skills Post-test mean standard score*
High scorers			
Experimental	108·19	103·91	101·97
Control	109·48	103·23	107·80
E—C	−1·29	0·68	−5·83
Medium scorers			
Experimental	88·90	89·02	86·85
Control	88·88	88·80	89·05
E—C	0·02	0·22	−2·20
Low scorers			
Experimental	76·48	74·98	77·26
Control	73·93	76·79	78·20
E—C	2·55	−1·81	−0·94

* Significantly different post-test score.

[1] See note 1 on page 182.
[2] See again Tables 4 and 5 in Appendix 5.
[3] By using the mean age at testing, the mean raw scores, and assuming that the group score is that of an individual child. For conversions see the *Manual for Administration of the Bristol Achievement Tests, Level 3.*

scores, into the highest, the average and the lowest performing groups.[1] Table 6 on page 185 summarises the results of analysis to test for this possibility. Only one pair of post-test scores was significantly different. The control group high scorers finished the year with a significantly higher performance on Study Skills than did the experimental high scorers.

Comparing the average performances of schools

There were significant differences on all the achievement tests between the schools in the Environmental Studies Scheme at its beginning; there were no differences between them at the end of the year.[2] The trend over the period, therefore, was towards greater homogeneity of scores between the schools taking part. A possible explanation of this result could be that the pre-test scores were false, that the post-test scores were closer to the true scores, and changes in score over time were regressions towards the true mean.

This does not seem a likely interpretation of the result, however. From Table 7 it can be seen that the average scores fell for all the schools on the Maths and Study Skills tests over the period; and that, on English, they fell in four out of six cases. Further, they fell by differing amounts: the median decline on English was only half a point, while on Maths it was approaching 6 points, and the range on all three tests was between 5 and 6 points of score. Thus it would need to be postulated, to sustain an explanation in terms of a regression to the mean, that all but two of the school-level measurement errors on the pre-test were inflations of the true scores: but inflations by differing amounts, on different tests, for different schools.[3]

There seems, on the other hand, to be a rank order in the relationship between a school's average pre-test score and its change in score, relative to the other experimental schools:[4] at least on English and Study Skills, the higher an experimental school's relative pre-test score, the greater the loss over time. This cannot be explained simply by losses in the scores of initially high performing children in the schools with the highest pre-test mean scores.[5] It would seem to be a general decrease in performance across all groups of children, rather than in a particular subgroup.

Thus, the strongest relationships that can be identified from a school level analysis, with the data available, are those between generally higher

---

[1] See Appendix 3 for the method.

[2] See Tables 10 and 11 in Appendix 5.

[3] There would be the further problem: of accommodating this position with the other findings. For instance, the following section (see particularly Table 8) shows the average scores for a sub-group of children at three points of time on the three tests. The experimental pre-test score is that measured at Time 2. If this score were inflated, so that regression to the mean occurred between Times 2 and 3, it would presumably also be out of line with the average scores at Time 1. This is not the case; the scores at Times 1 and 2 are similar.

[4] Kendall's rank correlation coefficient (see S. Siegel, *Non-Parametric Statistics*, McGraw-Hill) was calculated between the pre-test mean score on each test and change in score for the experimental schools. The results show a marked negative relationship between pre-test and change score in the case of English and Study Skills, see Table 7.

[5] See Table 7. The position cannot really be sustained that those schools with the highest proportion of high scoring children are those with the highest average scores (except perhaps on English); and, although the correlation between the high scorers in a school and the change in score for a school is higher than the orderings between pre-test mean scores and change scores for the English test, this is not so for the other two tests.

Table 7

The Pre-test Average Scores, Change Scores and Percentage of High Scoring Children on the Pre-test in Each of the Experimental Schools

	English			Maths			Study Skills		
	Pre-test mean score	Change score	% High scorers on the pre-test	Pre-test mean score	Change score	% High scorers on the pre-test	Pre-test mean score	Change score	% High scorers on the pre-test
0	93·84	−2·67	21	94·02	−3·89	21	92·60	−5·68	18
1	90·98	−0·82	18	95·44	−8·53	12	89·10	−2·25	11
2	93·82	−2·17	24	99·72	−8·01	29	93·73	−4·69	18
3	87·38	+2·52	6	93·30	−3·44	10	89·67	−3·19	10
4	86·83	+1·89	13	92·95	−5·05	17	92·16	−4·07	21
5	83·92	−0·21	7	90·13	−6·33	13	85·93	−0·07	—

		English	Maths	Study Skills
Kendall's rank correlation coefficient	Change score: Pre-test mean	$T = -0.60$	$T = -0.21$	$T = -0.73$
	Pre-test mean: % High scorers	$T = +0.60$	$T = +0.33$	$T = +0.20$
	Change score: High scorers	$T = -0.73$	$T = -0.06$	$T = -0.40$

performance initially and generally greater losses over time. In English and Study Skills, those schools that had most to lose by taking part in the scheme lost most over the period of the evaluation.

Performance of some children over a two year period[1]

A group of children taking part in the Environmental Studies Scheme during the evaluation year had been tested one year previously on a lower level of the Bristol Achievement Tests. This enabled measured changes in this group's performance over a year prior to the scheme to be compared with changes measured over their environmental studies year.

Table 8

Average School Performance Scores, and Significance of Different Changes in Score, for a Group of "Readers" Over Two Time Periods (N = 126)

	English		Maths		Study Skills	
	Mean score	SD	Mean score	SD	Mean score	SD
Time 1						
September 1969	91·3	14·1	93·8	14·0	92·5	12·8
Time 2						
October 1970 Pre-test	91·4	13·3	96·6	10·7	93·1	10·1
Time 3						
June 1971 Post-test	91·7	11·6	91·0	10·8	89·3	11·6
Significance of different score changes over the two time periods	Not significant		$p < 0.001$		$p < 0.001$	

Over the year immediately prior to this group's participation in the Environmental Studies Scheme, the children's English performance changed little, but their Maths and Study Skills improved slightly. Over the environmental studies period the English performance remained constant once again; but the average Maths score deteriorated by 6 points and finished relatively lower than it had been two school years before; and the Study Skills score fell by 4 points, again to a point below that achieved by the beginning of the children's third junior school year.

The differences in change score between the two times were significantly different on the Maths and Study Skills test,[2] and the conclusion must again be that a deterioration in aspects of school performance resulted from the environmental studies experience.

---

[1] These were children whose reading performance had been tested as part of the initial baseline testing programme, and who had been positively identified as able to read; they were, therefore, given the battery of Bristol Achievement Tests as part of that exercise. See Appendix 3 for a description of the group. See Volume II of the E.P.A. Series for an account of the baseline testing programme.

[2] See Tables 16, 17 and 18 in Appendix 5.

Summary of the Measured Effects on the Children

From all this it is possible to see a pattern of results. Their strength comes from their relative consistency; but the picture they create is depressing in the extreme.

1. On the school performance tests, both experimental and control children were performing below the national norms at the beginning of their fourth junior school year and fell further behind over that year. On the English test, which had a heavy reading component, this deterioration was slight; on the other two tests it was marked.
2. By the end of that year children taking part in the Environmental Studies Scheme preferred their day in the country to all the other things they did at school.
3. But the scheme had no effect on the attitudes or motivation of the subject children.
4. The scheme had no effect on English and Maths performance; there was no generally consistent pattern either of "opportunity cost" or of "spin off" from the experience.
5. The Study Skills of the children taking part in the Environmental Studies Scheme deteriorated more than those of the control group. Thus, a consequence of spending one fifth of the children's time on the scheme was a drop in Study Skills greater than otherwise could be expected.
6. A sub-group of children who could read by the middle of their second junior school year made slight gains in Maths and Study Skills over the year prior to the scheme (their third year), and then lost ground in these areas during the environmental studies year: relative to both national norms and to their own previous performance.
7. The experimental children, who were defined as the highest performers on the Study Skills test at the beginning of the period, lost ground significantly compared to a similar group in the control schools.
8. The experimental schools, which had achieved the best average scores on the Study Skills and the English tests by the beginning of the scheme, deteriorated most over the period.

A Balance of Evidence

How was a decision to be made about the viability of the Environmental Studies Project? And what can be said from the evidence available about rural environmental studies for urban E.P.A. children? At the least we can say that if the children take part frequently and regularly any scheme is likely to be costly. Without a radical restructuring of their budget, few local education authorities will be able to afford a scheme in which a significant number of children are involved. For such transformations to be worthwhile, a scheme would need to live up to expectations; can the field trial being assessed in this essay be said to have done that? Future schemes might also be regarded as field trials or experiments; but then surely some of the experience of the Environmental Studies Scheme run by the London E.P.A.

Project should be recognised? A judicious balancing of the evidence is needed.

There is a sense in which the E.P.A. Project's innovation was approved *before* it was ever tried out; and any subsequent evaluation of its effect on the children was superfluous to the way in which decisions about viability were made. Prior to taking part in, sanctioning or even being associated with any innovation, educational practitioners need to judge its appropriateness.[1] Therefore, a decision to be involved with a scheme demonstrably means to approve of it. If an innovation has been approved, there is no need to test its worthwhileness; it is approved of because it is seen to be worthwhile. The questions that remain are concerned with how to put it into practice, not with the effect of that practice. If it can be put into practice, then not only is it a good thing, it is viable. Seen in this way, field trials as aids to educational decision-making are part of a circular process. No teacher will try out an innovation unless she sees it to be educationally a good thing: if it is seen to be a good thing, then its worth need not be tried out. It should then be continued because it has been begun.

Clearly this is to parody reality: no process is as closed as that. Nevertheless, the Environmental Studies Scheme was seen to be a good thing. It was continued after the evaluation year with a change of sponsor. And one reason for continuing it was precisely that it was already there.

It is necessary then to ask what would have reversed any decision to continue with the scheme more or less without amendment? There are a series of exogenous factors like its costs which could, in principle, have prevented continued sponsorship. But, everything else being equal, the most significant and weighty evidence came from the teachers. They saw the scheme as one providing an environment in which they could work, and from which the children benefited. It was their unanimous verdict that the scheme had been successful during its evaluation year; and this was sufficient warranty for it.

It is still necessary to ask, however, in what sense it was seen to be successful. What was expected of the scheme? What should future sponsors expect of environmental studies in E.P.A. schools? (Some might say, what should they expect of any innovation in E.P.A. schools?) That the experience was of intrinsic worth and was enjoyed may be necessary, but can hardly be thought sufficient if it is provided by an educational institution. The teachers thought that their relationships with the children improved over the period; but when external measurement took place it was found that the children had become more hostile to their teachers, and that the Environmental Studies Scheme had not influenced this. The teachers thought that the children gained in school skills over the year. Clearly most of them did (although the West Indian immigrant group equally clearly did not): they gained in skills because they became older. The crucial question is whether they gained more than they would otherwise have done. Here also the test evidence is clear: the experimental children *lost* ground over the period relative to both national norms and to the control group.

The evidence on the score changes for the control group is highly significant. It is possible that the "natural" tendency in E.P.A. schools is for the children's

---

[1] See Part 4: The Peabody Language Development Kit was deemed inappropriate and, therefore, the nursery teachers would not use it. Thus an *a priori* decision was made before anybody tried it out and before its effect on the children was known.

school performance to deteriorate over time relative to national norms.[1] If this is so, then several things follow. The "normal" situation for teachers would be for their children to fall further behind over a school year; to say that the children gained in school skills might, in reality, mean that relative deterioration had stopped. Certainly intervention programmes would need to halt a relative decline before achieving any improvement. Seen in this way their rationale becomes dramatically different. Schools in educational priority areas "do their best" for the children: but this is inadequate when external standards of comparison are used because the children are losing ground. Therefore, before they can improve relative performance, curriculum intervention in these schools must stop it becoming worse. A certain consequence of this is that our expectations of innovations must become more moderate.

But we must still face the fact that the environmental studies children lost ground relative even to the control group. Two observations provide insight into why. In the first place there was a persistent belief that the scheme was basically good and therefore self-fulfilling. The I.L.E.A. Schools Sub-Committee Report once again states the position succinctly: "The children are more cared for because there are more people caring for them. Their enjoyment of valid educational experiences is being enlarged because there are more resources from which to provide them." [2] The environmental studies experience proves that this may be necessary but it is by no means sufficient. If children in educational priority areas are to be given an effective education, their teachers must teach them. Which leads to the second observation. The innovation was added to the extant curriculum with no plan or discussion about what it would replace. If innovations in a school curriculum are thought necessary, they must be seen and implemented in the context of all the other demands being made on curriculum time. Providing more resources to schools and leaving the rest to "good teaching practice" is insufficient on the basis of this evidence. A more systematic, perhaps a more radical, appraisal of what happens in our schools is necessary.

---

[1] This may not be the case for a specific skill like reading; but it would be more pronounced for more general school skills (like those measured on the study skills test). See pages 269–272 in Part 7 for an attempt to identify reading change over time.

[2] I.L.E.A. Report to Schools Sub-Committee. 12th October 1972. See note 1 on page 175.

THE COSTS OF THE SCHEME

The Financial Costs of the Environmental Studies Scheme

1. The costs of the scheme for the period May 1970 to July 1971 were:

	£
	£
Rent and rates for premises	1,346
Telephones	19
Sundries and Stationery	248
Caretaker for premises	662
Transport	5,160
	7,435
Salary of a Warden	1,435
(September 1970 to July 1971)	
Total	8,870

2. Thus, for a notional costing of the financial implications of the scheme one might say: The running costs for one school year (September to July) were £8,000.

3. Approximately *500 children* attended the study centre regularly. A full programme of activities comprised *30 visits*

(a) Thus the cost of the scheme per child was

$$\frac{8,000}{500} = £16$$

(b) Thus the cost of the scheme per child per visit was

$$\frac{800}{500 \times 30} = £0\cdot53 \text{ say } £0\cdot50$$

4. The I.L.E.A. allowance to junior schools for educational visits was £0·19 per child for the school year 1970–71.

5. The I.L.E.A. capitation allowance to a junior school was £3·82 per child for the school year 1970–71, plus £164·50 which was allocated directly to the school.

6. In addition to this, extra resources were available to schools with special difficulties. At the time the Environmental Studies Scheme was finishing, a new formula for deciding on the allocation of all extra resources was being devised. The formula under discussion was based on a weighting of the school roll and its "score" on an index of deprivation; thus the volume of extra resources available to a school would be a function of its size, its measured need and the total volume of resources available.

7. With a rough accounting procedure, it was calculated that approximately £2·5 million were being spent by I.L.E.A. to provide extra help to its primary schools at that period.

8. Assuming:
   (i) that the total volume of extra resources were "freed", to be reallocated to schools and spent by a school in any way it chose;
   (ii) that one calculated the volume of resources that would be available to I.L.E.A.'s 'most disadvantaged' school, i.e., the school receiving the maximum score on the need index;

then one could calculate the volume of current resources available to that school, given school size stated below.

School roll	Normal total capitation allowance plus school allowance	Extra help allowance for the top scoring school	Total	Amount per child in the school
	£	£	£	£
200	928·50	2,367	3,295·5	16·48
300	1,310·50	2,535	4,845·5	16·15
400	1,682·50	4,713	6,405·5	16·01
500	2,074·50	5,891	7,965·5	15·93

9. Thus, in order to pay for its children to take part in an environmental studies scheme costing £16 per head, I.L.E.A.'s most disadvantaged school would need to commit almost the total amount of current educational resources it had available for each child. (This excludes the salaries of the on-quota staff employed in the school.)

10. There were approximately 2,500 children in the ten plus age group in the I.L.E.A. schools which received the E.P.A. teacher's salary increment. If special provision were made to pay for these children to take part in an environmental studies programme costing £16 per head, a further £265,000 would be added to the educational budget.

EXAMPLES OF ENVIRONMENTAL STUDIES PRACTICE

Example 1: Of Good Practice Noted by the Project Director

The class from this school were particularly interested in geography. The class teacher, who was a countryman by origin, intended to develop a geographical thematic approach with his children and to use his visits to the country centre to complement a study of the local town environment undertaken the previous term. This young innovatory teacher believed in the value of comparative education and felt that it was absolutely necessary for his children to understand their own environment by studying a different one.

After discussion with the children it was agreed that a discussion about the type of investigation and the methods to be used should be left until preliminary probes at the country centre had suggested suitable areas for in-depth study.

When the children arrived back in school it was agreed that there was a great deal to be gained by studying the village near the country centre and its immediate surroundings. Teacher and child discussions led to the decision to work in groups and occasionally as individuals. Some children said that their mothers could accompany them on their countryside visits, and subsequently a good number did help with supervision and were gainfully employed in many learning situations.

Probably the most important decision made by the class was that, in order to gain the maximum benefit from visits to the country centre, thorough planning of the work should be done in the urban classroom before each visit. After each visit, follow-up work would extend and strengthen their direct country experience.

This class teacher believed in the critical importance of continual discussion with his class. Although the class consisted of 38 children of mixed ability and ethnic origin nevertheless a major factor in the pre-planning of the "action" programme and its implementation, were essential elements in a very successful piece of work. The following edited version of the year's "scheme of work" indicates that successful action may be related to early planning:

Aim: to look at the area around the country environmental studies centre and to make it a source of interest and intellectual stimulus.

Essential Materials

(a) Ordnance Survey route planning map of G.B.
(b) Local Ordnance Survey maps—6", 2½", 25".
    County Series Ordnance Survey map—6", 2½'.
(c) Geological map (County Series).

(d) Notebooks for field work/observation. Folders for recording visits, observations, etc.

Explanatory Geography

(a) Looking at the general appearance of the land form. Explaining factors responsible for its present form and appearance.
Work of rivers, seas. Geological history—fossils, chalk, etc.

(b) Explain relevant terms like: steep, undulating, gentle fold, valleys—wide or narrow, U-shaped, hilltop, brow of hill, crest, syncline, anticline, etc.

(c) Explain and illustrate practically, phrases like: swift flowing (river) gently flowing, meander, tributary, etc.

Villages and Towns

Aim: to recognise the *reason* for changes imposed by man on the landscape and to see how the landscape influences these changes.
Attempt to obtain up-to-date information on:

(a) Their earliest history—Roman, Saxon, Norman.

(b) Geographical significance and importance.
Why did this village/town grow up where it did?
Compare with the "home" urban area.
What purpose did it serve then? Now? Is it different from the urban area?
Is it an area of dense population?—if not, why not?
What do the people of the village do for a living? Is it different from the occupational structure of the urban area?

Agriculture

(a) What people grow (or reap) and why.

(b) Kind of soil—effect on crop yield.

(c) The countryside in winter compared with the town.

(d) The countryside in summer compared with the town.

Communications

(a) Traffic survey.

(b) Railway.

(c) Commuters.

(d) How do people get to work in the urban area? How does this compare with the country?

Nature Study

This aspect of the study will continually compare the city and countryside.

Plant Life

Looking at:
(a) general pattern of vegetation,
(b) kind of trees,
(c) kind of fruit trees and orchards,
(d) vegetable crops grown,
(e) seasonal effect on vegetation, e.g., autumn leaves, winter and spring appearances.

Practical work:

(a) Collecting, identifying and mounting samples of: wild flowers, shrubs and saplings, autumn leaves, twigs, cones and berries.
(b) Identifying and making rubbings of trees; estimating the height of trees, length of branches, circumference of trunks, etc.
(c) Using these as a basis for a wide range of mathematical work in the classroom.

This then is a brief outline of some of the work which it was anticipated the class should be engaged in. Where appropriate history, geography, English, mathematics and social studies were parts of the curriculum which might be covered during the investigation.

As visit followed visit, it became obvious that a continued weekly commitment to an environmental studies scheme could produce concrete evidence of success and achievement whatever statistical results may show. The classroom walls, indeed the corridors, were covered with charts, graphs, art work, models and folders. These were of such a high standard that the children became very critical of their previous lower standards. Remarks like: "I like this work, I know it is better than last term's" were commonplace. Parents who accompanied the children and visitors to the school commented on the purposeful behaviour of the class. One mother who left school at 14 years of age said her own standards of observation had improved.

What of the class teacher? When questioned, he believed that the social interaction of teacher, taught and parent had been the most successful part of the environmental studies scheme. He saw children reacting to another environment and this experience broadened and deepened his understanding of child development. Clearly there was much visible evidence of tremendously successful work by any standards, but the overriding impression of this young teacher and his colleagues was that the experience of the environmental studies scheme with its close relationships with disadvantaged children could be shown in increased verbal language; more creative writing; pride in achievement and standards of presentation; better attitudes towards work and people; improved attention span; and the ability to work individually and in a group.

Example 2: Good Practice, Report by a Class Teacher

When the environmental studies scheme venture was first mentioned my thoughts immediately went back to the Limehouse Playing Fields and Hainault Forest. How were we going to use it? So many valuable opportunities were wasted in those days. So much emphasis was put on games and P.E. There was so much more that could have been done. This time it had to be thought out and planned.

The first objective was a visit to the area. Unfortunately, this proved to be too brief and little was found out beyond the fact that there was a Roman villa and ruined castle within striking distance. Further visits were needed and these had to be done at weekends. These visits tended to show that if we kept to the main school area we would have several villages, parkland and woods to work on. This was all right for one term but in order that we might do the job properly we had to go much farther afield, as much as 4 or 5 miles. Then we could also take in the river, lakes, more interesting churches, the castle and villa and much more interesting countryside.

So the plan, as far as I was concerned, was beginning to take shape. Schools and teachers were left very much to their own devices, and, as it turned out, worked along very different lines. I myself know very little natural science; any teaching along these lines must be done by trial and error and would not be deeply involved. For nature study, it had to be kept simple and unadorned. We could, however, make quite a big stride in maths here. Distance, height, angles—general surveying, statistics. In language too, quite a lot could be done—watch, describe, explain,—tape recording and adventure. So that in the main was the general plan, and that is how it continued, with language gradually taking over as the main theme.

During the first few weeks the children found it difficult to settle down to anything constructive. The strangeness of the surroundings, the freedom from the city, all tended to keep the work rate down to a bare minimum and many curious features of behaviour pattern were noticed. They much preferred ball games on the hard playground, seldom venturing onto the playing field. Games had to be organised by the teacher to get them onto grass. Children would often be found, even on a bright day, around the dustbins, under the classrooms and in the old coke sheds. Indeed on several occasions the girls were found playing "shops" in an old unused covered passage, using old mineral water cans and cartons for goods. It was not until near the end of the environmental studies scheme that they began to drift away from this form of behaviour. But change they did, they now seem to be just as much at home in the country centre as they are in the urban area. I believe that there has been the most striking development. At first they needed to be led, shown and instructed, but now, both away and at home, they have a quiet, though sometimes noisy, confidence that will stand them in good stead. These visits to the country have helped them to grow up and stand on their own two feet. The standard of educational attainment has been little affected and I would say that for most of the children the advancement educationally is only slightly more than it would have been had they not taken part, but it is possible that the exception proves the rule and it might be as well if I discussed three exceptions.

1. John Z. was backward educationally, reading age of 6·8 years at 10 years old. He seldom spoke to adults, never of his own choosing. His family background is one of extreme difficulty, for his father is a permanent invalid, slowly and continuously becoming more and more ill. It was a loving, a caring family but always a worried family. Cash was constantly short and, at times, the shadow of death hung heavily over them.

   John only ever came alive when he had a ball at his feet. Whilst playing in a team if the ball was not with him, he was not with the game. He was often sullen and morose with all the troubles of mankind on his shoulders. John was helpful at home, but he always had to be cajoled and persuaded to do things.

   Today John is a good team man, eager to get up and go. He is still slow to converse with adults but is now willing and able to do so. When giving John an assignment, all that is needed now is to give him a simple instruction and leave him to work out his own pathway. He is still a very ordinary and somewhat backward boy, but he has now come to grips with his problems and is capable of overcoming them most of the time. Reading age now at 11 years old—9·2 years.

2. Wendy Y. was a rebel—at war with her own small world. Always at the centre of any storm that might break. It was in her written work that we saw the first signs of a breakthrough. Wendy was a cabbage intellectually, her spoken word restricted to that of the proverbial fish-wife. When spoken to she always went on to the defensive. That breakthrough I know was attributable to the environmental studies scheme. We were looking for any living thing—animal or insect—that we could find. When we returned Wendy wrote her first poem—about a butterfly. There is no doubt about this being the moment, for from that day Wendy wanted to talk and write. Mrs. Y. recently remarked; "She's always writing at home, I wouldn't mind but most of it is poetry."

3. Ann L. was shy, she was backward (R.A. 6·5 at 10). When spoken to, her face went beetroot red, she stammered and stuttered and almost looked for a place to hide. During the last few weeks she was interviewed by the headteacher for a place at her new secondary school. She had no qualms, no reticence, she spoke up pleasantly and unafraid. Last week she had the temerity to answer me back and then laugh!

These children have gained without doubt. How much of this is due to the environmental studies scheme I cannot gauge accurately, but only affirm the belief that most of it is, when comparing it with previous years.

The environmental studies scheme part of this project has been, to my mind, eminently successful. Its continuance for this school is, I believe, essential.

Example 3: Good Practice, Interview Responses of Class Teachers

* Our visit to the nursery and the church was particularly successful. We are trying to show them country life and it is important from a health point of view because that area has glorious air.

* It depends on good weather. Going out from the centre complete with sandwiches, waving to the local inhabitants, the children being in a good mood and this results in the development of personal relationships between the teacher and the children.

* We are trying to improve their lives and to make their school-days happier. Some of them are learning as fast as toddlers.

* We decide to visit a place, to see something or to look for things. The visit is spent looking, we stay outside as much as possible. On return to (the Project School) I try to teach, for example, about how plants work, what different plants are called. Once we saw a water-rat trapped on the barbed wire and we wrote poems about it and the art for that week was directed in that way.

* I try to find situations that the children haven't experienced before. I use these situations and events to stimulate the children to write about them . . . Rather than using them for sequenced, planned environmental studies, I use the new phenomena which the children experience as stimulators. I am not really interested in the new knowledge that can be built up about the country centre. I put the children in a situation; I let them deal with it; and then I let them write about it . . . I think the opportunities offered by (the environmental studies scheme) are to show the children that I care for them, and then they will care for me.

* Well, yesterday was a successful day where the children did two things: one of them is that we have forged links with a local school and played a return football match with them and therefore developed social relationships, and secondly the children spent some time digging on their own allotment under teacher supervision and this will give them the opportunity to grow things and observe their changes.

* We began in the classroom with a study on how to read a map which took place in the early part of the week, followed by a river study in the countryside (environmental studies centre). A bit of everything in the primary school timetable came out, particularly "drama in the wood" where the children enacted a variation of Robin Hood, which sprang from the wooded surroundings. These successful visits are one way of trying to raise academic standards, and this is my first aim.

* A successful day could be a day which we spent with the gypsies and the children were able to see at first hand the problems which afflict Travelling People. Another successful day was when we were collecting things in the countryside which could be used for signs in the wood for a form of nature trail exercise. As a follow-up we documented this the best way we could.

* We have this term in this school the students helping us. The children get more out of (the environmental studies scheme) than if the students weren't there. First of all there's one student for four children . . . On the other hand for us, the teachers, it makes life a bit chaotic. We find it difficult to keep in contact with what's going on. It makes it harder to keep in contact with each individual child—what they are doing and what they have seen. When the students have gone, I expect that some of the children will have done all the things that we would want to do.

* Well, there were two students and eight children and they were collecting insects. They looked in all the places insects could be found—under

stones for example. This went on for three weeks. The children got used to handling insects. By the end of the time the girls were not giggling when they handled a spider. They produced diagrams of this. One boy is doing—in school on his own—a topic book on insects.

* Let me see—something that went well—we haven't really had a failure yet. The fishing—the children wanted to fish in the river. At first— having ensured that they had spare socks and wellingtons, etc.—I let them play around in the river. I looked around for a child who was interested in something and asked questions about what they were doing. I didn't tell them answers—they were to find out. The children wanted to go to the stream again. Had they not wanted to, I would have let it drop. But they did. I then asked—on, say, the day before they went, what else they wanted to do in the river . . . We had some class discussion about it. Some said they wanted to count the fish in a partic- ular stretch of river—first it was only numbers. Then as we started talking we decided that the fish were found in different places in the river—some under stones, some in the weeds. So we decided to count the total number of fish and the different places in which they were found.

Example 4: Environmental Studies in the Urban E.P.A. Junior School–Teacher Responses

* It becomes civics straight away. The best approach would be to take a historical line. From time to time we do things like that—when it crops up. If we are doing anything in history, we relate it back to the history of the area (an example of Peter the Great was quoted). But (the country scheme) takes up a lot of time which could be used on a (local urban) study. Don't forget these children are in their fourth year and some time has to be spent on preparing them for their leaving examinations.

* Yes, environmental studies is the study of an area where the children live; I haven't got round to setting that up yet.

* In (the urban area) the supervision and organisation problems are too great. Now my class is too big and the behaviour of some of them is so odd that it often embarrasses me. I know that I risk the supervision rule when I take the class out. If one of them does a bunk I can't catch them. In (the urban area) the problems simply of getting the children from A to B, given the conditions we are expected to work in, make it impossible to do anything properly.

* I haven't done any of that kind of work because I have had students. However, last year we did a traffic census and charts and maps came from that—but I don't call that environmental studies. It was just part of my normal classroom work.

* It would include a study of the way people lived; you would meet people, for example in park visits and walks, but we don't do that here.

* Again as for (the country scheme) there is a need to integrate all studies. I cannot see that there is much difference in the way one studies in (the

urban area) or in the countryside although what the area has to offer may be different. In——, being an urban area, one would tend to study people and how they live. For example, history and geography, trade and occupations, transport and communications. Museum visits should be made and naval dockyards and so on. Yes. I have done this and used it as a form of comparative study and am beginning it again next term.

* I did this a couple of years ago. We did a land use survey, building types, communications, transport, historical connections. Then we ran out of time.

Question: Why do you not do that now?

Answer: Well, I had had that class for two years and I did it with them in the second of those two years. It was a three week project, a sort of holiday at the end of term. This year for this class there hasn't been enough time. Given (the country scheme) and the necessary follow-up. We have only $2\frac{1}{2}$ days left for pushing English and Maths; these children have to take the transfer profile and there's not very much time left.

Question: Why not push English and Maths through environmental studies?

Answer: Because we can't organise environmental studies to do this in the short time that is available. We have to teach English and Maths by the direct method rather than indirectly through environmental studies. If the whole school life . . . had been spent on environmental studies, then it would be possible, but given that they have only one term in this year before the profile, it takes time for anything definite to come out of it.

* I haven't thought about it. I don't know very much about (the urban area). I would like to tackle a (urban) project, but (the country scheme) takes all the time available for environmental studies. Given all the things that happen, there's not much time left to get the basics—maths and reading—in.

* I haven't done one. A different environment from the one the children are used to is important: either the children are so blasé about their own environment and anyway it is so sick—I mean by that sterile. As far as the children are concerned all the bad things the children experience are in this environment. I imagine if I did it, it would be basically the same way. But if I did try it, it would be more difficult to put across. There are many more problems—like traffic and supervision—in——. In the country the environment does the stimulating for you—all you have to do is guide the children. In (the urban area) you would have to do all the stimulating yourself—it must come from you with no help from the environment.

* I have done an environmental studies approach on my teaching practice . . . but in this school in my first two years I had first year children and they were too young, too inexperienced to have this kind of approach. This year as I have been teaching fourth years I aim to do it—but I don't see why it should be a comparison between (the country) and (the urban area). I would like to use the urban area as a starting-point for history and geography; in (the country) the obvious starting-point is through nature study.

APPENDIX 3

THE DESIGN OF THE EVALUATION AND THE TESTS USED

A. The design of the evaluation

The evaluation was designed to test for the following effects of the Environmental Studies Scheme.

  (i) A direct effect on preferences for school subjects, attitudes to school, motivation and Study Skills.

 (ii) A "spin off" effect, improving performance in more recognised school performance areas—English and Maths—and in other attitudinal areas.

(iii) An "opportunity cost" effect, depressing performance in English and Maths as attention and time were devoted to other things.

The comparisons made to estimate these effects were:

  (i) Between the experimental and control group over the scheme's "natural" period of operation, i.e., one school year. The control children came from the fourth year classes of the same schools as were controls for the language programme evaluation reported in Part 5 (pages 100 to 165).

 (ii) Comparisons with national norms on the school performance tests.

(iii) Comparisons on the school performance measures of standards over the year prior to the scheme and during the scheme for a "reading" sub-group of children. This sub-sample were defined as follows:

  a. They were present in their schools during March 1969 at the time of the baseline reading test for the National E.P.A. Study. (The full results of this test are included in Volume 2 of the E.P.A. Series.)

  b. They were operationally defined as readers as a result of achieving a standard score of 80+ on that test.

  c. They were in consequence tested during October 1969: on the same school performance tests as were used for the environmental studies evaluation (The Bristol Achievement Tests).

  d. They were present for both the pre- and post-test for the evaluation of the environmental studies scheme.

The design for the evaluation is shown in diagram form in Table 1. The numbers of children involved in the analysis is shown in Table 2.

As with the evaluation of the language programme, the possibility existed that the Environmental Studies Scheme would have a different effect on children depending on their school performance or attitude before taking part in the scheme. Accordingly, children were allocated to low, medium or high scoring groups as a result of their pre-test scores on a particular test, and the post-test scores of groups so defined were examined. On the performance tests children were allocated to a low, medium or high scoring group if their score on the particular test was minus one standard deviation, within one standard deviation or plus standard deviation of the combined experi-

Table 1

The Evaluation Design

	Time 1	Time 2 Pre-test	Time 3 Post-test
Experiment	Sub-sample of readers from the experimental schools	All children present in their experimental schools on on the days of testing	Those children from time 2 (pre-test) who were present in their schools on the days of testing
Control		All children present in their control schools on the days of testing	Those children from time 2 (pre-test) who were present in their schools on the days of testing

mental and control mean standard score on that test. Table 3 on page 205 shows the score ranges and the numbers of children in each range.

For the attitude data it was not possible to calculate meaningful standard deviations of pre-test mean scores. Rather, the distribution of scores at pre-test were inspected and as near as possible equal groups were created. Table 4 on page 205 shows the score ranges and the numbers involved.

B. The tests used

The following criteria were used to choose the tests:

(i) They should comprise a general battery of indicators, measuring as broad an area of both attitudes and school performance as possible.

(ii) They should be reliable.

(iii) They should be capable of measuring change.

(iv) They should be contemporary and sensitive to the most modern developments in junior school education. The adoption of an environmental studies curriculum would certainly mean integration of subjects, for example, and it could mean developing an ecological approach to learning.

(v) They should cover the correct age range of children and yet not be subject to ceiling effects. A proportion of the subject children were known to have very poor performance; and a spread of scores even among these groups was needed.

(vi) They should be relatively quick and easy to administer.

(vii) They should be valid and relevant measures for assessing the impact of an Environmental Studies Scheme. Although there was little prior knowledge of the specific educational contents of the scheme, an important consideration was to choose measures which were in some way conceptually related to what was likely to happen.

The following instruments were chosen:

1. For measuring attitude change: the *N.F.E.R. Streaming Study Children's*

Table 2

Numbers of Children Involved in the Analysis

	Time 1 (Prior to experiment)				Times 2 and 3 (The experimental period)			
	English	S. Skills	Maths		English	S. Skills	Maths	Attitude
Experimental	126	Readers 126	126	Boys	137	130	132	144
				Girls	116	120	117	126
				Non-immigrant	202	200	201	202
				West Indian immigrant	54	53	54	49
				Other immigrants	21	19	18	19
Control				Boys	68	65	68	77
				Girls	57	57	57	62
				Non-immigrant	121	120	116	113
				West Indian immigrant	7	7	7	7
				Other immigrants	10	9	10	10

Table 3

Pre-test Score Ranges and Frequency by Treatment Group of Children in Low, Medium and High Scoring Groups on the Three Bristol Achievement Tests

		Low scorers	Medium scorers	High scorers
Standard score	English	below 76	77 to 104	105 and above
range on pre-test	Maths	below 82	83 to 105	106 and above
	Study Skills	below 77	78 to 103	104 and above
Experimental	English	47	185	46
	Maths	52	174	47
	Study Skills	45	185	42
Control	English	16	103	25
	Maths	29	90	21
	Study Skills	20	98	26

Table 4

Pre-test Attitude Score Ranges and Frequency by Treatment Group of Children in Low, Medium and High Scoring Groups by the Attitude Scales.

	A	B	C	D	E	F	G	H	I	J
Score range										
High	5,6	5,6	9	8	5,6	4,5	4,5,6	4,5,6	4,5	7,8,9
Medium	3,4	3,4	7,8	6,7	3,4	2,3	2,3	2,3	2,3	5,6
Low	0,1,2	0,1,2	0–6	0–5	0,1,2	0,1	0,1	0,1	0,1	0–4
E. High	73	44	80	46	35	105	67	68	79	49
E. Medium	119	127	100	153	159	129	115	154	133	142
E. Low	78	99	90	71	76	36	88	48	58	79
C. High	65	25	43	27	31	65	34	29	38	24
C. Medium	43	78	53	79	83	52	63	79	58	67
C. Low	31	36	43	33	31	22	42	31	43	48

Column header above A–J: **Attitude scale**

Attitude Questionnaire which included items on motivation. This was chosen because:

(i) It was a broadly focused instrument measuring ten areas of children's attitudes to school. Table 5 below lists the ten scales in the questionnaire.

(ii) The items in it and techniques for its use had recently been standardised and used in the N.F.E.R. Streaming Study.[1]

(iii) It had been used in the N.F.E.R. Streaming Study to measure changes in attitude.

(iv) It had been used on roughly the right age range of children.

The same questionnaire was used for both pre- and post-tests. It was administered by us to small groups of children, taking particular care to deal with the problems of non-readers. The 64 statements on the questionnaire were read out, one at a time, to the children. The children were required to place a tick in one of three boxes to indicate their agreement, disagreement or neutrality to the statement in question.

[1] J. C. Barker Lunn, *Streaming in the Primary School.* E. Ferri, *Streaming two years later.*

Table 5

Scales in the N.F.E.R. Streaming Study Children's Attitude Questionnaire*

Scale	Area
A	Attitude to school
B	Interest in school work
C	Importance of doing well
D	Attitude to class
E	"Other Image" of class
F	Conforming versus non-conforming pupil
G	Relationship with teacher
H	Anxiety in the classroom situation
I	Social adjustment/getting on well with classmates
J	Academic self-image

* For full details see J. C. Barker Lunn, *Manual of Instructions for use of Primary Children's Attitude scales*, N.F.E.R.

2. For measuring change in the children's school performance the *Bristol Achievement Tests Level 3* were chosen because:

(i) They comprised a broadly focused battery measuring three areas of children's school performance—in English, Study Skills and in Maths.

(ii) They had parallel forms with high re-test reliabilities. The idea of administering Form A to half of the children at the pre-test stage and Form B to the other half was considered, but rejected because it was thought this would cause too much confusion and upset in the schools. Instead, Form A was used as the pre-test and Form B as the post-test.

(iii) The tests were designed to be, and were for the experimental evaluation, administered by the children's class teacher; they were marked and standardised by the researchers.

(iv) The tests had been constructed recently with the specific intention of being sensitive to modern junior school curricula.

(v) The tests, and Study Skills in particular, seemed to be the most valid measure of the aspects of school performance that the Environmental Studies Scheme was likely to act upon, i.e., the ability to inter-relate ideas and formulations from different parts of the traditional junior school curriculum.

The Analysis of Data

As with the evaluation of the language programme reported in Part 5, the two main statistical techniques used on the performance test material were the analysis of variance and covariance.[1] And as for Part 5 a 0·05 level of significance was accepted as statistically significant.

---

[1] See Appendix 2 of Part 5. As with the evaluation of the language programme, Miss Wendy Fader advised on the analysis and arranged for the computing.

For analysis of the attitude data, statistical control of initial differences between groups, through analysis of covariance, was inappropriate. Instead, differences in attitude between the experimental and control groups at pre-test were examined and subsequent analysis was performed without regard to initial differences. Firstly, changes in score between pre- and post-test on each of the attitude scales for each treatment group taken individually were examined. Secondly, differences in change score between the treatment groups were tested. The statistical tests used in this analysis were, in the first place, the Wilcoxon matched pairs sign test:[1] for whether the scores of a particular group of children changed in a particular direction over time. In the Wilcoxon test each child acts as his own control, i.e., the changes in score between pre- and post-test for individual children are separately calculated. Then the frequency of the various changes in a positive and in a negative direction is calculated for each group of children. The test takes into account both the direction and the magnitude of the change scores. The test of significance indicates whether or not the observed changes can be attributed to chance. In comparing the distribution of scores, or the distribution of change scores, for two sub-groups of children, the Komolgorov-Smirnov two-sample test[2] (the K.S. test) was used. For this test the distribution of scores are transformed into cumulative percentage distributions, and the distributions for one group are matched with those of another. If the two cumulative distributions are found to be "too far apart" at any point, then it can be said that the distributions are different. Depending on the end of the distribution at which the two become different, the group with the most positive distribution of scores can be identified. The test of significance indicates whether or not the observed differences can be attributed to chance.

---

[1] S. Siegal, *Non-Parametric Statistics*, McGraw-Hill, pp. 75–83.
[2] *Ibid.*, pp. 127–136.

THE RANKING OF PREFERENCES FOR
JUNIOR SCHOOL ACTIVITIES

E.P.A. Children's Ranking of Different School Activities

In addition to the evaluation of the impact of the Environmental Studies Scheme on the school performance and attitudes of the subject children, the *post hoc* preferences of a sample of both the experimental and control children for different school activities were assessed.

The sample of children

About two-thirds of the children from the experimental and control treatment cells were sampled at random from each class in all schools included in the evaluation. (Eighteen children were taken from each class. One experimental class did not have enough children. Therefore every available child in this class was questioned: a total of 14.)

The ranking instrument

The object of the exercise was to discover which activities children most preferred doing at school and to monitor any distortions in preferences that could be attributed to the Environmental Studies Scheme. In doing this the following difficulties had to be overcome:

(i) The primary school day is not timetabled into distinct areas of the curriculum.
(ii) There is considerable variation between schools over which activities children take part in.
(iii) A list of all possible activities would be too long for young children to remember and to order into a list of preferences.
(iv) The reading and ability level of many of the children was extremely low. One could expect them neither to be able to remember a verbal description of an activity nor to be able to read such a description.

There were thus three sorts of operational difficulties: to select a realistic and relevant variety of school activities for the children to choose from; to present the children with a task which was within their range of competence; to establish an order of preferences between the choices available to the children.

Although there was considerable variation between schools over the activities offered to children, and the relative importance given to them in the school timetable, the variation existed at the margin. There were a number of core activities which were accorded commonly high priority in all junior schools. In addition to these core activities, a number of others were identified which, although not all children were able to take part in them with equal frequency, could be used to contrast with aspects of the Environmental Studies Scheme.

In order to overcome the problem of operating within the children's ranges of competence it was decided to show them photographs of the selected school activities.

The relationship between the preferences was established by asking the children to rank a closed list of school activities.

The whole exercise was piloted in a junior school in another part of London. About twenty 9″ × 7″ black and white photographs of school activities were made and shown in various combinations to the pilot children. Initially the children were not asked to rank the activities but merely to identify each one. The pilot children identified all the photographs easily; and photographs were given titles chosen by them.[1] From the twenty initial photographs thirteen were chosen which gave the range of activities wanted. (See Table 1 for the final list.) The pilot children seemed to be able to search

Table 1

Activities Presented to the Children

Activity inscription	Description of the photographs
A Local studies	Children doing a traffic census near a main road.
B Outside visits	Children sitting on the steps leading up to the *Cutty Sark*.
C Model making	Children making a paper and material collage.
D Maths lesson	The rear view of children sitting at desks with maths problems written on the blackboard.
E Measuring the playground	Two children with a tape measure in a school playground.
F Painting	A child painting.
G Games	A group of children playing with a ball and a bean bag.
H Playtime	Groups of children in the playground.
I Trip to the Park	A group of children walking in Greenwich Park.
J Swimming	Children at an indoor swimming pool.
K School in the country	Photograph of the Environmental Studies Centre.
L Science experiment	Child working with water and beakers.
M Reading	A group of children reading at a desk.

through that number of photographs and to make positive choices between them, i.e., not many reversals of choice took place, choices were made with no more than a 10 second delay and the children recognised the activities as being distinct from one another.

For the children in the assessment the photographs were presented in the following way:

(i) Each child was seen individually by the research worker in a room or space removed from the rest of the class.

(ii) The thirteen photographs were displayed in front of the child on a

---

[1] There was no consensus among the pilot children for the identifying title of three activities: Local studies, Outside visits and the environmental studies school in the country. These photographs were nevertheless retained and labels given them by the researchers.

table. The child could see all the photographs before him. The order of the display was rotated between children. The research worker sat on the opposite side of the table.

(iii) The research worker said to the child "Here we have some photographs of things children might be doing at school. I will tell you what each of them is and then I would like you to tell me which you would most like to be doing at school".

(iv) The title under each photograph was then read in turn while the research worker pointed to the picture itself. For the photographs of Outside visits, Local studies and the School in the country the research worker quickly established that the child recognised the content of the photograph and to cater for the unfamiliarity of these activities the possibility of their occurrence was emphasised.

(v) The child then made his first choice by pointing to or saying the title of one of the photographs. In either case the research worker checked the child's response by getting it to do the other operation also and then recorded the choice. The research worker then turned the first picture over and asked "Which would you like best to do now?" The process was repeated until all the pictures had been turned over.

Results

School activity preferences of the total sample

Table 2 gives the order of ranked preferences for the thirteen activities. It should be borne in mind that this is only a generalised picture of E.P.A. children's preference for school activities. In particular it is important to note that there are more experimental children than control children in the total sample, and since, as is shown later, there are differences in the preference for activities A, B and K between these two groups, the place in the ranked order of these three activities is uncertain.

The order of preference is:

1. J—Swimming
2. B—Outside visits
3. K—School in the country
4. G—Games
5. M—Reading
6. C—Model making
7. F—Painting: Median Rank
{8. L—Science experiment
{8. D—Maths lesson
10. I—Trip to the park
11. H—Playtime
12. A—Local studies
13. E—Measuring the playground

Although the differences in mean score for the activities are not very great the two extremes of preference do seem to be of interest. J—Swimming is consistently highly ranked: a low ranked position for it often reflects the child's inability to swim. This raises a general point when dealing with these preferences: different children tended to interpret the exercise in different ways.

During the pilot phase, the children were unsystematically questioned about their choices and it became obvious that the relative preference for any particular activity depended on the application of a range of criteria:

(i) *Familiarity*
If the child had not experienced a particular activity he tended to give it a low rank. Closely associated with familiarity was the child's perception of something as a *possible* school activity; this factor particularly affected the ranking of K—School in the country by the control children. The familiarity factor might account for the bottom ranked position of A—Local studies and E—Measuring the playground.

(ii) *Competence*
As mentioned above for J—Swimming, a child's ability at a particular activity seemed to affect the ranked preference for it. So, for example, children who gave a low rank to D—Maths lesson, sometimes said afterwards that they quite liked it as an activity but were not very good at it.

(iii) *Expectations*
A more intangible influence on the ranking of activities concerned what the child thought a school's function to be. Subjects like D—Maths lesson and M—Reading tended to receive a higher rank from some children than I—Trip to the park or C—Model making for this reason.

Despite these various facets of influence on the actual rank given to an activity, certain definite conclusions can be drawn.

Although there are sex differences in the ranking of H—Playtime, both sexes give it a low rank. Children said that there was nothing to do at playtime and that they were bored by it. Some also said that the playground of their school could be a frightening place. B—Outside visits was the second favoured activity across the total sample. Even though the activity shown was in the geographical area of most of the schools (the *Cutty Sark*) and had probably been visited by most of the children in their non-school time, perhaps these trips represent a sufficient break from the sometimes drab atmosphere of school to be popular with the children.

Comparison of the experimental and control groups' preference

As explained above the only assumed difference between the experimental children and the control children was that the experimental children had experienced the Environmental Study Scheme centred around K—School in the country, while the control children could only conjecture as to its attractiveness. It would be expected therefore, that the ranking of K—School in the country would be different for these two groups.

From an inspection of Table 3 below it can be seen that significant differences occur between the experimental and control groups in their ranking of A—Local studies, B—Outside visits and K—School in the country. In the case of K—School in the country, the experimental group ranked it higher;

Table 2
Summary of Rankings of All Children

	N =	A	B	C	D	E	F	G	H	I	J	K	L	M	Coefficient of concordance = W
		Mean rank of activity													
All children	286	8·96	5·39	6·84	7·42	9·77	7·20	5·95	8·74	7·57	4·02	5·57	7·42	6·07	0·1694

Table 3
Comparison of the Rankings of the Experimental and Control Children

	N =	A	B	C	D	E	F	G	H	I	J	K	L	M	Coefficient of concordance = W
		Mean rank of activities													
Experimental	180	9·33	5·88	6·87	7·09	9·86	7·39	5·88	8·55	7·81	4·42	4·28	7·57	5·97	0·1908
Control	106	8·35	4·55	6·70	7·99	9·61	6·88	6·05	9·08	7·18	3·34	7·75	7·15	6·24	0·1954
t (df = 284)		2·7944	3·6141	0·4013	1·7857	0·7791	1·1633	0·3617	1·3900	1·6967	2·3684	9·2336	0·9217	0·6125	
p*		$0·01 > p > 0·001$	$p < 0·001$	(ns)	(ns)	(ns)	(ns)	(ns)	(ns)	(ns)	(ns)	$p < ·001$	(ns)	(ns)	

* (ns) = $p > 0·05$.

activities A—Local studies and B—Outside visits were ranked higher by the control group. The Environmental Studies Scheme had two major components; it took place on the whole away from the physical building of a school and its content was the study of the environment. For the experimental group, given a relatively greater interest in K—School in the country over the control group, some other activities must have been ranked relatively lower. Rather than every activity being ranked lower by the experimental children, however, they showed a relative decrease in the preference for the two activities most closely related to K—School in the country, i.e., A—Local studies and B—Outside visits.

Comparison of boys and girls

The t-tests presented in Table 4 show that there are no significant differences between experimental boys and girls in their ranking of K—School in

Table 4

Ranking of K—School in the Country by Boys and Girls in Both Treatment Groups

	N	Mean rank
1. Experimental boys	98	4·45
2. Experimental girls	82	4·08
3. Control boys	60	8·03
4. Control girls	46	7·37

t-Tests

	Degrees of freedom	t	p
Within experimental group Boys:Girls	168	0·6630	(ns)
Within control group Boys:Girls	104	2·1030	$0·05 > p > 0·02$
Boys—between experimental and control groups	156	7·0854	$p < 0·001$
Girls—between experimental and control groups	126	9·7367	$p < 0·001$

the country: both prefer it equally. Within the control group K—School in the country is significantly more favoured by girls than by boys.

Both experimental boys and experimental girls rank K—School in the Country significantly higher than their control counterparts.

Comparison of classes within the experimental group

With the data from Table 5 below comparisons are made between the relative preference of K—School in the country of the classes which took part in the Environmental Studies Scheme. Classes with a common first digit come from the same school. One can see that not only are there significant differences between the ranking of K—School in the country by different classes, but that there are significant differences between classes within the same school (i.e., between classes 01 and 00).

The factors affecting inter-class differences in the ranking of K—School in the country are complex and there is insufficient information to isolate their influences. Factors contributing to differences could be a function of (i) the *class teacher*—her interests and relationship with the children irrespective of the scheme, (ii) the teacher's *approach to the environmental studies work*—one observed differences in approach ranging from treating the day's trip as an outing which was worthwhile in itself, to regarding it as an opportunity to intensify and broaden the character of school "work", (iii) the experience of *scheme irrespective of the teacher*—for example classes were assigned a day of the week to go to the country centre, the teachers at least were happier to go on Tuesday than they were on Friday, (iv) the arrangements for *teaching the children at the centre*—some classes were taught always and only by their class teachers (classes 00 and 01), some classes rotated teachers, some classes took extra teachers with them from their London schools, some had students, some had parents with them. The combination of factors is extreme. All one is able to say from this exercise is that there are differences—some of them statistically highly significant—between classes from the experimental group in their preferences for activity K—School in the country.

Table 5

Comparison of Classes from the Experimental Group on their Ranking of K—School in the Country

Mean rank of K

Class no.	N	Mean rank of K	Class no.	N	Mean rank of K
01	18	3·05	21	18	4·78
50	14	3·50	41	18	5·00
12	18	3·61	00	18	5·11
10	18	3·67	20	18	5·56
40	18	3·72	30	18	6·22
11	18	3·83			

t—Tests on the Class Comparisons

Class no.	01	50	12	10	40	11	21	41	00	20	30
01	—										
50†	0·5348	—									
12	0·9247	0·3938	—								
10	1·3561	0·2436	0·1279	—							
40	0·8077	0·2272	0·1329	0·0684	—						
11	1·0422	0·3341	0·2931	0·2492	0·1174	—					
21	2·3047	1·2855	1·5431	1·7059	1·1243	1·0848	—				
41	2·3126*	1·3692	1·6364	1·7614	1·2580	1·2241	0·2288	—			
00	2·7373***	1·6126	1·9721	2·2032*	1·4714	1·4582	0·3732	0·1142	—		
20	3·3245***	2·0565*	2·5534**	2·8763***	1·9426	1·9648	0·8795	0·5797	0·5062	—	
30	3·6485****	2·4173*	2·9784***	3·2476***	2·4036*	2·4393**	1·4612	1·1539	1·1242	0·6669	—

† For this row the degrees of freedom = 30. For all other df = 34.

* = $0.05 > p > 0.02$: ** = $0.02 > p > 0.01$: *** = $0.01 > p > 0.001$: **** = $p < 0.001$: All others $p > 0.05$ ∴ Not significant.

APPENDIX 5

THE RESULTS OF THE EVALUATION

This appendix contains tables of descriptive statistics and the results of the analysis of change scores for the school performance tests and the pupil attitude data. The ordering of the tables conforms more closely to the logic of the analysis than does the account in the text. Since the full data on the total experimental and control groups are included in the text they are not reproduced here.

The descriptive tables for the school performance tests record mean raw and standard scores for each sub-group in question. The analysis of variance and co-variance was in each case performed on changes in raw scores: there were no significant differences in age between any of the groups.

Since the distributions of attitude score are of little value in themselves, only the results of the Wilcoxon and Komolgorov-Smirnov tests are presented. Barker Lunn's study *Streaming in the Primary School* has shown significant differences between a national sample of boys and girls on all the attitude scales. Barker Lunn's findings indicate significantly "better" attitudes for girls on Scales A–G, girls are more anxious than boys (Scale H), and boys are more socially adjusted and have a better academic self-image than girls (Scales I and J). Analysis of the pre-test results of the E.P.A. groups showed differences between E.P.A. boys and girls only on Scales A—Attitude to school, B—Interest in school work, D—Attitude to class, F—Conformity and G—Relations with teacher. On the other scales there were no significant differences. It would appear that E.P.A. girls' attitudes are less positive than girls in general, in a number of areas, and this should be borne in mind when studying the pattern of results.

Table 1

Mean Scores at Pre- and Post-test of Boys and Girls in the Two Treatment Groups on the School Performance Tests

A. Experimental boys

	English (137)		Maths (132)		Study Skills (130)	
	Mean	SD	Mean	SD	Mean	SD
Pre-test						
Standard score	87·85	11·88	94·44	12·09	91·28	11·75
Raw score	17·88	14·16	20·22	14·28	15·66	10·57
Post-test						
Standard score	87·55	12·03	87·33	13·51	86·92	12·72
Raw score	31·32	18·82	26·89	17·19	18·62	11·49

B. Experimental girls

	English (116)		Maths (117)		Study Skills (120)	
	Mean	SD	Mean	SD	Mean	SD
Pre-test						
Standard score	92·71	16·01	96·07	10·59	91·73	10·72
Raw score	24·08	18·34	21·35	12·61	16·02	9·93
Post-test						
Standard score	92·42	13·60	90·51	11·43	88·53	10·08
Raw score	37·29	20·33	30·01	15·30	19·79	9·33

C. Control boys

	English (68)		Maths (65)		Study Skills (68)	
	Mean	SD	Mean	SD	Mean	SD
Pre-test						
Standard score	91·25	11·55	92·80	10·55	92·78	12·77
Raw score	21·68	14·37	18·08	11·65	17·21	11·44
Post-test						
Standard score	90·76	13·14	88·71	11·48	91·10	11·92
Raw score	34·96	20·27	27·29	14·42	21·66	11·00

D. Control girls

	English (58)		Maths (57)		Study Skills (57)	
	Mean	SD	Mean	SD	Mean	SD
Pre-test						
Standard score	92·63	12·66	93·83	11·12	91·62	14·62
Raw score	26·69	18·09	21·72	14·50	16·58	10·91
Post-test						
Standard score	91·30	13·22	89·13	11·54	91·30	12·27
Raw score	37·97	20·54	29·30	15·70	22·92	11·61

Table 2

Summary of Results of Analysis of Covariance Comparing Boys and Girls School Performance Scores Both Within and Between Treatment Groups

A. Experimental boys:experimental girls

	English	Maths	Study Skills
Pre-test variance			
F value	9·1933	0·4402	0·0746
	$0.005 > p > 0.001$	(ns)	(ns)
Post-test variance			
F value	5·8746	2·2571	0·7819
	$0.025 > p > 0.01$	(ns)	(ns)
Differences in regression			
F value	5·1754	0·9715	4·9391
	$0.025 > p > 0.01$	(ns)	$0.05 > p > 0.025$
Pooled regressions			
F value	411·6040	295·9344	209·7695
	$p < 0.001$	$p < 0.001$	$p < 0.001$
Difference in intercepts			
F value	0·2084	3·0201	1·1992
	(ns)	(ns)	(ns)

B. Control boys:control girls

	English	Maths	Study Skills
Pre-test variance			
F value	3·007	2·3639	0·0971
	(ns)	(ns)	(ns)
Post-test variance			
F value	0·6816	0·5409	0·3807
	(ns)	(ns)	(ns)
Differences in regression			
F value	7·3346	0·0331	1·8764
	$0.01 > p > 0.005$	(ns)	(ns)
Pooled regressions			
F value	242·2606	125·5236	158·2438
	$p < 0.001$	$p < 0.001$	$p < 0.001$
Difference in intercepts			
F value	2·4133	0·8549	2·7602
	(ns)	(ns)	(ns)

Table 2 (continued)

C. Experimental boys: control boys			
	English	Maths	Study Skills
Pre-test variance			
F value	3·2400	1·1017	0·9001
	(ns)	(ns)	(ns)
Post-test variance			
F value	1·6095	0·0259	3·2303
	(ns)	(ns)	(ns)
Differences in regression			
F value	1·7392	0·6503	1·0547
	(ns)	(ns)	(ns)
Pooled regressions			
F value	349·4482	247·4378	199·6033
	$p < 0.001$	$p < 0.001$	$p < 0.001$
Differences in intercept			
F value	0·4348	3·8726	3·1344
	(ns)	$0.05 > p > 0.025$	(ns)

D. Experimental girls: control girls			
	English	Maths	Study Skills
Pre-test Variance			
F value	0·7913	0·0282	0·1162
	(ns)	(ns)	(ns)
Post-test variance			
F value	0·0420	0·0812	0·1162
	(ns)	(ns)	(ns)
Differences in regression			
F value	0·0350	0·0572	5·7050
	(ns)	(ns)	$0.025 > p > 0.01$
Pooled regressions			
F value	302·7443	175·6540	162·0485
	$p < 0.001$	$p < 0.001$	$p < 0.001$
Difference in intercepts			
F value	1·5155	0·5425	7·6785
	(ns)	(ns)	$0.01 > p > 0.005$

Table 3

Change Scores on the Attitude Questionnaire for Boys and Girls in Both the Experimental and Control Treatment Groups

A. Summary of the Wilcoxon test for significance of change scores between pre- and post-tests

	Experimental treatment		Control treatment	
Attitude scale	Boys	Girls	Boys	Girls
A. Attitude to school	(ns)	(ns)	(ns)	(ns)
B. Interest in school	(ns)	(ns)	(ns)	(ns)
C. Importance of doing well	B 0·008	(ns)	(ns)	(ns)
D. Attitude to class	(ns)	(ns)	(ns)	(ns)
E. "Other" image of class	W 0·0014	(ns)	B 0·0444	(ns)
F. Conformity	(ns)	(ns)	(ns)	(ns)
G. Relations with teachers	(ns)	W 0·012	(ns)	(ns)
H. Anxiety	(ns)	(ns)	(ns)	(ns)
I. Social adjustments	(ns)	(ns)	(ns)	B 0·0018
J. Academic self-image	(ns)	(ns)	(ns)	(ns)

B. Summary of the Komolgorov-Smirnov test for significance of different change scores between boys and girls within and between treatment groups

	Experimental	Control	Experiment : control	
Attitude scale	Boys : Girls	Boys : Girls	Boys	Girls
A. Attitudes to school	(ns)	(ns)	(ns)	(ns)
B. Interest in school	(ns)	(ns)	(ns)	(ns)
C. Importance of doing well	(ns)	(ns)	(ns)	(ns)
D. Attitude to class	(ns)	(ns)	(ns)	(ns)
E. "Other" image of class	(ns)	(ns)	(ns)	(ns)
F. Conformity	(ns)	(ns)	(ns)	(ns)
G. Relations with teachers	(ns)	(ns)	(ns)	(ns)
H. Anxiety	(ns)	(ns)	(ns)	(ns)
I. Social adjustment	(ns)	$0·05 > p > 0·01$	(ns)	(ns)
J. Academic self-image	(ns)	(ns)	(ns)	(ns)

N.B. B = Better,   W = Worse.

Immigrant and Non-Immigrant Groups

Table 4

Mean Scores at Pre- and Post-test on the School Performance Tests for Groups of Children of Different Immigrant Status

A. Experimental group: Non-immigrant

	English (202)		Maths (201)		Study Skills (200)	
	Mean	SD	Mean	SD	Mean	SD
Pre-test						
Standard score	91·53	14·78	96·91	11·30	93·23	11·30
Raw score	22·59	17·12	22·50	13·65	17·24	10·46
Post-test						
Standard score	91·14	13·59	90·76	12·34	89·63	11·28
Raw score	36·14	20·34	30·70	16·29	20·78	10·39

B. Experimental group: West Indian immigrant

	English (54)		Maths (54)		Study Skills (53)	
	Mean	SD	Mean	SD	Mean	SD
Pre-test						
Standard score	87·63	9·70	91·00	9·22	86·49	8·46
Raw score	17·07	11·63	16·04	9·91	11·83	7·26
Post-test						
Standard score	87·30	9·13	83·80	9·49	81·79	7·69
Raw score	30·17	15·18	21·65	11·14	14·06	7·07

C. Experimental group: Other immigrants

	English (21)		Maths (18)		Study Skills (19)	
	Mean	SD	Mean	SD	Mean	SD
Pre-test						
Standard score	86·76	14·56	88·11	13·46	85·21	12·63
Raw score	17·19	18·66	14·67	16·44	10·74	11·12
Post-test						
Standard score	85·86	13·88	83·67	15·68	82·47	13·99
Raw score	28·38	21·07	22·94	20·14	15·33	12·51

D. Control group: Non-immigrant

	English (121)		Maths (116)		Study Skills (120)	
	Mean	SD	Mean	SD	Mean	SD
Pre-test						
Standard score	92·60	11·87	94·36	10·83	91·78	14·80
Raw score	23·64	15·61	20·41	13·05	17·10	11·21
Post-test						
Standard score	91·07	12·82	89·17	11·44	91·80	11·94
Raw score	35·87	19·66	28·35	15·11	22·70	10·91

Table 4 (continued)

E. Control group: West Indian immigrant

	English (7)		Maths (7)		Study Skills (7)	
	Mean	SD	Mean	SD	Mean	SD
Pre-test						
Standard score	94·00	14·49	86·86	10·87	89·86	6·62
Raw score	25·14	18·67	11·57	9·59	14·00	6·35
Post-test						
Standard score	92·57	13·96	88·43	8·50	87·29	10·32
Raw score	38·00	21·98	25·71	11·22	18·29	10·40

F. Control group: Other immigrants

	English (9)		Maths (10)		Study Skills (9)	
	Mean	SD	Mean	SD	Mean	SD
Pre-test						
Standard score	81·89	14·55	86·40	10·80	81·44	9·03
Raw score	13·33	16·25	11·60	10·28	7·67	7·65
Post-test						
Standard score	81·78	15·78	80·00	12·81	78·78	9·30
Raw score	22·56	23·63	17·50	13·44	11·11	8·10

Table 5

Summary of Results of Analysis of Covariance Comparing School Performance Scores of Children of Different Immigrant Status Within and Between Treatment Groups

A. Children of different immigrant status within the experimental group

	English	Maths	Study Skills
Pre-test variance			
F value	3·0837	7·1192	8·7237
	$0·05 > p > 0·025$	$p < 0·001$	$p < 0·001$
Post-test variance			
F value	3·0769	8·2282	10·7730
	$0·05 > p > 0·025$	$p < 0·001$	$p < 0·001$
Difference in regression			
F value	0·0800	1·0257	0·8459
	(ns)	(ns)	(ns)
Pooled regressions			
F value	306·3603	199·0945	137·9404
	$p < 0·001$	$p < 0·001$	$p < 0·001$
Difference in intercepts			
F value	0·4718	1·9393	3·2082
	(ns)	(ns)	$0·05 > p > 0·025$

Table 5 (continued)

B. Children of different immigrant status within the control group

	English	Maths	Study Skills
Pre-test variance F value	1·8490 (ns)	3·5617 $0.05 > p > 0.025$	3·3333 $0.05 > p > 0.025$
Post-test variance F value	1·9277 (ns)	2·5095 (ns)	5·2501 $0.01 > p > 0.005$
Difference in regression F value	0·7681 (ns)	0·5604 (ns)	1·5288 (ns)
Pooled regressions F value	131·5232 $p < 0.001$	91·2644 $p < 0.001$	98·1361 $p < 0.001$
Difference in intercepts F value	0·1733 (ns)	2·0585 (ns)	1·8638 (ns)

C. Experimental non-immigrants : control non-immigrants

	English	Maths	Study Skills
Pre-test variance F value	0·3091 (ns)	1·7780 (ns)	0·0125 (ns)
Post-test variance F value	0·0135 (ns)	1·6029 (ns)	2·4659 (ns)
Difference in regression F value	0·1579 (ns)	0·0796 (ns)	0·2346 (ns)
Pooled regressions F value	531·3021 $p < 0.001$	331·6434 $p < 0.001$	276·9729 $p < 0.001$
Difference in intercepts F value	1·5673 (ns)	0·0861 (ns)	7·5420 $0.01 > p > 0.005$

D. Experimental West Indian immigrants : control West Indian immigrants

	English	Maths	Study Skills
Pre-test variance F value	2·5708 (ns)	1·2671 (ns)	0·5655 (ns)
Post-test variance F value	1·4843 (ns)	0·8237 (ns)	1·9746 (ns)
Difference in regression F value	0·0241 (ns)	0·3769 (ns)	5·1799 $0.05 > p > 0.025$
Pooled regressions F value	49·0444 $p < 0.001$	42·4125 $p < 0.001$	41·0060 $p < 0.001$
Difference in intercepts F value	0·0081 (ns)	7·4247 $0.01 > p > 0.005$	1·6791 (ns)

Table 5 (continued)

E. Experimental other immigrants: control other immigrants

	English	Maths	Study Skills
Pre-test variance			
F value	0·2891	0·5551	0·2835
	(ns)	(ns)	(ns)
Post-test variance			
F value	0·4482	0·9257	0·5814
	(ns)	(ns)	(ns)
Difference in regression			
F value	2·2775	0·0032	0·0104
	(ns)	(ns)	(ns)
Pooled regressions			
F value	91·0429	29·8918	62·7209
	$p < 0·001$	$p < 0·001$	$p < 0·001$
Difference in intercepts			
F value	0·2116	0·3493	0·4557
	(ns)	(ns)	(ns)

Table 6

Change Scores on the Attitude Questionnaire for Children of Different Immigrant Status in Both the Experimental and Control Groups

A. Summary of the Wilcoxon test for significance of change scores between pre- and post-test with each group treated independently

	Experimental			Control		
Attitude scale	Non-immigrant	West Indian immigrant	Other immigrants	Non-immigrant	West Indian immigrant	Other immigrants
A Attitude to school	(ns)	(ns)	(ns)	(ns)	(ns)	(ns)
B Interest in school	(ns)	(ns)	(ns)	(ns)	(ns)	(ns)
C Importance of doing well	(ns)	(ns)	(ns)	(ns)	—*	(ns)
D Attitude to class	(ns)	(ns)	W 0·01	(ns)	(ns)	B 0·05
E "Other" image of class	W 0·0244	(ns)	W 0·05 > p > 0·02	(ns)	—*	(ns)
F Conformity	B 0·0038	(ns)	(ns)	(ns)	(ns)	(ns)
G Relations with teacher	W 0·0168	(ns)	(ns)	W 0·0082	—*	(ns)
H Anxiety	(ns)	(ns)	(ns)	(ns)	(ns)	(ns)
I Social adjustment	(ns)	(ns)	B 0·01	B 0·0332	—*	(ns)
J Academic self-image	B 0·0012	(ns)	B 0·01	B 0·0012	B 0·05	(ns)

Table 6 (continued)

B. Summary of the Komolgorov-Smirnov test for significance of different change scores between children of different immigrant status within treatment groups

Attitude Scale	Experimental			Control		
	Non-immigrant: West Indian immigrant	Non-immigrant: Other immigrant	West Indian immigrant: other immigrant	Non-immigrant: West Indian immigrant	Non-immigrant: other immigrant	West Indian immigrant: other immigrant
A Attitude to school	(ns)	(ns)	(ns)	(ns)	(ns)	(ns)
B Interest in school	(ns)	(ns)	(ns)	(ns)	(ns)	(ns)
C Importance of doing well	(ns)	(ns)	(ns)	(ns)	(ns)	(ns)
D Attitude to class	(ns)	(ns)	(ns)	(ns)	(ns)	(ns)
E "Other" image of class	(ns)	(ns)	(ns)	(ns)	(ns)	(ns)
F Conformity	(ns)	(ns)	(ns)	(ns)	(ns)	(ns)
G Relations with teacher	(ns)	(ns)	(ns)	(ns)	(ns)	(ns)
H Anxiety	(ns)	(ns)	(ns)	(ns)	(ns)	(ns)
I Social adjustment	(ns)	(ns)	(ns)	(ns)	(ns)	(ns)
J Academic self-image	(ns)	(ns)	(ns)	(ns)	(ns)	$0.05 > p > 0.02$

C. Summary of the Komolgorov-Smirnov test for significance of different change scores between children of different immigrant status between treatment groups

Attitude scale	Non-immigrants Experimental : control	West Indian immigrants Experimental : control	Other immigrants Experimental : control
A Attitude to school	(ns)	(ns)	(ns)
B Interest in school	(ns)	(ns)	(ns)
C Importance of doing well	(ns)	(ns)	(ns)
D Attitude to class	(ns)	(ns)	(ns)
E "Other" image of class	(ns)	(ns)	(ns)
F Conformity	(ns)	(ns)	(ns)
G Relations with teacher	(ns)	(ns)	(ns)
H Anxiety	(ns)	(ns)	(ns)
I Social adjustment	(ns)	(ns)	(ns)
J Academic self-image	(ns)	(ns)	(ns)

* —Indicates insufficient cell size to complete the test. B = Better, W = Worse.

Initially Low, Medium and High Scoring Groups

For Tables 7, 8 and 9 below children were allocated to a low, medium or high performing group as a result of their pre-test score and analysis was performed on post-test scores (see Appendix 3, pages 202 to 205).

Table 7

Post-test Mean Scores for High, Medium and Low Scoring Groups at Pre-test on the Three School Performance Tests*

	English			Maths			Study Skills		
	Count	Post-test standard score	SD	Count	Post-test standard score	SD	Count	Post-test standard score	SD
High scorers at pre-test									
Experimental	46	108·19	11·93	47	103·91	7·67	42	101·97	10·84
Control	25	109·48	6·68	21	103·23	7·20	26	107·80	10·35
Difference in score: E–C		−1·29			0·68			5·83	
Medium scorers at pre-test									
Experimental	185	88·90	8·59	174	89·02	9·34	185	86·85	8·92
Control	103	88·88	9·23	90	88·80	8·59	98	89·05	7·82
Difference in score: E–C		0·02			0·22			−2·20	
Low scorers at pre-test									
Experimental	47	76·48	7·45	52	74·98	7·93	45	77·26	6·64
Control	16	73·93	7·36	29	76·79	8·34	20	78·20	6·77
Difference in score: E–C		2·55			−1·81			−0·94	

* The analysis of variance was again conducted on raw scores, but standard scores are used in this table also to ease comparison.

Table 8

*Summary of Results of Analysis of Variance on Post-test Raw Scores for
High, Medium and Low Scoring Groups on the School Performance Tests*

	English	Maths	Study Skills
High: Experimental/Control	0·284 (ns)	0·003 (ns)	5·586 $0·025 > p > 0·01$
Medium: Experimental/Control	0·006 (ns)	0·301 (ns)	2·884 (ns)
Low: Experimental/Control	1·412 (ns)	0·947 (ns)	0·531 (ns)

Table 9

*Summary of Komolgorov-Smirnov Test on Post-test
Scores for High, Medium and Low Scoring Groups
on the Attitudes Scales*

Attitude scale	Low E:C	Medium E:C	High E:C
A	(ns)	(ns)	(ns)
B	(ns)	(ns)	(ns)
C	(ns)	(ns)	(ns)
D	(ns)	(ns)	(ns)
E	(ns)	(ns)	(ns)
F	$0·05 > p > 0·02$	(ns)	(ns)
G	(ns)	(ns)	(ns)
H	(ns)	(ns)	(ns)
I	(ns)	(ns)	(ns)
J	(ns)	(ns)	(ns)

Table 10

Mean Scores at Pre- and Post-test for the Experimental and Control Schools on the School Performance Tests

Experimental group

	English			Maths			Study Skills		
	Count	Mean	SD	Count	Mean	SD	Count	Mean	SD
0: Pre-test S.S.	39	93·84	13·42	38	94·02	12·12	38	92·60	10·50
Post-test S.S.		91·17	11·72		90·13	13·27		86·92	11·94
Difference in score		-2·67			-3·89			-5·68	
1: Pre-test S.S.	66	90·98	13·83	59	95·44	9·09	56	89·10	11·26
Post-test S.S.		90·16	13·93		86·91	12·33		86·65	11·77
Difference in score		-0·82			-8·53			-2·25	
2: Pre-test S.S.	67	93·82	12·77	66	99·72	10·67	66	93·75	10·73
Post-test S.S.		91·65	12·75		91·71	10·54		89·06	10·38
Difference in score		-2·17			-8·01			-4·69	
3: Pre-test S.S.	31	87·38	11·09	30	93·30	10·60	31	89·67	11·91
Post-test S.S.		89·90	10·62		89·86	14·29		86·48	12·37
Difference in score		+2·52			-3·44			-3·19	
4: Pre-test S.S.	61	86·83	13·92	65	92·95	13·02	66	92·16	12·22
Post-test S.S.		88·72	14·52		87·90	12·44		88·09	11·53
Difference in score		+1·89			-5·05			-4·07	
5: Pre-test S.S.	14	83·92	21·40	15	90·13	10·60	15	85·93	7·91
Post-test S.S.		83·71	8·98		83·80	12·77		85·86	10·58
Difference in score		-0·21			-6·33			-0·07	

Control group

	English			Maths			Study Skills		
	Count	Mean	SD	Count	Mean	SD	Count	Mean	SD
0: Pre-test S.S.	76	90·28	12·83	73	91·27	10·88	73	90·00	15·99
Post-test S.S.		88·88	13·23		86·87	11·66		89·45	11·78
Difference in score		-1·40			-4·40			-0·55	
1: Pre-test S.S.	21	91·14	11·91	19	93·78	10·73	21	93·33	15·93
Post-test S.S.		90·76	13·63		87·73	13·73		91·38	14·46
Difference in score		-0·38			-6·05			-1·95	
2: Pre-test S.S.	47	95·78	10·69	48	96·72	10·30	50	92·14	9·83
Post-test S.S.		93·91	12·00		91·20	9·93		92·90	10·99
Difference in score		-1·87			-5·52			+0·76	

Table 11

Summary of Results of Analysis on School Performance Tests Comparing Control Schools

	English	Maths	Study Skills
Pre-test variance			
F value	2·3841	3·5941	0·4091
	(ns)	0·05 > p > 0·025	(ns)
Post-test variance			
F value	1·8438	1·8786	1·1200
	(ns)	(ns)	(ns)
Difference in regression			
F value	0·0625	1·7886	1·4605
	(ns)	(ns)	(ns)
Pooled regressions			
F value	140·9259	92·8311	114·1820
	p < 0·001	p < 0·001	p < 0·001
Difference in intercepts			
F value	0·2544	0·2311	1·9642
	(ns)	(ns)	(ns)

Table 12

Summary of Results of Analysis on School Performance Tests Comparing Experimental Schools

	English	Maths	Study Skills
Pre-test variance			
F value	2·5172	3·8215	2·8503
	0·05 > p > 0·025	0·005 > p > 0·001	0·025 > p > 0·01
Post-test variance			
F value	1·8149	2·0264	0·6666
	(ns)	(ns)	(ns)
Difference in regression			
F value	0·9204	2·0264	2·8685
	(ns)	0·05 > p > 0·025	0·025 > p > 0·01
Pooled regressions			
F value	165·0197	115·8558	80·0918
	p < 0·001	p < 0·001	p < 0·001
Difference in intercepts			
F value	4·1017	4·4153	1·1146
	p < 0·001	p < 0·001	(ns)

Table 13

Attitude Change Scores by Experimental School

Attitude Scale		School 00 %	01 %	02 %	03 %	04 %	05 %
A	+*	23·67	49·07	47·79	33·33	34·41	27·89
	0	26·31	25·45	24·63	33·33	22·95	25·58
	−	49·98	25·44	27·52	33·33	42·60	46·49
B	+	28·94	45·43	37·67	27·27	27·85	27·89
	0	28·94	20·00	31·88	27·27	27·86	25·58
	−	42·10	34·53	30·42	45·45	44·24	46·50
C	+	39·46	45·43	40·54	30·30	32·76	43·00
	0	23·68	38·18	30·43	39·39	42·62	29·06
	−	36·83	16·34	28·95	30·30	24·56	27·88
D	+	42·09	50·88	28·95	24·24	27·83	38·34
	0	26·31	30·90	30·43	27·27	19·67	25·58
	−	31·56	18·16	40·55	48·48	52·42	36·01
E	+	15·78	21·80	34·75	33·33	26·22	40·68
	0	34·21	40·00	28·98	18·18	19·67	31·39
	−	49·99	38·16	36·20	48·48	54·08	27·89
F	+	21·04	49·07	36·21	27·27	24·58	26·73
	0	23·68	40·00	42·02	39·39	37·70	40·69
	−	55·25	10·90	21·73	33·33	37·68	32·54
G	+	21·04	43·43	30·41	30·30	9·81	18·59
	0	26·31	18·18	40·57	21·21	34·42	32·55
	−	52·62	36·35	28·97	48·48	55·71	48·81
H	+	31·57	41·79	44·91	30·30	36·04	33·71
	0	31·57	29·09	27·53	45·45	32·78	31·39
	−	36·83	29·08	27·51	24·24	31·13	34·87
I	+	52·60	27·25	44·90	42·42	37·68	38·36
	0	23·68	32·72	23·18	30·30	22·95	31·39
	−	23·67	39·97	31·86	27·27	39·32	30·22
J	+	39·46	25·45	36·20	36·36	27·85	37·19
	0	36·84	34·54	34·78	36·36	29·50	29·06
	−	23·67	39·99	28·97	27·27	42·59	33·70

* + = In a positive direction.
  0 = No change.
  − = In a negative direction.

Table 14

Chi-square Probabilities of Difference Between Schools on the Attitude Pre-test

	A	B	C	D	E
Schools within experiment	$p < 0.001$	$0.01 > p > 0.001$	(ns)	$0.01 > p > 0.001$	$p > 0.001$
Schools within control	(ns)	(ns)	(ns)	(ns)	(ns)

	F	G	H	I	J
Schools within experiment	$p < 0.001$	$0.01 > p > 0.001$	(ns)	$p < 0.001$	(ns)
Schools within control	$0.02 > p > 0.01$	$0.05 > p > 0.02$	(ns)	(ns)	$0.05 > p > 0.02$

Table 15

Summary of the Results of Comparison of Each Experimental School's Attitude Change Score with the Total Experimental Distribution on the Komolgorov-Smirnov Test, and of the Results of a Kruskall-Wallis One-way Analysis of Variance Across All Experimental Schools.

Attitude scales	Schools						Kruskall-Wallis
	00	01	02	03	04	05	
A	(ns)	(ns)	(ns)	(ns)	(ns)	(ns)	$0.05 > p > 0.02$
B	(ns)	(ns)	(ns)	(ns)	(ns)	(ns)	$p < 0.001$
C	(ns)	(ns)	(ns)	(ns)	(ns)	(ns)	$p < 0.001$
D	(ns)	(ns)	(ns)	(ns)	(ns)	(ns)	(ns)
E	(ns)	(ns)	(ns)	(ns)	(ns)	(ns)	(ns)
F	$0.05 > p > 0.02$	(ns)	(ns)	(ns)	(ns)	(ns)	$p < 0.001$
G	(ns)	(ns)	(ns)	(ns)	(ns)	(ns)	$0.01 > p > 0.001$
H	(ns)	(ns)	(ns)	(ns)	(ns)	(ns)	(ns)
I	(ns)	(ns)	(ns)	(ns)	(ns)	(ns)	(ns)
J	(ns)	(ns)	(ns)	(ns)	(ns)	(ns)	(ns)

The Group of Readers

Tables 16 and 17 below show scores on the school achievement tests for a group of children who were confirmed as able to read at the beginning of their second junior school year. The children were tested one year prior to their environmental studies year (Time 1) and then twice during the experimental year (Times 2 and 3). A modified *t*-test was used to find possible differences in scores over the two periods.

For the English test there were no statistically significant changes in score. For the other two tests there were significant differences in change scores, however. On the Maths test the performance children's improved by almost three standard points over the first period (prior to the Environmental Studies Scheme) and deteriorated by 5.5 standard points over the period of the scheme (Table 16). On the Study Skills test the children's performance again improved slightly during the year prior to the Environmental Studies Scheme and deteriorated by nearly four standard points during it.

Table 16

Mean School Performance Scores for the Sub-group of "Reading" Experimental Children at Three Points in Time

	English			Maths			Study Skills		
	Count	Mean	SD	Count	Mean	SD	Count	Mean	SD
Time 1 September 1969	126	91·341	14·066	126	93·786	13·959	126	92·452	12·767
Time 2 October 1970 Pre-test		91·397	13·255		96·564	10·743		93·103	10·192
Time 3 June 1971 Post-test		91·683	11·601		90·984	10·778		89·310	11·601

Table 17

Changes in Score for the "Reading" Sub-group Over the Two Periods

	English	Maths	Study Skills
Time 2 − Time 1	0·056	2·778	0·651
Time 3 − Time 2	0·286	− 5·579	− 3·793

Table 18

Summary of Results of t-test to Examine the Differences in Change Scores Between the Two Time Periods (The Calculations for this Table are Presented in the Note Below)

Comparison	Results of *t*-test
Time 2 − Time 1 and Time 3 − Time 2 on B.A.T. English	$t = -0·1591$; d.f. $= n - 1$; (ns)
Time 2 − Time 1 and Time 3 − Time 2 on B.A.T. Maths	$t = 6·9592$; d.f. $= n - 1$; $p < 0·001$
Time 2 − Time 1 and Time 3 − Time 2 on B.A.T. Study Skills	$t = 3·8914$; d.f. $= n - 1$; $p < 0·001$

Note to Table 18

t-tests on mean scores for the reading group of children at the three points in time ($A = 1$, $B = 2$, $C = 3$)

$$t = \frac{2\bar{B} - \bar{A} - \bar{C}}{se}$$

where

$$se^2 = 4se(\bar{B})^2 + se(\bar{A}^2) + se(\bar{C}^2) - 4AB\frac{AB}{n} - 4BC\frac{BC}{n} + 2AC\frac{AC}{n}$$

where $n =$ the number of children,

$\bar{A}, \bar{B}, \bar{C}$ = the mean scores for the children for the test at that point in time,

A, B, C = the standard deviation of scores on the test at that point in time,

AB, BC, AC = the intercorrelations of scores on the tests in question.

For the English B.A.T. comparisons:

$$\bar{A} = 91·34, \quad A = 14·07, \quad AB = 0·75825$$
$$\bar{B} = 91·40, \quad B = 13·26, \quad BC = 0·78483$$
$$\bar{C} = 91·68, \quad C = 11·60, \quad AC = 0·84741$$
$$n = 126$$

then

$$t = -0·1591 \text{ (with degrees of freedom} = n - 1)$$
$$\text{ns} = \text{not significant.}$$

For the B.A.T. Maths comparisons:

$$\bar{A} = 93{\cdot}78572, \quad A = 13{\cdot}95857, \quad AB = 0{\cdot}72260$$
$$\bar{B} = 96{\cdot}56350, \quad B = 10{\cdot}74318, \quad BC = 0{\cdot}82961$$
$$\bar{C} = 90{\cdot}98413, \quad C = 10{\cdot}77848, \quad AC = 0{\cdot}75535$$
$$n = 126$$

then

$$t = 6{\cdot}9592 \text{ (with degrees of freedom } = n - 1)$$
$$p < 0{\cdot}001.$$

For the B.A.T. Study Skills comparisons:

$$\bar{A} = 92{\cdot}45239, \quad A = 12{\cdot}76658, \quad AB = 0{\cdot}75824$$
$$\bar{B} = 93{\cdot}10318, \quad B = 10{\cdot}19162, \quad BC = 0{\cdot}81723$$
$$\bar{C} = 89{\cdot}30952, \quad C = 11{\cdot}60113, \quad AC = 0{\cdot}78362$$
$$n = 126$$

then

$$t = 3{\cdot}8914 \text{ (with degrees of freedom } = n - 1)$$
$$p < 0{\cdot}001$$

List of Results

1. The pre-test mean scores of both experimental and control groups are below the national standard mean on all the school performance tests.

2. Neither the experimental nor the control groups make any substantial progress between the pre-test and the post-test, and at the end of the school year are performing less well than at its beginning.

3. *For English and Maths there is no statistically significant difference in the change scores between the experimental and control groups.*

4. *For Study Skills, the experimental group's score deteriorated more than that of the control group ($0{\cdot}005 > p > 0{\cdot}001$).*

5. On only one attitude scale were there significant differences at pre-test between the experimental and control groups. On scale A—Attitude to school, the experimental children have a significantly worse attitude to school than the control children ($0{\cdot}01 > p > 0{\cdot}001$).

6. On five attitude scales the experimental children's attitudes changed significantly between the pre-test and the post-test:

(a) On Scale C—Importance of doing well—they became *better* ($p = 0{\cdot}0046$).

(b) On Scale E—Other image of class—they became *worse* ($p < 0{\cdot}0006$).

(c) On Scale G—Relations with teacher—they became *worse* ($p < 0{\cdot}001$).

(d) On Scale H—Anxiety—they became *worse* ($p = 0{\cdot}006$).

(e) On Scale I—Social adjustment—they became *better* ($p = 0{\cdot}0086$)

7. On three scales the control children's attitudes changed significantly between pre-test and post-test:

(a) On Scale A—Attitude to school—they became *worse* ($p = 0{\cdot}0434$).

(b) On Scale G—Relations with teacher—they became *worse* ($p < 0{\cdot}0006$).

(c) On Scale I—Social adjustment—they became *better* ($p = 0{\cdot}0244$).

8. *There is no significant difference between the change scores of the experimental and control groups on the attitude questionnaire.*

9. On the school performance English B.A.T. sub-test the experimental girls perform better than the experimental boys at both the pre-test ($0.005 > p > 0.001$) and at the post-test ($0.025 > p > 0.01$).

10. There were no differences at pre-test, post-test or in school performance change scores between boys and girls in the control group.

11. *On only one school performance sub-test was there a statistically significant difference between the experimental boys and control boys; the experimental boys deteriorated more on the Maths test than did the control boys ($0.05 > p > 0.025$).*

12. *On neither the English, Maths nor Study Skills were there statistically significant differences in change score between experimental girls and control girls.*

13. The total sample of boys and girls replicated the N.F.E.R. Streaming Study findings of sex differences in attitude, but only for 5 scales; A—Attitude to school, B—Interest in school work, D—Attitude to class, F—Conformity and G—Relations with teacher. In each of these cases girls had a better attitude than boys ($p < 0.05$).

14. There were no significant differences in attitude change scores between experimental boys and experimental girls.

15. On only one attitude scale was there a significant difference in change score for control boys and control girls: Scale I—Social adjustment, where the girls improved more than the boys ($0.05 > p > 0.01$).

16. The experimental boys' attitudes changed significantly on 2 scales:
   (a) Scale C—Importance of doing well—they became *better* ($p = 0.008$).
   (b) Scale E—Other image of class—they became *worse* ($p < 0.0014$).

17. The control boys' attitudes changed significantly on one scale. Scale E—Other image of class—they became *better* ($p = 0.0444$).

18. *There were no significant differences between the attitude change scores of experimental boys and control boys.*

19. The experimental girls' attitudes changed significantly on only one scale: Scale G—Relations with teacher, where they became *worse* ($p = 0.012$).

20. The control girls' attitudes changed significantly on only one scale: Scale I—Social adjustment, where they became *better* ($p = 0.0018$).

21. *There were no significant differences in the attitude change scores between experimental girls and control girls.*

22. There were significant differences on school performance measures between the experimental non-immigrant, West Indian immigrant and other immigrant groups at both pre-test and post-test on English, Maths, Study Skills.

23. *For only one test (Study Skills) was there a significant difference in change score between these experimental groups ($0.05 > p > 0.025$): with the West Indian immigrant group deteriorating more than the other two groups.*

24. There were no significant differences in changes in school performance scores between the control non-immigrants, West Indian immigrants and other immigrants.

25. *Only on Study Skills was there a significant difference between the performance change score of the experimental non-immigrants and control non-immigrants. The experimental non-immigrants deteriorated more than the control non-immigrants ($0.01 > p > 0.005$).*

26. *On Maths there were significant differences between the change scores of the experimental and control West Indian immigrants. The experimental West Indian immigrants deteriorated more than the control group ($0·01 > p > 0·005$).*

27. *There were no significant differences between the performance change scores of the experimental and control other immigrant groups.*

28. There were no significant differences between the total sample non-immigrant, West Indian immigrant and other immigrant groups' attitude scores on the pre-test.

29. There were no significant differences between the attitude change scores of the experimental non-immigrant, West Indian immigrant and other immigrant groups.

30. There were no significant differences between the attitude change scores of the control non-immigrant, West Indian immigrant and other immigrant groups.

31. *There were no significant differences between the attitude change scores of non-immigrant, West Indian immigrant and other immigrant groups compared across treatments.*

32. *On the school performance tests, comparing high, medium and low performing children across treatments, there was only one significant difference on post-test scores. On the Study Skills tests the high performing experimental children were significantly worse than the control children ($0·025 > p > 0·01$).*

33. Only on Maths is there a significant difference on the pre-test for the control schools ($0·05 > p > 0·025$).

34. There are no significant differences between the control schools on post-test or on changes in performance score.

35. There are significant differences in English, Maths and Study Skills on pre-test between the experimental schools.

36. There are no significant differences in performance scores at post-test between the experimental schools.

37. *There are high negative correlations for experimental schools between pre-test score on English and Study Skills and negative change scores for the tests ($= -0·60$ and $-0·73$ respectively).*

Part Seven

Positive Discrimination in Education: Individuals, Groups and Institutions

J. H. Barnes and H. Lucas

)

Positive Discrimination in Education: Individuals, Groups and Institutions

The Policy of Positive Discrimination

A dominant theme of policy research in education has been the documentation of how far schools reflect, rather than affect, their social context. Educational institutions seem to produce an academic ranking of each generation which follows closely the socio-economic ranking of their parents.[1] This observed performance is seen to be in painful contradiction with the moral implications of a democratic ideology—that educational opportunities should be equal, and educational experiences should be universal and open. And reformers are devoting enormous efforts to change it and to make equality of opportunity a more cogent reality.[2]

But the tensions for educational policy and for research have neither been resolved nor receded with time. If anything, they have become more severe as the disparity between the performance of schools and the developing demands on them has grown. The old search for equality of opportunity, seen in terms of individuals fulfilling some notion of their potential and gaining access to the more selective levels of education, has moved on. Some see the issues now to be concerned more with equality of *results* between groups, than with opportunities for *access* open to individuals. It is argued that education should not reflect the divisions current in society, simply providing opportunities for some to ascend the ladder of privilege; it should, in fact, be judged by the extent to which it transcends those divisions, and provides convergent experiences for its subjects.[3] Thus, in its performance, education seems to persist as a means whereby society perpetually renews the conditions of its own existence, reflecting the extant and dominant distribution of adult roles. Yet many believe that it ought to be an agency of social reform, redistributing access to and transforming the nature of adult roles.

In this paper we report our attempts to clarify the nature and identify the possible outcomes of one series of policies which have been designed to promote greater equality in British primary education: "positive discrimination in the allocation of educational resources . . . in favour of areas and schools where children are most severely handicapped by home conditions".[4]

The policy was first proposed by the Plowden Council in 1967 in its report on "primary education in all its aspects".[5] Their formulations were designed to encompass an extremely complex series of interactions, many of which they imply rather than specify. Children in educational priority areas were seen to be surrounded by a "seamless web of circumstance",[6] where everything was causing everything else. Individuals and institutions were interacting together in a downward spiral of deprivation, making identification of cause or consequence redundant—perhaps impossible. The basic dynamic appears to have been as follows: various non-educational characteristics of groups of children—the colour of their skin, the occupation of their father, the financial circumstances of their family—are determinants of their

239

educational performance. The effect of combinations of these attributes on a child's capacity to perform successfully at school is cumulative. The Council identified this as "cumulative deprivation", a situation which, they said, occurred when one deprivation "reinforced" another. Children subject to these cumulative deprivations are not scattered at random across the population. They are concentrated in certain (primarily urban) areas and schools where their interaction together, and with an environment "ingrained with the grime of generations", increased the cumulative effect of disadvantage. Situations in the schools are thus a consequence, and then become a further cause of disadvantage for the children attending them. The concentration of disadvantaged families in poor neighbourhoods has consequences for their community institutions, which lack coherent organisation and suffer from poor leadership. And to complete the circle, disorganisation at the community and family level contributes further to the educational effects of initially non-educational circumstances: race, social class, income, etc.

In some respects the policy proposed by the Council to deal with this situation was clear and unambiguous. It was to be an educational policy; and one which had relatively moderate resource implications. Marginal increments to the total volume of resources available to education were to be diverted to educational priority areas and their children and schools. The main weapon in the attack on multiple deprivation was to be more effective schools.[7] Secondly "objective criteria for the selection of educational priority schools and areas" were provided.[8] The policy would be focused on the poor; but it would not require poor people to identify, and to risk stigmatising themselves in order to receive help. The target for the policy was to be disadvantaged areas and the schools in them.

In other respects the Council's recommendations are less easy to understand. In particular, although their concern for disadvantaged schools and areas is unequivocal, it occasionally becomes muddled with a further concern: for disadvantaged groups and individuals and their families. Certainly the Report moves very easily from one to the other without recognising the consequences of the change of focus. And further, it is not clear what the effects of positive discrimination on its recipients are intended to be. The Council advised, for instance, that "the first step must be to raise the schools with low standards to the national average. The second quite deliberately to make them better."[9] The target for the policy here is schools; but it is not clear whether "better" refers specifically and only to the volume of resources going to the schools, to the opportunities available to, or to the actual performance of the children in them. Initial priority should, they urged, be given "to the schools which by our criteria contain the ten per cent of most deprived children";[10] but for a longer term programme they envisaged an extension of positive discrimination beyond "an arbitrary figure of ten per cent of the population".[11] (Notice that the target for the policy has moved from schools to people.) Both in the long and the short term, a national policy of positive discrimination should "favour *schools* in *neighbourhoods* where *children* are most severely handicapped by *home* conditions"[12] (authors' italics).

Our analysis has been directed towards a clarification of these two issues: of who can be helped, and of what can be achieved by a policy of positive discrimination in favour of educational priority area schools. In the first section of text below we examine the concept of educational disadvantage itself. We attempt to identify the disadvantaged children in one inner city population. We ask whether the notion of disadvantage is a meaningful way to characterise their social and educational situation. And we attempt to place the phenomenon in the context of its social geography by exploring how far disadvantaged or poor children are concentrated in disadvantaged or poor areas. From this we are able to estimate possible upper limits to the scope of the policy expressed in terms of who can be helped. In the second section of text we examine what effect a discriminatory policy can have. This necessarily involves an attempt to identify an effect from the social and educational context of schools which exists independently of the circumstances of individual children. Presuming that a discriminatory policy will operate in some way to counteract this contextual effect, we once again estimate the upper limits to the scope of the policy. The data we use were largely gathered at the individual level; and we would contend that such a heterogeneous concept as educational disadvantage can only be studied in this way. But at the same time our concern is largely with the policy consequences for groups of children and for schools. We would contend in this respect that, while educational policies might be designed to help particular groups of individuals (and these groups might be very small and homogeneous), policies can hardly be expected to accommodate the unique life situations of particular individuals. Teachers do this while teaching children; we are unsure what a policy for it would look like other than in some very general and perhaps rhetorical sense.

Sources of Data

The data used were all derived from work undertaken by the Research and Statistics Group of the Inner London Education Authority (the I.L.E.A.) during the period 1968–71. It should be remembered that the original data were collected in order to provide the Authority with descriptive material on its primary schools and their children. Certainly the child data are in a number of ways unreliable and inadequate for our purposes.[13] And our findings can only be applied with confidence to Inner London. We were aware of these limitations throughout the analysis, and have taken account of them when presenting our conclusions.

1. *Information on the Schools: From the Index of Relative Institutional Deprivation*

During 1967–68 the Research and Statistics Group of the I.L.E.A. developed an Index to identify primary schools which answered to the Plowden Council's definition of educational priority area schools.[14] The criteria included in the Index were either those recommended by the Plowden Council or conveniently near equivalents. The measures of each of the criteria were either school-based or collected for a notional catchment area for all primary schools in the I.L.E.A.[15] School scores on each of the measures were scaled to conform to a distribution between 0 and 100; and these scaled scores were summed to derive an equally weighted, composite, institutional score. Schools were then ranked, according to their composite score, to create an Index of Relative School Deprivation.

A basic premise of our analysis is that the logic of this Index is an adequate and acceptable way to identify educational priority area schools. We offer no defence of the Index, except to say that there was substantial agreement between the schools' rank positions on it and practitioner assessments of their relative positions. It was, and still is, used by the I.L.E.A. as one basis for allocating extra resources to schools thought to need help; and in spite of its limitations which are discussed in the account of its construction, it appears to have few rivals as an attempt to identify disadvantaged schools or areas as targets for positive discrimination.

2. Information on the Children: From the I.L.E.A. Literacy Survey

At the same time as the construction of its Index of E.P.A. Primary Schools, the I.L.E.A. conducted the first stage of a survey of reading performance in one age cohort of children in its junior schools. All junior schools in the Authority were asked to test all children who were in their second junior school year (the 8+ group) on a reading test (the Sentence Reading Test A).[16] In addition, class and head teachers were asked to complete a questionnaire giving a range of background information on each child.[17] Towards the end of the school year 1970–71 all junior schools in the Authority were again asked to test all children in the same cohort on a parallel form of the original reading test. The cohort was then in its last year in primary school (the 11+ group).

Table 1 below shows the absolute size of that cohort of I.L.E.A. children from their birth year in 1960 to their year of transfer to secondary school in 1971. The table shows, firstly, that the cohort was growing smaller at a net

Table 1
Changes in the Size of the Age Cohort over Time

Year		Size	Change	% Change
1960	Birth cohort	56,642		
			− 18,499	− 32·7
1965	Cohort 5+ years old	38,143		
			− 864	− 2·3
1966	Cohort 6+ years old	37,279		
			− 1,001	− 2·7
1967	Cohort 7+ years old	36,278		
			− 1,152	− 3·2
1968*	Cohort 8+ years old	35,126		
			− 977	− 2·8
1969	Cohort 9+ years old	34,149		
			− 980	− 2·9
1970	Cohort 10+ years old	33,169		
			− 803	− 2·4
1971†	Cohort 11+ years old	32,366		
Mean Net Percentage Change 1965–1971				− 2·7

* Time of initial reading survey: *31,308* children tested.
† Time of second reading survey: *31,731* children tested.
Derived from I.L.E.A. Statistics.

rate of 2·7 per cent per annum for each year it was in I.L.E.A. primary schools and, secondly, that a reading test score was achieved for a very high proportion of the universe of children. We nevertheless need to be extremely careful when speaking about the performance of the whole cohort.[18],[19]
A file was created containing both school and child-based data. We set out

Table 2

Main Data Items Used in the Analysis

1.	Data on the schools	Data we used

A. *Source: I.L.E.A. Schools Index*
(i) School's scaled score on the E.P.A. Index
(ii) School's rank position on the E.P.A. Index
(iii) School's scaled score on the E.P.A. Index amended by removing factors of overcrowding of houses and housing stress
(iv) School's rank position on the amended Index

To identify the E.P.A. Schools and to arrange schools into Quartiles. (See Tables 4A, 4B, and 6.)
To characterise schools for the regression analysis. (See Tables 9, 11 and 12.)

B. *Data from the Literacy Survey averaged over all the children in the same school*
(i) Percentage of children whose parent or guardian was a semi-skilled or unskilled manual worker

To characterise schools for the regression analysis. (See Table 8.)

(ii) Percentage of children who were immigrant (i.e., stated country of origin was not the United Kingdom or the Republic of Ireland)

To characterise schools for the regression analysis. (See Table 8.)

2.	Data on the Children	

C. *Source 1968 Literacy Survey*

	For the Index of Disadvantage (see note 21). Tables 3, 4A, 4B, 6, 7A and 7B	For the regression analysis. Only if the following data were available. Tables 5, 8, 9, 10, 11 and 12
(i) Country of origin of the child	×	×
(ii) Number of schools attended by the child	×	
(iii) Number of teachers who had taught the child	×	
(iv) Number of absences during one term	×	
(v) Family size	×	×
(vi) Whether the child received free school meals	×	×
(vii) Occupation of parent or guardian (a proxy measure for social class)	×	×
(viii) Child's standardised score on the S.R.A. Reading Test		(×)

D. *Source 1971 Literacy Survey*
(i) Child's standardised score on the S.R.B. Reading Test
(ii) Child's rank position on a Verbal Reasoning Test completed prior to transfer to secondary school   × *

* Children whose position was unknown were dropped for the analysis presented in Table 6.

the main data items placed on this file in Table 2 above. But briefly, all infant schools were excluded together with any junior schools on which there were no data from the schools' Index of Deprivation. As we had measures from the child data on only eight of the ten variables in the initial schools' Index, a new eight variable Index of Schools was constructed for the file. To the new file, already containing both the school scores and their rank position on this new Index, were added equivalent variables for each individual child, together, where they were available, with the reading test scores. We then added three other pieces of data to characterise schools: the proportion of semi-skilled and unskilled workers' children in each school, the proportion of immigrant children in each school and the score and rank position of each school on the original I.L.E.A. Schools' Index of Relative Deprivation.

I   Disadvantaged Children: The Ecological Fallacy[20]

It is our conclusion that, in as far as they were concerned to help poor children or children in disadvantaged or deprived circumstances, the analysis of the Plowden Council which led it to advocate an educational priority area or school programme was based on a methodological fallacy. The fallacy occurs when ecological methods of analysis are used—when aggregated or averaged data are used to characterise areas or institutions. It is caused by a concentration on the principal or dominant pattern, and a failure to recognise the variation or heterogeneity. The fallacy in this particular case does not take account of the diversity within any group of educational priority schools, of the wide distribution of circumstances to which children outside any such group of schools are subject, nor does it recognise the logical jump between a counting of separate problems and the identification of a condition of cumulative disadvantage or deprivation. In advocating a priority area or school programme to meet the needs of poor children, the Council went beyond conclusions which could have been borne out by analysis of its data.

The policy consequences are that, as a device for helping poor children, positive discrimination through schools can only be disappointing. Most poor families do not live in poor areas; they are widely scattered throughout the population. A policy which discriminated in favour of the most disadvantaged 10 per cent of schools, could only help a relatively small proportion of the total number of poor or disadvantaged children. And trying to bring help to more of them by expanding the number of schools would run into diminishing returns: as more schools were added into the programme, so the rate at which relatively privileged children were included would increase faster than the rate for disadvantaged children. In effect, positive discrimination in favour of the most disadvantaged schools establishes for itself criteria which limit the number of disadvantaged people that can be reached.

1. Children at Risk

We came to this conclusion once we had found the numbers and the various proportions of children, inside and outside priority area schools, who were at risk on criteria equivalent to those which had been used to identify the schools. Tables 3, 4A and 4B summarise our findings. For each of the school criteria on which we had individualised data, children were assigned an at-risk or not at-risk score; and these scores were added together to create a cumulative index.[21] For analysis using the individual items, we said simply that children were either at-risk or not at-risk. For the analysis using the cumulative index, we said that children with high scores (five or more out of a maximum of eight) were at risk of being disadvantaged. For the sake of clear exposition we call these the disadvantaged children, but we think there should be more investigation of a "condition of disadvantage" before a positive diagnosis is made. We said children with low scores on the index (zero or one) were not at risk. We call these the non-disadvantaged children. They cannot be called a privileged group because their "objective" circumstances have been defined by a series of negatives: they were not immigrants, not unskilled or semi-skilled workers' children, they were not from large families, etc. Schools are grouped in two ways for tables 3 and 4A and 4B. The "Least Privileged Group" are those junior schools which were included in the 150 primary schools having the highest scores on the I.L.E.A. Index of Schools. We call these the E.P.A. schools in the text below, because they are the group which conform most strongly to the Plowden Council's definition of educational priority area schools.[22] The second way in which schools are grouped (for Table 4B) is into approximate quartiles on the I.L.E.A. Index of Schools; this enables us to illustrate the effect, in terms of the individual children who would be encompassed, of extending the range of schools in any educational priority area programme.

The proportions of the total population at-risk on the individual items in the analysis varies from 16 per cent, in the case of high pupil mobility, to 50 per cent in the case of low social class (see Table 3 on page 246). The overall pattern is that, in each case, between one in five and one in three of the cohort are at risk on these items, although the proportions are higher for social class and low verbal reasoning.

As could be expected, the proportions of children at risk in the E.P.A. schools are higher than in the total population; but they only go above 50 per cent on those two items whose incidence in the population is also significantly high. On two items—pupil mobility and high absenteeism—the incidence in the E.P.A. schools is similar to that which could be expected in any other group of schools in this population.

Although children with these individual at-risk characteristics are a higher proportion of the population of E.P.A. schools than they are of the population generally, their total number is far greater outside the E.P.A. schools. For instance, we might wish to say that immigrant children are concentrated in under-privileged E.P.A. schools; but from our evidence, for every immigrant child that is in an E.P.A. school three are not. There are five times as many children at-risk because they come from large families outside the E.P.A. schools than there are inside them. There are five times as many unskilled and semi-skilled workers' children, three and a half times as many children receiving free school meals and four and a half times as many children with low verbal reasoning scores outside the E.P.A. schools than there are in them.[23]

It might be argued that, although the incidence of individual situations of need is widely spread throughout the population, cumulative disadvantage is

Table 3

Proportion of Children at Risk and Not at Risk on the Single Items of Risk (per cent)

	Immigrant children	High pupil mobility	High teacher mobility	High absenteeism	Large families	Free meals	Low verbal reasoning scores	Low social class
Least privileged group of schools (E.P.A. Schools) (N = 4,158)								
Not at risk	67·75	81·48	70·66	73·71	57·96	68·22	49·86	37·45
At risk	30·57 }32·25	14·14 }18·52	23·74 }29·34	17·27 }26·29	34·53 }42·03	29·56 }31·76	30·47 }50·14	50·07 }62·55
Don't know	1·68	4·38	5·60	9·02	7·5	2·2	19·67	12·48
All other schools (N = 26,338)								
Not at risk	83·55	84·20	81·65	75·67	67·46	82·79	64·09	52·11
At risk	16·45 }16·45	13·03 }15·80	15·15 }18·34	17·59 }24·33	27·59 }32·53	16·57 }17·21	17·80 }35·91	38·40 }47·89
Don't know	—	2·77	3·19	6·74	4·94	0·64	18·11	9·49
Total (N = 30,496)								
Not at risk	81·56	83·99	79·97	75·48	65·90	80·73	62·19	49·98
At risk	18·22 }18·44	13·05 }16·00	16·53 }20·03	17·52 }24·52	28·55 }34·10	18·42 }19·27	19·52 }37·81	39·96 }50·20
Don't know	0·22	2·95	3·50	7·00	5·55	0·85	18·29	10·06
Number of cases of risk in the least privileged schools:all other schools	1:3·2	1:5·4	1:4·0	1:5·9	1:4·9	1:3·4	1:4·5	1:4·9

246

Table 4A

Individuals at Risk on the Cumulative Child At-risk Index of Disadvantage in the Least Privileged Group of Schools

i. By school group by level of risk
ii. By level of risk by school group

Level of risk	Least privileged schools (%)	All other schools (%)	Total (%)
i. Least privileged group of schools: the E.P.A. schools			
0	6·0	14·5	13·3
1	15·4	25·5	24·1
2	22·1	24·7	24·3
3	21·8	18·0	18·5
4	17·9	10·6	11·6
5+	16·8	6·7	8·1
Base (= 100)%	4158	26338	30496
ii. By level of risk			
0%	6·1	93·9	100
1%	8·7	91·3	100
2%	12·4	87·6	100
3%	16·1	83·9	100
4%	21·0	79·0	100
5+%	28·2	71·8	100
Total %	13·6	86·4	100

Table 4B

Individuals at Risk on the Cumulative Child At-risk Index of Disadvantage in the Schools Grouped into Approximate E.P.A. Quartiles

i. By school group by level of risk
ii. By level of risk by school group

Level of risk	Least privileged quartile (%)	Second quartile (%)	Third quartile (%)	Most privileged quartile (%)
i. Schools grouped into quartiles				
0	6·7	11·4	14·0	22·2
1	17·5	22·3	26·9	30·4
2	23·0	24·5	25·4	24·0
3	21·6	20·3	18·0	13·5
4	16·8	12·4	10·1	6·6
5+	14·3	9·0	5·5	3·3
Base (= 100%)	7029	9122	7670	6675
ii. Level of risk				
0%	11·6	25·6	26·4	36·4
1%	16·8	27·6	28·0	27·6
2%	21·9	30·2	26·3	21·6
3%	26·8	32·8	24·5	15·9
4%	33·6	32·0	21·9	12·6
5+%	40·5	33·3	17·1	9·0
Total%	23·0	29·9	25·2	21·9

a phenomenon more common to the E.P.A. schools. Tables 4A and 4B above show our findings on this matter. (See note 21 for the way in which the index of disadvantage was constructed.) In the total cohort 11,400 children—one in three—had scores of zero or one. We can say that these children are not disadvantaged. However, two and a half thousand children—one in every twelve—were multiply disadvantaged on our measures and according to our definition.

As with the single at-risk items, these children comprise a significantly higher proportion of the E.P.A. schools than of the total population: 16.8 per cent as opposed to 8·1 per cent (Table 4). Even so, even in the E.P.A. schools, the disadvantaged group are outnumbered by children who are not disadvantaged: for every three children in these schools who are at risk of being disadvantaged, four are not.

Perhaps most significantly, less than one third of the multiply disadvantaged children are in the E.P.A. schools. In other words, resources going to these schools reach 13·6 per cent of all the children in the cohort, but only 28·2 per cent (two out of every seven) of the disadvantaged children in it. It would clearly be unrealistic to expect all the disadvantaged children to be in the disadvantaged E.P.A. schools. And it is an open question what proportion of them it would be regarded as satisfactory for any schools' programme to pick up. Indeed, given limited resources, a school or area policy acts as an effective rationing device.

But what seems to us to be important is that the logic of discriminatory school or area policies constrains the upper limit to their effectiveness seen in this way. The policy can only be discriminatory if some schools are excluded; but excluding some schools excludes some disadvantaged children. Table 4B illustrates the point. By encompassing half the schools in this analysis, a school programme of positive discrimination could bring benefit to 74 per cent of the disadvantaged children; but 40 per cent of the children who were not disadvantaged would also be included. By expanding to three quarters of all schools (78 per cent of all children), 90 per cent of high risk children could be reached but so also would nearly two thirds of the non-disadvantaged group. Nine per cent of disadvantaged children are in the most privileged quartile of schools, where they comprise 3 per cent of the population. To help this group, a schools' programme would need to include all schools and all children; it could hardly then be discriminatory according to the conventional definitions.

We believe that the results of this part of our analysis confront the policy of discrimination in favour of E.P.A. schools with a paradox. It seems likely that the majority of disadvantaged children are not in disadvantaged areas, and the majority of children in disadvantaged areas are not disadvantaged. At the least this means that policies to assist disadvantaged schools or areas should not be seen as alternatives to policies which are focused on groups of children, whether these groups are to be identified in terms of single or combined indicators of need.

Further, we might wish to develop the policy by saying that any help for disadvantaged children which was channelled through a positively biased schools' programme should be differentially weighted according to the proportion of disadvantaged children in each school. But if such a programme were to be sensitively adjusted to the needs of different groups of children, it would need to take account of their relative positions within a school as well as the presence of their disadvantage measured on "objective" indicators of need. In other words, once the policy moves from one which simply discriminates among schools to one which accommodates intra school differences, it must recognise other parameters. We illustrate something of what we mean by this in the text below, when we move from analysis of the children's circumstances to say something about their behaviour.

2. Reading Performance and Objective and Relative Disadvantage

We used performance on the reading test, given at the beginning of the children's second year in the junior school, to compare their objective and their relative situations seen in behavioural terms. We used this because, effectively, there was no other available measure of the children's behaviour.[24] Clearly it provides a narrow view of a child's relative position in a school and other measures might have given different results. But every primary school tries to teach this skill, and its acquisition is seen to be particularly important for children of this age.[25] Given this, it seems to us that reading performance is a powerful indicator of the degree to which a child is being assimilated into the main academic culture of the school.

Tables 5 and 6 provide basic descriptive statistics on the reading performance of the children in this analysis. For Table 5 groups of children are organised according to categorisations on four objective need indicators (see note 27). In Table 6 children are ranked according to their level of risk of being disadvantaged and by the previous school groupings.[26] It is important to be clear what can be inferred from these tables. They represent the extant reading performance of groups of children: performances which are a consequence of the interaction of all kinds of factors. In the second section of the paper we attribute variations in reading performance to possible "effects": but for the moment we wish to illustrate the actual situation, at one point in time, *whatever* the apparent reason for it.

Not surprisingly our broad findings are that, as children's objective circumstances become more disadvantaged, so their reading performance tends to be lower. But the actual size of the differences found between privileged and underprivileged children do seem to be disturbingly large. The performance of disadvantaged children in the E.P.A. schools is slightly below that of similar children in the privileged schools. But at the same time, there are senses in which the relative position of disadvantaged children in privileged schools is actually worse than it is in E.P.A. schools. In absolute terms disadvantaged children appear to be poor readers whatever sort of school they are in. In privileged schools, where average reading performances are high, low performing disadvantaged children are therefore relatively worse off.

Table 5 shows the average reading scores for groups of children as various home background factors or characteristics of family circumstance are controlled for.[27] The average reading score for the whole group of children, for instance, is 95·5. When the occupation of the children's father (our proxy for social class) is controlled, the averages range from 107·4, for the children of professional and managerial workers, to 89·1, for unskilled workers' children. The range of average scores, when all four of the factors have been

9*

Table 5

Mean Reading Scores for Groups of Children

A. according to social class
B. for West Indian immigrant and groups born in the United Kingdom
C. according to family size
D. according to receipt of free school meals

	N	Mean Score	SD
Total	22,614	95·5	15·28
A. Social class			
Social class I	1,872	107·4	14·59
Social class II	3,539	100·4	14·43
Social class III	7,662	96·0	14·29
Social class IV	5,073	92·5	13·72
Social class V	4,468	89·1	13·95
B. Non-immigrant and West Indian immigrant groups			
Non-immigrant			
Social class I	1,845	107·5	14·64
Social class II	3,425	100·7	14·45
Social class III	7,113	96·6	14·35
Social class IV	4,432	93·3	13·81
Social class V	3,793	90·2	14·19
West Indian immigrant			
Social class I	27	—	—
Social class II	114	91·8	13·78
Social class III	549	88·9	13·47
Social class IV	641	87·2	13·04
Social class V	675	83·1	12·55
C. Family size			
Small families			
Non-immigrant			
Social class I	1,512	107·9	14·74
Social class II	2,765	101·4	14·49
Social class III	5,381	97·4	14·40
Social class IV	3,117	94·1	13·94
Social class V	2,430	91·5	14·53
West Indian immigrant			
Social class I	17	—	—
Social class II	71	93·5	14·12
Social class III	295	89·1	13·46
Social class IV	290	87·5	13·60
Social class V	294	83·8	12·81
Large Familes			
Non-immigrant			
Social class I	333	105·7	14·18
Social class II	660	97·7	14·28
Social class III	1,732	93·9	14·20
Social class IV	1,315	91·3	13·48
Social class V	1,363	87·9	13·55
West Indian immigrant			
Social class I	10	—	—
Social class II	43	88·8	13·22
Social class III	254	88·6	13·49
Social class IV	351	86·8	12·56
Social class V	381	82·6	12·35

Table 5 (continued)

	N	Mean Score	SD
D. Receipt of free meals			
No free meals small families			
Non-immigrant			
Social class I	1,469	108·1	14·70
Social class II	2,647	101·7	14·52
Social class III	5,187	97·6	14·40
Social class IV	2,910	94·5	13·92
Social class V	2,099	92·1	14·60
West Indian immigrant			
Social class I	15	—	—
Social class II	59	93·0	14·04
Social class III	252	89·7	13·61
Social class IV	247	88·0	13·72
Social class V	215	84·4	12·88
No free meals large families			
Non-immigrant			
Social class I	282	106·0	13·92
Social class II	505	99·0	14·06
Social class III	1,220	94·7	14·35
Social class IV	836	92·4	13·66
Social class V	693	89·5	13·70
West Indian immigrant			
Social class I	5	—	—
Social class II	25	—	—
Social class III	164	89·0	13·70
Social class IV	206	87·1	13·08
Social class V	193	82·4	12·80
Free meals small families			
Non-immigrant			
Social class I	43	99·0	15·84
Social class II	118	95·4	13·64
Social class III	194	92·2	14·26
Social class IV	207	89·6	14·23
Social class V	331	87·4	14·13
West Indian immigrant			
Social class I	2	—	—
Social class II	12	—	—
Social class III	43	86·2	12·52
Social class IV	43	84·7	12·93
Social class V	79	82·0	12·59
Free meals large families			
Non-immigrant			
Social class I	51	103·9	15·53
Social class II	155	93·3	14·99
Social class III	512	91·8	13·85
Social class IV	479	89·4	13·18
Social class V	670	86·2	13·40
West Indian immigrant			
Social class I	5	—	—
Social class II	18	—	—
Social class III	90	87·9	13·12
Social class IV	145	86·3	11·79
Social class V	188	82·7	11·87

controlled, is twenty six points of reading score (more than two years of reading age): between the average score of professional and managerial workers' children, who were born in the United Kingdom, who do not receive free school meals and who come from small families and the children of West Indian immigrant unskilled workers, whether or not they receive free school meals and irrespective of their family size.

A simple comparison of mean scores does not recognise that, in every case, there is nearly as much variation in score within one of these groups as there is within the whole population. In order to illustrate the size of the differences among groups, therefore, we prefer to use a measure of the extent to which the various distributions of score overlap each other.[28]

The reading performance of 50 per cent of the whole population represented in Table 5 falls below 95.5. The performance of 86 per cent of West Indian immigrant unskilled workers' children falls below this point. In other words, 86 per cent of this group of West Indian immigrant children score below the

Table 6

Individuals at Risk on the Cumulative Child Index of Disadvantage: Mean Reading Score and Standard Deviation

a. By the least privileged group of schools by level of risk
b. By the schools grouped into "quartiles" by level of risk

a. Least privileged group of schools

Level of risk	Least privileged group of schools (N = 3284)		All other schools in the index of privilege (N = 21360)		Total (N = 25952)	
	Mean	SD	Mean	SD	Mean	SD
0	98·8	12·7	104·1	13·3	103·8	13·3
1	94·4	13·2	99·6	13·6	99·1	13·7
2	90·6	13·3	94·9	14·4	94·4	14·3
3	85·7	12·2	90·3	13·9	89·6	13·7
4	82·5	13·3	85·7	13·7	85·0	13·7
5+	80·7	12·1	81·9	12·5	81·5	12·4
Total	88·0	14·0	95·5	15·2	94·6	15·2

b. Schools grouped into "quartiles"

Level of risk	Least privileged quartile (N = 5581)		Second quartile (N = 7292)		Third quartile (N = 6291)		Most privileged quartile (N = 5480)	
	Mean	SD	Mean	SD	Mean	SD	Mean	SD
0	99·6	13·3	101·8	12·9	103·9	13·3	106·5	13·1
1	95·6	13·1	98·1	13·1	99·2	13·6	102·2	14·0
2	91·2	13·5	93·1	13·9	95·3	14·1	98·2	15·0
3	86·6	13·0	88·6	13·3	91·3	13·7	94·1	14·6
4	83·1	13·3	84·8	13·7	85·9	13·5	89·6	14·1
5+	80·6	12·1	81·4	12·2	83·2	12·7	84·2	13·3
Total	89·2	14·4	93·0	14·7	95·9	14·8	100·4	15·1

average for the population. Seventy-five per cent of all West Indian immigrant children score below the average for the non-immigrant children in the analysis. Seventy-seven per cent of non-immigrant professional workers' children score above the average for all non-immigrant children. Ninety-seven per cent of West Indian immigrant unskilled workers' children score below the average for non-immigrant professional workers' children; and 71 per cent of West Indian immigrant unskilled workers' children score below the average for non-immigrant unskilled workers' children. For whatever reason, differences in reading performance between privileged and disadvantaged children appear to be very large indeed.

A similar calculation from the mean and standard deviation of scores in Table 6 simply confirms this. The differences in mean score between zero risk children and children with a score of five or more on the index of disadvantage is of the order of twenty-two points (nearly two years of reading age); and 96 per cent of the high risk children score below the average for the zero risk group.

The average reading performance of high risk children in E.P.A. schools is only one point of score below their average performance in all other schools, while high risk children in the most privileged quartile of schools do slightly better in an absolute sense: the difference of mean scores between disadvantaged children in E.P.A. and in the most privileged quartile of schools is therefore of the order of three and a half points. In other words, 53 per cent of high risk children in E.P.A. schools score below the average for high risk children in all other schools, but 61 per cent fall below the average for high risk children in the privileged schools. On the other hand, looking at intra school differences, high risk children in privileged schools are worse off relative to their classmates. Again the point can be illustrated with reference to distributions of score. Eighty per cent of high risk children score below the average for the total population; 70 per cent score below the average for E.P.A. schools; and 86 per cent score below the average for the most privileged group of schools.

Clearly disadvantaged children in privileged schools have potentially more access to privileged children. But from this piece of analysis we do not know whether either of the groups take advantage of whatever opportunities this offers or whether, if they did, either would benefit from it. We do know that high risk children in privileged schools do slightly better than similarly defined groups of children in E.P.A. schools. But it should be remembered that, in every case, the reading performance of groups of disadvantaged children is extremely low, that the difference between their scores in different sorts of school are relatively small, and that the performance of high risk children is more deviant for privileged schools and closer to the average in E.P.A. schools.

We have previously demonstrated that there is only a loose correlation between the objectively measured and accepted distribution of disadvantaged schools and the spread of similarly identified groups of children. The geographical distribution of children at risk of being disadvantaged is not confined to a particular sample of schools; and school programmes of positive discrimination cannot be alternatives to other programmes of help for children in need. We can now also say with some confidence that educationally disadvantaged circumstances are themselves diverse.[29] The behaviour—measured in terms of reading performance—of groups of disadvantaged children is different from that of privileged groups, and from groups that are not disadvantaged. But we have also illustrated that groups of children whose circumstances are identical on objective indicators (they are all at risk of being disadvantaged) can be in quite different social and educational situations. It may be that it is more pleasant in some way for disadvantaged children to be in privileged schools; it is certain that their group performance is low wherever they are. Once again we can ask what follows. At the very least programmes of positive discrimination must face the low performance of groups of disadvantaged children wherever they are: with concentrations of low performance in E.P.A. schools and extreme diversities in performance between groups of children in privileged schools.

3. The Nature of Child Disadvantage

We had established that child disadvantage can only be studied adequately with data gathered at the individual and not the aggregated level. Our empirical evidence at least raised the possibility that, in addition to its objective dimensions, there were relative and possibly therefore subjective aspects to disadvantage. We tried, lastly, to investigate the content of disadvantage as it was identified by the objective indicators. We wanted to discover whether a series of relationships could be established between the objective measures in the child index which approximated to a latent variable (of deprivation or disadvantage).

When people talk of seeing disadvantaged or deprived children they mean that they can *see* poor or black or badly clothed or dirty children. We think they *mean* something more however. They mean that some children are subject to a particular substantive condition. This may need to be observed or measured through observable criteria; but it is thought to exist in the same way that, say, productivity in factories, or bravery in soldiers, or aggression in a species or even intelligence in human beings is thought to exist. Our findings indicate that, in as far as this phenomenon of disadvantage is to be identified through the at-risk criteria we had constructed, people who believe this are probably wrong. The at-risk index is a definition of need rather than an approximation to a latent variable of multiple deprivation.

Table 7A below shows the relationships between any two at-risk indicators for the total population.[30] By far the strongest relationship exists, unsurprisingly perhaps, between the large families and the free school meals indicators ($r = 0.333$). A second level of relationships exist between the social class, large families, free meals, low verbal reasoning and immigrant items: the correlation coefficients in this case range between 0.107 and 0.225. The other relationships are extremely weak; and we decided to concentrate the later stages of our analysis on only those variables that were strongly related together.[31]

Table 7B below summarises the results of a principal components analysis to test directly for the existence of a latent variable of multiple deprivation.[32] The largest factor has, as could be predicted, a high weighting for free school meals, family size, low verbal reasoning, low social class and immigrants. It accounts for only 21 per cent of the variance, however; and in such an analysis, on any eight variables, at least 12.5 per cent must be explained by the first component.

Table 7A

Correlations Between Individual At-risk Items in the Total Population (N = 25949)

Immigrants	1·0						
High number of schools attended	0·078	1·0					
High number of different teachers	0·059	0·074	1·0				
High absentee rate	−0·053	0·086	0·113	1·0			
Large family	0·133	0·066	0·022	−0·005	1·0		
Free meals	0·107	0·096	0·041	0·022	0·333	1·0	
Low social class	0·108	0·047	0·032	0·046	0·143	0·225	1·0
Low verbal reasoning score	0·109	0·043	0·022	0·036	0·110	0·146	0·168	1·0

Table 7B

Principal Components Analysis on Individual At-risk Items on the Total Population

Component	1	2	3	4	5	6	7	8
Component variance	1·7044345	1·1416622	0·9910582	0·9593481	0·9159591	0·8226776	0·8126737	0·6521867
Percentage added to total variance	21·31	14·27	12·38	12·00	11·45	10·28	10·16	8·15
Accumulated value of total variance (%)	21·31	35·58	47·96	59·96	71·41	81·69	91·85	100
Immigrants	0·324301	0·114425	0·597226	0·433012	0·039429	−0·066769	0·564314	0·114427
High number of schools attended	0·233239	−0·385418	0·408864	0·325134	0·664119	0·041089	−0·274751	0·077072
High number of different teachers	0·013665	−0·580760	0·284987	0·215164	−0·612530	−0·028984	−0·372091	0·045182
High absentee rate	0·090471	−0·066531	−0·433303	−0·692644	0·067294	−0·062081	0·588555	0·043019
Large family	0·474388	0·197956	−0·024917	−0·431875	−0·256472	−0·025709	0·166910	−0·619840
Free meals	0·526151	0·125984	−0·202766	−0·344021	−0·168198	−0·023548	−0·090910	0·073585
Low social class	0·425316	0·038550	−0·324700	0·240905	0·058862	0·762065	−0·142564	−0·222762
Low verbal reasoning score	0·361657	0·043547	−0·301289	0·541104	0·274653	−0·584608	−0·254490	−0·421115

There appears thus to be a large degree of heterogeneity in the population. Any linear construct of "multiple deprivation" using these variables would strictly involve adding together measures of *separate* conditions of need. It could hardly be said that they were estimating a series of underlying factors of deprivation.

From this evidence, although we would concede that the terms disadvantage and deprivation provide a convenient shorthand for the many different social situations that they might cover, it should be clear that shorthand devices cannot replace more precise and, if necessary, more elaborate understanding of those situations.

II School Context and Family Circumstance

The first stage of our analysis was focused on the concept of child disadvantage, and was concerned to establish upper limits to what school and area based programmes can achieve as devices for rationing and allocating resources. But there is a second proposition implied by the policy of positive discrimination in favour of schools: that disadvantaged schools themselves somehow affect performance irrespective of the home circumstances of children. Certainly there was some evidence for this from the first stage of our analysis; the average reading performance of disadvantaged children in privileged schools was slightly higher than their performance in E.P.A. schools (see Table 6). In the text below we report our conclusions from an attempt to investigate this more directly. We first of all attempted to identify an "effect" of school context on reading performance, which was independent of the family circumstances of children; and we secondly converted our findings into statistics which establish upper limits to the effectiveness of discriminatory policies to overcome this effect.

Schools in the United States

The question of how far differences among different school situations have independent effects on the distribution of educational performance is a matter of debate in the United States. The main source of data for the debate is the 1965 "Survey of Equality of Educational Opportunity" conducted and initially analysed by Coleman and associates.[33] Many of the major findings of the initial Coleman Report have been confirmed by later re-analysis: the differences seem to have arisen over their interpretation and significance.[34] Our findings, although similar to those on the American school system, are different in a number of important respects. A brief outline of the main evidence on inequalities of conditions and performance in American elementary schools may be helpful, therefore, to set our results in context.

It seems clear that the 1965 Coleman Survey was conducted in order to document that there were dramatic inequalities in school facilities in the United States, particularly for minority groups, and further, that these inequalities in resources were directly related to school performance. Analysis of the data revealed that there were inequalities in resources between regions and states; but that, within regions, school resources were more similar than had been supposed. Since those regions which had relatively poor resources tended to be those with higher concentrations of minority group children, there were overall differences between the volume of educational resources available to minority group and to white children. But the larger part of the difference was accounted for by a regional effect. In any case it was found that differences in traditional resource levels bore little or no relationship to differences in school performance levels.

The average school performance of minority group or poor children was found to be lower at every stage of schooling than that of the average white pupil. Family circumstances were found to have the strongest explanatory power over performance levels.[35] But the "human resources" available to schools were found to have a significant impact on levels of performance, even when the family characteristics of individual children and levels of expenditure had been controlled. Subsequent re-analysis of the data has found that family background factors are, if anything, more strongly related to achievement levels than Coleman and associates originally asserted.[36] But the re-analysis has not destroyed the main Coleman findings on the effect of schools—that it is the resources contributed to a school by the other people in it that most affect levels of performance. Further, the effect of schools on performance is strongest for those groups of children whose family circumstances are likely to be the most disadvantaged. Coleman has succinctly restated the case: ". . . the strongest inference that can be drawn from the results is that the resources most important for a child's achievement in school are the cognitive skills in his social environment in school, including his fellow students as well as his teachers, and that these effects are strongest for the children with least educational resources outside school . . . Other resources, on which school systems spend much money, appear unimportant; and lower class students do better in absolute terms rather than worse (as one might have predicted) in schools where their *relative* achievement is low due to the presence of higher-performing middle-class students".[37]

The major American findings of interest to us for this analysis, therefore, are above all that we should be moderate in our expectations of what schools can do to overcome adverse extra-school circumstances. Secondly, we should expect evidence that variation in the human resources available to schools—in particular the mixture of pupils in the school—affect performance levels more than variations in more traditional expenditures or resources; and thirdly we should expect schools to have more effect on the performance of children from poor homes than they have on privileged children.

The Effect of Environmental Disadvantage

Our concern was to identify the effect of poor environmental conditions on the school performance of groups of children. We used three measures of school environment for this the first two of which depicted characteristics of the pupils in each school (the proportion of immigrants and the proportion of unskilled and semi-skilled workers' children). The third was a composite measure of the relative circumstances of each school according to the logic of the original I.L.E.A. Schools' Index (see pages 241 and 242 and Table 2 on page 243); we call this the measure of school context.

In order to avoid possible misunderstandings, it is important to be clear what our analysis cannot show about the behaviour of schools. We had no measure of the relative volume of resources going to different schools; and we can say nothing about an effect on the performance of children from variations in traditional school resources. In only one sense (namely teacher mobility),[38] did we have data on the characteristics of the teaching force; and we do not identify the characteristics or the behaviour of teachers as a separate variable. We had no data on the attitudes or affective behaviour of teachers, children or their parents; and we can say nothing about how these might mediate among family circumstance, reading performance and schools as we characterised them. We can say nothing from this analysis about intra school processes or the possible effect of different curriculum or teaching methods.

We wished to find answers to five related but conceptually distinct questions: all of which can be answered at the macro level and all of which relate to the justification for a priority area or school strategy.

(i) Can an independent contextual effect (of relative institutional disadvantage) on reading performance be identified and its strength measured?

(ii) If there is such a contextual effect, are different groups of children differently affected by it?

(iii) Irrespective of any contextual effect across all schools, is there a significantly strong effect on the performance of groups of children in the most disadvantaged schools?

(iv) In addition to any contextual effect which might be identified among groups of children in their second year in junior school, is there an effect on the changes in reading performance taking place between the beginning of the second and the end of the fourth year in junior school?[39]

(v) How strong is the independent effect of schools compared to the effects of various measured characteristics of the circumstances of families?

Children were included in the analysis to establish the school contextual effect only if four pieces of information were available on their family circumstance: the occupation of their father, whether they were children born in the United Kingdom or were immigrants from the West Indies, whether or not they came from large families and whether or not they received free school meals.[40]

The method of analysis used was to compute how far the measured variation in reading performance for groups of children could be "explained" by the measured characteristics of schools. We wished to avoid assuming that the effect of schools on different groups of children was the same or homogeneous. Indeed, given the American findings that schools have most effect on disadvantaged children and the argument of the Plowden Council that the effect of environmental disadvantage was most strongly felt by the most deprived children, this assumption was one we wanted to investigate. Therefore, the explained variation was computed separately for each group of children defined by social class, immigrant and family status, etc.[41]

The regression coefficient given in the tables below is a line of best fit between the measured school characteristic and the reading score of each child, calculated separately within each group. In virtually all cases it has a negative value, indicating that as the school context becomes less advantaged so reading performance tends to deteriorate, even when various family characteristics have been controlled. The explained variance (the R^2 value) is a measure of the improvement that can be made in the prediction of a child's actual reading score by using the characteristic of the schools, rather than the average score of the group of children in that particular regression equation. It is, therefore, a measure of the strength of the independent effect of school context on the reading performance of children, when the various characteristics of family circumstance have been controlled for (see note 41).

The proportion of the total variation in reading scores explained by any of the factors included in the analysis never reaches above 20 per cent and most of the time it is below 10 per cent. In other words we always fail to explain more than 80 per cent of the total variation in scores. We do not consider this to be surprising. The regression analyses were attempts to discover how far the derived, standardised distribution of scores was biased, or could be attributed to various family, or group, or institutional factors which educational policies might hope to affect. Included in the unexplained variances are errors in the measurement of reading scores, of child background characteristics and of school context. The unexplained variation would, in addition, be due to possibly random factors like the alertness and motivation of particular children on the day of the test, and also to variables which were not measured—the most significant of which would probably be the intelligence of individual and groups of children. More of the variation in reading performance could in principle be explained by the inclusion of more data in the analysis.[42] But to repeat, we were interested in that part of the variation which can be explained or controlled; and which therefore, if they are to increase equality of opportunity or of performance, educational policies must do something about.

A School Effect Due to the Social Class and Immigrant Status Characteristics of a Child's Peers

We found no significant pattern of independent effects on variations in reading performance from the social or immigrant mix of pupils in the school.

A proportion of the overall variation in reading performance could be explained by the concentration of unskilled and semi-skilled workers' children in schools. But this was reduced to between 1 and 2 per cent when occupation of father had been controlled (see Table 8 below). We doubt the educational significance of apparent "effects" of this size.

There was virtually no independent effect on overall variations in reading performance from the concentrations of immigrant children. This is hardly a surprising finding when most schools have very few immigrant children in them. Sixty-five per cent of the non-immigrant children in the analysis are in schools where less than 10 per cent of the children are immigrant; 44 per cent of them are in schools where less than 5 per cent of the children are immigrant; and only 3·4 per cent are in schools which contain more than 40 per cent immigrant children. (Appendix Table 3.)

Table 8

Reading Score and Social and Immigrant Mix Regression Series

Reading score regressed against:
1. Concentration of low social class children in the school
2. Concentration of immigrant children in the school

For groups of children controlling:
A. By social class (I and V only are displayed)
B. By West Indian immigrant and groups born in the United Kingdom
C. By family size
D. By receipt of free school meals

	1. Class concentration		2. Immigrant concentration	
	Regression coefficient	R^2	Regression coefficient	R^2
Total	−0·18	0·0429	−0·17	0·0229
A. Social class				
Social class I	−0·12	0·0203	−0·11	0·0062
Social class V	−0·10	0·0133	−0·15	0·0227
B. Non-immigrant and West Indian immigrant groups				
Non-immigrant				
Social class I	−0·12	0·0195	−0·09	0·0038
Social class V	−0·10	0·0134	−0·11	0·0085
West Indian immigrant				
Social class I	—	—	—	—
Social class V	−0·07	0·0052	−0·00	0·0000
C. Family size				
Small families				
Non-immigrant				
Social class I	−0·13	0·0216	−0·08	0·0032
Social class V	−0·11	0·0150	−0·09	0·0057
West Indian immigrant				
Social class I	—	—	—	—
Social class V	−0·11	0·0219	−0·02	0·0037
Large families				
Non-immigrant				
Social class I	−0·09	0·0104	−0·18	0·0117
Social class V	−0·08	0·0094	−0·15	0·0171
West Indian immigrant				
Social class I	—	—	—	—
Social class V	−0·04	0·0017	+0·01	0·0002
D. Receipt of free meals				
No free meals small families				
Non-immigrant				
Social class I	−0·13	0·0214	−0·08	0·0032
Social class V	−0·11	0·0150	−0·09	0·0054
West Indian immigrant				
Social class I	—	—	—	—
Social class V	−0·14	0·0226	−0·07	0·0071
No free meals large families				
Non-immigrant				
Social class I	−0·08	0·0078	−0·14	0·0069
Social class V	−0·08	0·0082	−0·14	0·0133
West Indian immigrant				
Social class I	—	—	—	—
Social class V	−0·00	0·0000	−0·02	0·0005

Table 8 (continued)

	1. Class concentration		2. Immigrant concentration	
	Regression coefficient	R^2	Regression coefficient	R^2
Free meals small families				
Non-immigrant				
Social class I	—	—	—	—
Social class V	−0·11	0·0185	−0·06	0·0031
West Indian immigrant				
Social class I	—	—	—	—
Social class V	—	—	—	—
Free meals large families				
Non-immigrant				
Social class I	—	—	—	—
Social class V	−0·08	0·0091	−0·16	0·0203
West Indian immigrant				
Social class I	—	—	—	—
Social class V	−0·08	0·0089	+0·04	0·0030

Using the same body of data but a different method of analysis, Little and Mabey found that for children born in the United Kingdom . . . "there is a marked fall in attainment of children in schools with more than 60 per cent immigrants; (and) . . . there is very little difference . . . in the mean scores of children in schools between 10 and 50 per cent immigrant concentration". They also found that "immigrant children were only marginally affected by the immigrant concentration in the school".[43]

Our analysis obscured identification of the presence of any such "tip-off" concentrations of immigrant children. We would point out, however, that the Little and Mabey method of comparing mean scores, without regard for variations of score around the mean, tends to dramatise the strength of relatively small differences. Further, even if the differences in score which they found are seen to be educationally significant, relatively small numbers of children are involved. For instance, 0·1 per cent of the non-immigrant population which remain in the cohort for our analysis are in schools with more than 60 per cent immigrant children—the point at which a strong deterioration in the reading score of non-immigrant children was found; and two out of three non-immigrant children are in schools with less than 10 per cent immigrant children—the point at which some deterioration in the attainment of non-immigrant children began. With the overall net size of the cohort of children falling at the rate of 2 per cent per annum, class sizes will tend to become smaller as the cohort becomes older. In this situation, relatively small movements of children could obviate any possible impact of certainly the heaviest concentrations of immigrant children on the reading performance of non-immigrant children.

A School Effect Due to the Environmental Context

We found that there was an effect on reading performance from the total school context. Reading performance was significantly lower the more disadvantaged the school—at least for groups of children from the United Kingdom.

It makes a difference to the reading performance of groups of non-immigrant children whether they go to schools which are privileged or disadvantaged on the measure we used. The differences exist irrespective of the family circumstances of the children. They tend to become unstable when groups are homogeneous with respect to the four characteristics of family circumstance, but the overall pattern remains and the instability leads to high as well as low proportions of explained variation. This independent contextual effect is slightly stronger for United Kingdom children from non-manual workers' homes than for children from manual workers' homes: 6 per cent and 4 per cent respectively of the variation in reading performance is explained by it (see Table 9 below).

There is no significant school contextual effect on the variation in reading scores for groups of West Indian immigrant children. We had found that the average reading performance of West Indian immigrant children in this cohort was low irrespective of the occupation of their father (see Table 5 on page 250). From this subsequent finding we must say, further, that whether they are in privileged or disadvantaged schools makes far less difference to the reading performance of West Indian immigrant children than it does to non-immigrant children.

With this evidence we can answer the first two of our questions concerning the justification for programmes to combat the effect of relatively disadvantaged school environments. There *is* an effect of relative institutional deprivation on the school performance of children. It *does* affect different groups of children in different ways: but in ways contrary to the forecast of the Plowden Council and expectations from the American data analysis. Across the whole population, the more privileged the home circumstances of groups of children, the more their performance is depressed by the apparent effect; and the less advantaged their home circumstances, the less children are affected by school context.

We can illustrate these points by establishing what, in principle, would be the upper limits to the impact of a programme of positive discrimination through schools. We can ask, first of all, what would be the impact on the distribution of individual scores of a policy which overcame the effects of the school context. Clearly the distribution of scores would be reduced by the amount now attributable to it.[44] But the effect, in this case, would be to reduce the spread of individual scores in the population by a maximum of only 3·4 per cent. And so we must say that policies of positive discrimination which successfully overcame the total effect of school context would do little to reduce the spread of performance among individual children.

But the target for the Plowden Council's programme of positive discrimination was to be more specific than this. The programme was to bring help to the most disadvantaged 10 per cent of the population—initially raising them to the national average and subsequently improving their position even more (see page 240 above). We might ask, therefore, what would be the effect of a policy which did this for groups of children in the bottom 10 per cent of schools—bearing in mind that the measured effect of school context is different for different groups of children.[45]

We are speculating here about a possible future situation from evidence on the present; we do not identify what could be done to bring about that situation. We are providing theoretical upper limits to the impact of discriminatory policies and not positive forecasts or practical recommendations.

Table 9

Reading Score and School Privilege Regression Series

Reading score regressed against relative privilege score of school for groups of children controlling:
- A. By social class
- B. By West Indian immigrant and groups born in the United Kingdom
- C. By family size
- D. By receipt of free school meals

	Regression Coefficient	R^2
Total	−0·34	0·0674
A. Social class		
Social class I	−0·26	0·0378
Social class II	−0·29	0·0485
Social class III	−0·26	0·0418
Social class IV	−0·18	0·0218
Social class V	−0·27	0·0478
B. Non-immigrant and West Indian immigrant groups		
All non-immigrant children	−0·31	0·0579
Non-immigrant		
Social class I	−0·26	0·0367
Social class II	−0·26	0·0408
Social class III	−0·24	0·0352
Social class IV	−0·16	0·0163
Social class V	−0·25	0·0409
All West Indian immigrant children	−0·16	0·0140
West Indian immigrant		
Social class I	—	—
Social class II	−0·02	0·0009
Social class III	−0·19	0·0194
Social class IV	−0·14	0·0118
Social class V	−0·16	0·0148
Non-immigrant non-manual	−0·30	0·0581
Non-immigrant manual	−0·24	0·0366
West Indian immigrant non-manual	−0·14	0·0098
West Indian immigrant manual	−0·15	0·0135
C. Family size		
Small families		
Non-immigrant		
Social class I	−0·24	0·0333
Social class II	−0·24	0·0368
Social class III	−0·23	0·0324
Social class IV	−0·15	0·0143
Social class V	−0·24	0·0378
West Indian immigrant		
Social class I	—	—
Social class III	—	—
Social class III	−0·15	0·0129
Social class IV	−0·10	0·0053
Social class V	−0·23	0·0271
Large families		
Non-immigrant		
Social class I	−0·31	0·0556
Social class II	−0·29	0·0550
Social class III	−0·25	0·0396
Social class IV	−0·16	0·0189
Social class V	−0·24	0·0456

Table 9 (continued)

	Regression Coefficient	R^2
West Indian immigrant		
Social class I	—	—
Social class II	—	—
Social class III	−0·24	0·0308
Social class IV	0·08	0·0037
Social class V	−0·12	0·0096
D. Receipt of free meals		
No free meals small families		
Non-immigrant		
Social class I	−0·24	0·0326
Social class II	−0·24	0·0351
Social class III	−0·22	0·0302
Social class IV	−0·15	0·0141
Social class V	−0·24	0·0359
West Indian immigrant		
Social class I	—	—
Social class II	—	—
Social class III	−0·15	0·0129
Social class IV	−0·12	0·0075
Social class V	−0·27	0·0365
No free meals large families		
Non-immigrant		
Social class I	−0·31	0·0533
Social class II	−0·25	0·0418
Social class III	−0·23	0·0308
Social class IV	−0·12	0·0104
Social class V	−0·25	0·0475
West Indian immigrant		
Social class I	—	—
Social class II	—	—
Social class III	−0·37	0·0626
Social class IV	−0·06	0·0020
Social class V	−0·05	0·0018
Free meals small families		
Non-immigrant		
Social class I	—	—
Social class II	−0·11	0·0085
Social class III	−0·28	0·0514
Social class IV	−0·08	0·0035
Social class V	−0·21	0·0292
West Indian immigrant		
Social class I	—	—
Social class II	—	—
Social class III	—	—
Social class IV	—	—
Social class V	—	—
Free meals large families		
Non-immigrant		
Social class I	—	—
Social class II	−0·37	0·0893
Social class III	−0·28	0·0563
Social class IV	−0·19	0·0288
Social class V	−0·21	0·0346
West Indian immigrant		
Social class I	—	—
Social class II	—	—
Social class III	—	—
Social class IV	−0·08	0·0057
Social class V	−0·20	0·0280

N.B. See Table 5 for mean scores for these groups of children.

To do even this we must assume that any transformation in scores brought about by a successful policy would be linear: that to make the most disadvantaged group of schools as good as the average would, in principle, be to make their effects on reading performance the same as those currently produced by the average schools. The validity of the assumption may be questioned; but it is necessary to ask what would be the consequences of not accepting it. All that could be said, if it were unacceptable, would be that improving schools will cause them to have as yet unknown effects on the performance of the children in them. Clearly in all policy there is an element of what we hope will happen in addition to what might reasonably be predicted. These transformations establish the reasonable predictions from evidence on schools as they operate at present; the creation of new futures is beyond their scope.

If, therefore, we say that the purpose of a programme of positive discrimination through schools was to overcome the disadvantages they currently impose on the children in them, then we can assess the maximum reduction in the spread of scores that would result from a successful policy. In this case we would need to say that the differences in score between groups of children in the most disadvantaged 10 per cent of schools and groups, with the same home situation, but in the average school would be reduced by:

$$(z) \times (r) \times (s)$$

where z is equal to the number of standard deviations between the overall group mean and the mean of the bottom 10 per cent of children in that group (1·9), r^2 is equal to the amount that the total variation in scores would be reduced if the effect now attributable to school context for the group of children in question were removed, and s is equal to the standard deviation of scores for the group in question (see note 45).

Thus, policies of discrimination which overcame the effect of school context in the most disadvantaged 10 per cent of schools would narrow the gap in performance between groups of children in those schools, and similarly defined groups in the average school, by the following amounts:

For the children of non-immigrant non-manual workers	by 6·90 points of score or months of reading age.
For the children of non-immigrant manual workers	by 5·28 points.
For the children of West Indian immigrant non-manual workers	by 2·70 points.
For the children of West Indian immigrant manual workers	by 2·93 points.

The effect of such policies, far from tempering differences between groups which resulted from factors outside the school situation, would be to reinforce them. Positive discrimination which made the most disadvantaged schools as good as the average schools would increase the differences in performance between groups of children defined in terms of their family circumstances.

4 School Effect Due to Different Magnitudes of Contextual Disadvantage

We investigated whether the most disadvantaged schools had effects on the performance of groups of children in them, which were different to the

Table 10

Reading Score and School Privilege Group Regression Series

Reading score regressed against relative privilege score of school with schools grouped into the most, mid and least privileged third of scores for groups of children controlling:
A. By social class
B. By West Indian immigrant and groups born in the United Kingdom

	N	Mean	Regression Coefficient	R^2
Most privileged third of scores—the lowest scores for disadvantage on the schools index				
Total	3,452	102·4	−0·44	0·0144
A. Social class				
Social class I	664	110·3	−0·35	0·0103
Social class II	797	104·9	−0·45	0·0194
Social class III	1,096	100·6	−0·36	0·0106
Social class IV	519	97·0	−0·10	0·0010
Social class V	376	95·4	−0·16	0·0014
B. Non-immigrant and West Indian immigrant groups				
Non-immigrant				
Social class I	663	110·3	−0·34	0·0101
Social class II	790	105·0	−0·45	0·0192
Social class III	1,007	100·8	−0·32	0·0086
Social class IV	498	97·1	−0·12	0·0013
Social class V	362	95·6	−0·16	0·0014
West Indian immigrant				
Social class I	—	—	—	—
Social class II	—	—	—	—
Social class III	—	—	—	—
Social class IV	—	—	—	—
Social class V	—	—	—	—
Mid Privileged Third of Scores				
Total	16,084	95·2	−0·30	0·0180
A. Social class				
Social class I	1,105	106·2	−0·27	0·0130
Social class II	2,449	99·7	−0·20	0·0085
Social class III	5,592	96·0	−0·21	0·0100
Social class IV	3,738	92·6	−0·12	0·0033
Social class V	3,200	89·7	−0·32	0·0227
B. Non-immigrant and West Indian immigrant groups				
Non-immigrant				
Social class I	1,083	106·4	−0·26	0·0115
Social class II	2,377	100·0	−0·19	0·0075
Social class III	5,214	96·5	−0·17	0·0068
Social class IV	3,296	93·3	−0·10	0·0025
Social class V	2,733	90·7	−0·26	0·0148
West Indian immigrant				
Social class I	—	—	—	—
Social class II	72	92·1	—	—
Social class III	378	89·5	−0·30	0·0195
Social class IV	442	87·5	+0·11	0·0030
Social class V	467	83·6	−0·24	0·0119

Table 10 (continued)

	N	Mean	Regression Coefficient	R^2
Least privileged third of scores—the highest scores for disadvantage on the schools index				
Total	3,208	89·3	−0·24	0·0059
A. Social class				
Social class I	113	101·8	−0·16	0·0016
Social class II	312	94·3	−0·08	0·0006
Social class III	1,006	90·6	−0·02	0·0000
Social class IV	840	89·3	−0·16	0·0028
Social class V	937	84·9	−0·24	0·0080
B. Non-immigrant and West Indian immigrant groups				
Non-immigrant				
Social class I	109	101·6	−0·12	0·0010
Social class II	277	94·8	−0·07	0·0004
Social class III	847	91·3	−0·03	0·0001
Social class IV	661	90·4	−0·24	0·0062
Social class V	736	85·8	−0·22	0·0071
West Indian immigrant				
Social class I	—	—	—	—
Social class II	35	90·4	—	—
Social class III	159	86·9	+0·01	0·0011
Social class IV	179	85·3	+0·06	0·0004
Social class V	201	81·7	−0·35	0·0162

effects of the least disadvantaged schools: whether there were different apparent contextual effects at different concentrations of institutional disadvantage.

For this analysis schools were grouped into thirds according to their score on the eight variable school index, and the variations in reading performance for the groups of children were regressed against variations in school contextual score for the three groups of schools.

The small numbers of West Indian immigrant children in each regression equation makes confident interpretation of the results for these groups impossible, and we focused on the pattern of results for children born in the United Kingdom grouped by the occupation of their father. From Table 10 above it can be seen that the variations within the three groups of schools are dramatically smaller than for the total population of schools. Further, the variations remain roughly similar for heavily disadvantaged and for privileged schools. In other words, there are no significant differences between the effects from the most disadvantaged and the least disadvantaged group of schools on the reading performance of the children in them.

In one sense this is not a surprising result. For this analysis the groups of schools were in each case relatively homogeneous with respect to variations in measured levels of contextual disadvantage; and so their independent effects became correspondingly smaller. But it could have been otherwise. The logic of the Plowden principle of "cumulative disadvantage" means that as schools become more disadvantaged so the consequences for children attending them become progressively more detrimental. To repeat: we did not find this. There is an effect of school context operating across the whole population of schools in this analysis; but it is not confined to, and it is not especially powerful in, a particular group of heavily disadvantaged schools.

Although for this piece of analysis the explained variances were in every case below 2 per cent and were below 1 per cent for most cases, there is the semblance of a pattern to the situations where the variance is between 1 and 2 per cent. Children born in the United Kingdom, whose fathers are semi-skilled and unskilled workers and who are in the most disadvantaged schools, and United Kingdom children whose fathers are non-manual and skilled manual workers but who are not in the most disadvantaged schools, are the groups for whom the proportions of explained variation in reading score are strongest. This by itself proves nothing; but it opens up an interesting specula-tion. For instance, we might say that although privileged groups of children are affected by their school context in most schools, they are not further affected by the most disadvantaged schools: in other words, once privileged children are in heavily disadvantaged schools it does not matter how much more disadvantaged the schools become. Similarly we could speculate that, although disadvantaged non-immigrant children appear to be affected by the degree of institutional disadvantage in the most disadvantaged schools, it matters less to them once they are in relatively more privileged schools.

Effects of Family Circumstance

In order to provide a further framework within which the relative size of the overall independent school effects might be seen, we calculated the varia-tion in reading performance which could be attributed to the measured characteristics of home circumstances. Table 11 below presents our findings.[46]

Table 11

Variations in Reading Scores Independently Explained by Home Background Characteristics of Groups of Children

	Explained variation (%)
Occupation of father	9·35
Whether the child was of United Kingdom or West Indian immigrant origin	3·01
Contribution of all four family background characteristics: father's occupation, immigrant status, size of family, receipt of free school meals.	14·30
Cumulative child at-risk index	19·06

With school effects explaining between 4 and 6 per cent of the variations in reading score for groups of United Kingdom children and 1 per cent for West Indian immigrants, it is clear from Table 11 that the circumstances of families explain more of the variation in reading performance than do the circumstances of schools.

These again are perhaps not surprising findings but their implications for educational policy remain highly significant. To begin with, the measure of the socio-economic status of the children's father dominates the other measures—both of school context and of other family characteristics. Secondly, there is an effect of the immigrant status of groups of children which is independent of social class. The distinction in this cohort between West Indian immigrants and children born in the United Kingdom "explains" a 3 per cent variation in reading performance which cannot be attributed to the father's occupation. Thirdly, once these two factors—social class and immigrant status—are taken into account, the remaining variance explained by the characteristics of home circumstances—family size and free school meals—appears far less important.

Making the same assumptions as were made over the calculation of the maximum impact of discriminatory policies operating against the apparent effect of schools on groups of children, we used the variances explained by family circumstance to estimate upper limits to the impact of policies on these effects. Thus in principle, the impact of policies which removed the effect of socio-economic status on the reading performance of groups of children would narrow the gap in performance between children in the bottom 10 per cent on that dimension of inequality and the average child in the population by *8·7 points* of reading score: an amount equivalent to the same number of months of reading age. Similarly, the removal of differences attributable to a distinction between West Indian immigrant children and children born in the United Kingdom would mean that differences in reading performance between the bottom 10 per cent of children and the average child on that dimension would become smaller by *4·9 points*. Policies operating against effects of all four family circumstance characteristics could have an effect of *10·8 points* on the gap between the bottom 10 per cent and the average child; and the upper limit to a totally effective policy against cumulative disadvantage (as it was measured on the at-risk index) would narrow the gap in performance between the most disadvantaged 10 per cent of children and the average child by *12·5 points* of score, or over a year of reading age.

Changes in Score

We attempted, lastly, to examine the changes in score taking place in the cohort over time, and to relate these to measured characteristics of family circumstance and school context.

Analysis of the "Equality of Opportunity" cross-sectional data in the United States had shown that the differences among the average verbal ability levels of groups of children were greater in the higher than in the lower school grades.[47] Cohort studies in this country had similarly shown that both vocabulary and reading performance of groups of low working class children deteriorated with reference to national norms between the ages of eight and eleven.[48] These findings were highly significant for us because they implied that schools provide divergent experiences for children and that, in consequence, the longer children attend school the more the average performances of privileged and underprivileged groups are likely to differ.

Comparison of the average scores of the total age groups in I.L.E.A. schools at the time of the first and second reading surveys showed them to be remarkably similar.[46] We isolated the children who were present at

Table 12

Changes in Reading Score and School Privilege

Changes in reading score regressed against relative privilege score of original school for groups of children controlling:

A. By social class
B. By West Indian immigrant and groups born in the United Kingdom
C. By family size
D. By receipt of free school meals

	N	Mean	SD	Regression Coefficient	R^2
Total	18,596	+0·25	10·6	−0·01	0·00
A. Social class					
Social class I	1,438	+1·48	10·8	+0·01	0·00
Social class II	2,853	+0·54	10·3	0·00	0·00
Social class III	6,354	+0·10	10·6	−0·02	0·00
Social class IV	4,224	+0·14	10·6	+0·01	0·00
Social class V	3,727	−0·07	10·9	+0·01	0·00
B. Non-immigrant and West Indian immigrant groups					
All non-immigrant children	16,907	+0·28	10·6	−0·01	0·00
Non-immigrant					
Social class I	1,421	+1·48	10·9	+0·01	0·00
Social class II	2,757	+0·55	10·3	−0·01	0·00
Social class III	5,871	+0·13	10·6	−0·02	0·00
Social class IV	3,686	+0·18	10·6	−0·01	0·00
Social class V	3,172	−0·08	10·9	0·00	0·00
All West Indian immigrant children	1,689	−0·09	10·7	+0·07	0·00
West Indian immigrant					
Social class I	—	—	—	—	—
Social class II	96	+0·08	11·4	—	—
Social class III	483	−0·27	10·5	+0·04	0·00
Social class IV	538	−0·12	10·4	+0·12	0·02
Social class V	555	−0·01	11·0	+0·04	0·00
C. Family size					
Small families					
Non-immigrant					
Social class I	1,154	+1·65	11·1	+0·02	0·00
Social class II	2,222	+0·57	12·1	−0·01	0·00
Social class III	3,948	+0·32	11·2	+0·13	0·00
Social class IV	2,582	+0·39	10·7	0·00	0·00
Social class V	2,042	+0·21	10·9	+0·01	0·00
West Indian immigrant					
Social class I	—	—	—	—	—
Social class II	59	−0·98	10·7	—	—
Social class III	248	−0·59	10·4	−0·06	0·00
Social class IV	233	+0·60	9·4	−0·03	0·00
Social class V	232	+0·85	10·5	+0·02	0·00
Large families					
Non-immigrant					
Social class I	267	+0·73	10·0	−0·01	0·00
Social class II	535	+0·49	10·4	0·00	0·00
Social class III	1,428	−0·35	10·7	−0·02	0·00
Social class IV	1,104	−0·31	10·4	−0·01	0·00
Social class V	1,130	−0·59	10·8	−0·01	0·00
West Indian immigrant					
Social class I	—	—	—	—	—
Social class II	34	+1·78	12·5	—	—
Social class III	235	+0·07	10·7	+0·11	0·03
Social class IV	305	−0·06	11·1	+0·04	0·00
Social class V	323	−0·62	11·3	+0·05	0·00
D. Receipt of free meals					
No free meals small families					
Non-immigrant					
Social class I	1,120	+1·66	11·03	+0·02	0·00
Social class II	2,130	+0·68	10·22	0·00	0·00
Social class III	4,269	+0·29	10·59	−0·02	0·00
Social class IV	2,416	+0·38	10·74	0·00	0·00
Social class V	1,769	+0·28	10·89	0·00	0·00

Table 12 (continued)

	N	Mean	SD	Regression Coefficient	R^2
West Indian immigrant					
Social class I	—	—	—	—	—
Social class II	48	+0·27	10·59	—	—
Social class III	212	−0·73	10·36	−0·07	0·01
Social class IV	197	+0·80	9·48	−0·03	0·00
Social class V	168	+0·60	10·66	+0·02	0·00
No free meals large families					
Non-immigrant					
Social class I	226	+0·98	10·14	−0·04	0·00
Social class II	409	−0·61	10·58	−0·01	0·00
Social class III	1,021	−0·18	10·76	−0·02	0·00
Social class IV	699	−0·25	10·56	0·00	0·00
Social class V	583	−0·27	10·87	−0·02	0·00
West Indian immigrant					
Social class I	—	—	—	—	—
Social class II	—	—	—	—	—
Social class III	145	−0·74	10·49	+0·20	0·07
Social class IV	180	+0·31	12·14	+0·04	0·00
Social class V	171	−0·06	12·08	+0·06	0·01
Free meals small families					
Non-immigrant					
Social class I	34	+1·26	11·83	—	—
Social class II	92	−1·19	10·03	—	—
Social class III	174	+0·10	10·22	+0·05	0·00
Social class IV	166	+0·58	10·52	−0·01	0·00
Social class V	273	−0·28	10·67	+0·06	0·01
West Indian immigrant					
Social class I	—	—	—	—	—
Social class II	—	—	—	—	—
Social class III	36	+0·25	10·46	—	—
Social class IV	36	−0·47	8·41	—	—
Social class V	64	+1·52	9·93	—	—
Free meals large families					
Non-immigrant					
Social class I	41	−0·66	8·93	—	—
Social class II	126	+0·07	9·95	+0·04	0·00
Social class III	407	−0·75	10·53	−0·03	0·00
Social class IV	405	−0·41	10·25	−0·04	0·00
Social class V	547	−0·93	10·78	0·00	0·00
West Indian immigrant					
Social class I	—	—	—	—	—
Social class II	—	—	—	—	—
Social class III	90	+1·39	10·83	—	—
Social class IV	125	−2·06	9·31	+0·07	0·00
Social class V	152	−1·25	10·39	+0·05	0·00

both test times, and on whom there was adequate family circumstance data, and calculated individual change scores over the period.[50]

Our first finding was that average change scores are very small no matter how we define each group of children. The children of United Kingdom professional and managerial workers improved by an average of one and a half standard points; and the children of West Indian immigrant unskilled workers, who came from large families and received free school meals, lost ground by an average of one and a quarter standard points over the period (see Table 12). The second finding makes it necessary to be extremely circumspect about conclusions to be drawn from even these small changes in score. The variations about the average scores are considerable for each group and they nullify any straight comparison of average scores.

It is necessary to be clear what kind of results an analysis of the kind we performed could, in principle, give. We examined differences between two standardised scores.[51] Essentially, therefore, consideration could only be given to those changes which would result in a reordering of the children's relative performance between the two test times. A change in rank position relative to peers could be estimated; absolute changes in reading performance had already been accommodated by the standardisation process.

On this basis we were able to find no contributions of importance from either school context or family circumstance to changes in children's relative positions over time (school contextual contribution explained none of the variance whatsoever and the home background variables explained 0·5 per cent of the variation). Thus we must conclude that, while on average the more privileged groups appear to improve their position and the less privileged groups appear to lose ground, any pattern is swamped by random variations which are associated with neither school context nor family circumstance.

Conclusions

In this paper we have reported our attempts to analyse data on one cohort of junior school children in Inner London, in order to say something more about educational disadvantage and about policies of positive discrimination through schools in order to meet it. In particular, we have tried to establish upper limits to those policies both in terms of their potential coverage and their possible effects. From the data available to us we have come to fourteen specific major conclusions:

1. Using single item indicators: between one in four and one in six of the children in need are in the E.P.A. schools. (See pages 245 and 248 and Table 3)

2. Using an indicator of cumulative disadvantage: for every two disadvantaged children who are in EP.A. schools, five are outside them. And in the E.P.A. schools themselves, disadvantaged children are outnumbered by children who are not disadvantaged. (See page 248 and Table 4.)

3. Irrespective of the schools they attend, there is about two years difference in the average reading age of disadvantaged and non-disadvantaged children, when those children are between eight and nine years old. (See pages 249 and 252 and Tables 5 and 6.)

4. The average reading performance of disadvantaged children in the E.P.A. schools is approximately three months behind that of disadvantaged children in the most privileged schools. The two groups are nineteen months and sixteen months respectively behind a national norm, and eight months and sixteen months behind the average for their group of schools. (See page 253 and Table 6.)

5. We could find no evidence of a substantive content to a condition which people call disadvantage. It seems to refer to many different situations of need. (See pages 254 and 256 and Tables 7A and 7B.)

6. Once the occupation of father has been controlled for, there is no effect on variations in reading performance of either the low social class composition or the concentration of immigrant children in a school. (See page 259 and Table 8.)

7. There is a pattern of independent effects on variations in reading performance from the overall context of a school. This pattern holds

up even when groups of children are homogeneous with respect to the occupation of their father, their immigrant status, the size of their family and whether or not they receive free school meals. (See page 262 and Table 9.)

8. This is not a school contextual effect which is concentrated in a particular group of E.P.A. schools. It operates across the whole population. (See page 267 and Table 11.)

9. Policies of discrimination which overcame this effect would do little to equalise performance between *individual* children. (See page 262 and note 44.)

10. Policies which overcame it would substantially reduce the gap in performance between identically defined groups of children in different sorts of school. The strongest impact of such a policy would be felt by the children of professional and managerial workers who were born in the United Kingdom. For that group, the gap between their performance in the most disadvantaged 10 per cent of schools and in the average school would be closed by 7 points of score or months of reading age. (See page 265 and note 45.)

11. The group of children least affected by discriminatory policies which overcame the effects of school context would be West Indian immigrants. This group is significantly less affected by its school context than are non-immigrant children. (See page 265 and Table 9.)

12. The effect of school context on variations in reading performance is considerably less than the effect of characteristics of family circumstance. (See page 269 and Table 11.)

13. In addition to having average reading performances which were below their non-immigrant contemporaries when they were aged between eight and nine, in addition to being less affected by school context than their contemporaries at that stage, the average change in score of the West Indian immigrant group remained virtually constant between the two test times, while the score of the non-immigrant group improved slightly. (See pages 252, 265 and 271 and Tables 5, 9 and 12.)

14. There were no changes in the relative ordering of reading scores taking place in the cohort between the second year and the last year in the junior school which could be attributed to the effect of school context or to family circumstance. (See page 271 and Table 12.)

The validity and general applicability of these findings can be criticised in a series of ways and it is instructive to list some of the main ones here. The data were only for one age group of children from Inner London, mainly for one point of time, five years ago. The information is in some senses faulty. It is also inadequate (see notes 13 and 18). In particular we must be careful of what can be inferred from measured performance on one reading test. There is no information on intra school processes, or on teacher skills, or on schools which have effects on their children which are quite different from the measured dominant pattern. Quite possibly, policies which improved schools would change their impact on the performance of the children. For determined critics the list can go on. We think that these points should be considered carefully and we have tried to qualify our findings in the text without littering it with apologies.

At the same time two issues seem to us of overriding importance. The first comes from the logic of the data rather than from its precise quantification. Educational disadvantage is a very heterogeneous concept. School and area policies to tackle it set for themselves limits which prevent complete coverage. In order to bring discriminatory help to disadvantaged or needy children such policies will need to become substantially more complex, accommodating both intra school and area processes and other dimensions to the phenomenon. If school and area policies are to retain their original simplicity, they must be complemented with other, perhaps new and different policies which help the disadvantaged children who will inevitably be left out.

The other issue does rely on accurate measurement and correct analysis. But we think here that the questions we raise should be taken seriously even by those who may wish to question our findings. Consider the conclusions we derive from the analysis. Policies which successfully overcame the effect of school context and improved the performance of schools, would equalise performance between schools. But they would do little to equalise performances between individuals—perhaps nobody would expect them to; but also, therefore, equalising the performance of schools could do little to equalise opportunities between individuals. In addition, because the effect of school context is stronger for privileged groups than for less privileged ones, equalising the performance of schools would increase inequalities in performance between groups.

At the very least this raises questions about what it is appropriate and realistic to expect from schools. If what is desired is to maximise the opportunities available to all children irrespective of which school they go to, then, on this evidence, inequalities in performance between groups will increase. If what is desired is to reduce inequalities in performance between all children then, again on this evidence, more powerful policies than school reform will be needed. If what is desired is to reduce inequalities in performance between groups, then on this evidence, reforms will be needed which transform the relationships between schools and their social context. Further, a community of interest could not be assumed between all the families whose children attend the most disadvantaged schools; whether the policy is to improve or to transform those schools, again on this evidence, different groups will have different amounts to gain (and to lose) by it. It seems reasonable to ask the question, both of schools as they operate now and of a policy of positive discrimination to change them, who is expected to benefit?

NOTES

(1) Those institutions which appear to have strong redistributive functions are also those which are privileged in terms of selective restrictions on access to them. For instance, the *Robbins Committee* on higher education in Great Britain found that once they were in higher education, working class children did at least as well as those from middle class homes—whether this was measured in terms of the type of degree achieved or in terms of wastage rates. On the other hand, there were large variations in rates of access to higher education: 41 per cent of children from non-manual families who were born in 1940–41 and had measured IQs of 130+ entered full time higher education, whereas 30 per cent of such children from manual workers' families did so. 17 per cent of non-manual workers' children with IQs below 114 went into full time higher education, whereas 6 per cent of manual workers' children with similar measured intelligence did so. *Westergaard and Little's* 1964 collation of data on class differences in access to education showed the

grammar schools effectively to be selecting for access to higher education—"one in four (of the cohort they studied) was at a secondary grammar school at 13; one in ten was still at school at 17; while one in twenty-five went on to university. . . . At 11–13 a professional or managerial family's child had nine times as high a chance of entering a grammar school or independent school as an unskilled worker's child. Some years later, at 17, he had nearly thirty times as high a chance as the others of still being at school. . . . One in every four of the non-manual, middle class children who entered a grammar school type course at 11 + eventually went to a university; but only one in fifteen, to one in twenty of the grammar school entrants from unskilled working class homes did so."

(2) See Passow (ed.), *Urban Education in the 1970's* and Smith and Little, *Strategies for Compensation* for surveys of the United States programmes. See Halsey (ed.), *Educational Priority* for an account of the educational priority area programmes in British primary schools, and Benn and Simon, *Half Way There* and Rubinstein and Simon, *The Evolution of the Comprehensive School* for accounts of the reform of British secondary education.

(3) See Evetts, "Equality of educational opportunity: the recent history of a concept", *British Journal of Sociology*, December 1970 for a discussion of the development of the concept of equality of opportunity in Britain. See Coleman, "The Concept of Equality of Educational Opportunity", *Harvard Educational Review*, Winter 1968 for an analysis leading to advocacy of equality of performance between groups. See Jencks, *Inequality* for a conceptual and empirical analysis of the opportunities for equality between individuals. Halsey, in *Educational Priority*, advocates a further development of the concept. He sees the need for diversity of educational contents between schools and areas. Education should, he argues, be one of the means which would enable local communities to transform their own local situation. This further development assumes an actual or potential community of interest in particular schools and areas; we comment in the conclusions to this paper on how far our analysis would lend support to such an assumption.

(4) See *The Plowden Report*, Chapter 5, *passim*.

(5) The terms of reference of the *Plowden Council* were "to consider primary education in all its aspects, and the transition to secondary education." Although this reference was enormously wide, in a strictly formal sense the Council was not allowed to investigate all aspects of child socialisation and child poverty. Its recommendations for positive discrimination through the agency of schools should perhaps be seen in this light.

(6) *The Plowden Report*, paragraph 131.

(7) The research commissioned by the Council found that a relatively small amount of the variation in children's educational performance could be attributed to "the state of the school" (a variable composed largely of the characteristics of the teachers in the school). The regression analysis of this material found respectively 28 per cent, 20 per cent and 17 per cent of the between school variance explained by "Parental Attitudes", "Home Circumstances" and "School Variables": See Appendix 4, Table 3, Volume 2, *Plowden Report*. In other chapters in the Report, the Council stressed the importance of parental attitudes to children's performance at school. Yet only one of the thirteen specific and precise recommendations for an educational priority area policy is related to parental attitudes; at least nine of them, on the other hand, are recommendations for extra resources to be chanelled to schools in priority areas.

(8) The objective criteria were:

(a) Occupation,
(b) Size of families,
(c) Supplements in cash or kind from the state,
(d) Overcrowding and sharing of houses,
(e) Poor attendance and truancy,
(f) Proportions of retarded, disturbed or handicapped pupils,
(g) Incomplete families,
(h) Children unable to speak English.

The Plowden Report, paragraph 153

(9) *Ibid.*, paragraph 151.
(10) *Ibid.*, paragraph 169.
(11) *Ibid.*, paragraph 171.
(12) *Ibid.*, paragraph 174.
(13) Undoubtedly the main problem of using the I.L.E.A. Literacy Survey as a research

source was the understandable reliance on uncorroborated teacher information and opinion. One difficulty was the probable lack of informity between teachers and schools in their intepretation of the questions. This, we suggest, arose not only for questions involving child relationships at school and the degree of home stimulation (only a tiny proportion of immigrant homes were thought to be "stimulating"), but also for supposedly factual items such as country of origin and parental occupation (the proportion of semi-skilled manual occupations in many schools was so low as to give rise to the speculation that some teachers misplaced this category). Secondly, it was precisely those groups in which we were most interested, those with high at-risk scores, for which information was often not available (for West Indian immigrant children there was no information on the guardian's occupation in some 20 per cent of cases) See Goodacre *Teachers and their pupils home backgrounds* for a discussion of teacher perceptions of the home background of the children they teach.

Secondly, the data were inadequate for our purposes. For instance, it would have been most interesting to have had some measure of the children's IQ. However, the only available measure—the child's rank position on a verbal reasoning test—although designed to measure something akin to IQ was also, in part, a measure of child vocabulary. We could see no way of using this variable without considerably confusing any interpretation of our analysis. Further, the measure was not taken directly from an individual's test performance. Tests administered to all children were marked anonymously; schools were subsequently told the number of children which they could place in particular categories and individual children were then assigned a rank score for purposes of secondary school selection. The "goodness of fit" between a child's actual performance on the initial test and subsequent assignment to a rank position were not known. Lastly the data were available for children two and half years after the initial reading test. We used this information for the at-risk index, but excluded it from the regression analysis (see notes 18, 21, 26 and 27).

(14) A full account of the construction of the index of schools is given by Little and Mabey in Shonfield and Shaw, *Social Indicators and Social Policy*.

(15) Of the 10 variables in the I.L.E.A. Index, four were area based and collected from Census material (unskilled employed males, overcrowding of houses, housing stress and family size). The remaining six (proportion of immigrants, incidence of receipt of free school meals, high pupil absenteeism, high teacher mobility, high pupil turnover, low verbal reasoning scores) were all school based. A notional catchment area of the schools was calculated, for county schools, as an area within one quarter of a mile radius from the school. When the Index was constructed the density of population in Inner London was 40·6 people per acre. Broadly then, the population in the notional catchment area of a London primary school at the time was slightly more than 5,000 people.

(16) This test, and its parallel version, was constructed for use in the National Foundation for Educational Research's study of streaming in primary schools. See Barker Lunn: *Streaming in the Primary School*. The Sentence Reading Test A is standardised on a national sample of English children to have a mean of 100, a standard deviation of 15, a range from 70 to 140 points and a standard error of measurement of approximately 3·5 points.

(17) It has not proved possible to print the questionnaire. Copies may be obtained from the authors at the Centre for Studies in Social Policy, London.

(18) The overall response rate was very high, but the amount of missing data caused serious problems (see note 13). We needed to adopt different methods to deal with this at different stages of the analysis. For the regression analysis, we only dealt with cases on which there was complete data (see note 27). For the calculation of the at-risk scores, we counted a case with unknown data on a specific item as at-risk (see note 21). This caused problems when we wished to calculate the reading performance of at-risk groups, particularly with regard to the verbal reasoning scores. Not only were these indirect measures, but a substantial proportion of the children who were present in I.L.E.A. schools in 1968 (when the initial reading performance was measured) had left by 1971 (when the verbal reasoning rank assignments were allocated) (see Table 3). We therefore discounted children whose verbal reasoning position was unknown for the calculation of mean reading scores (Table 6).

(19) There was an additional problem: the S.R.A. reading test was standardised by N.F.E.R. on a sample from the whole of England. When used for the I.L.E.A. children it was found that many more of them than expected scored the minimum possible standardised score of 70. To have included these children, and used the 70 score for them,

would have considerably biased the mean score for disadvantaged groups as these had a high proportion of 70 scorers. To have eliminated such children from the analysis would have had a similar effect. Our resolution to this problem was as follows:

(i) We assumed that scores between 71 and 139 (the true range of the S.R.A. test) were from a truncated normal distribution.

(ii) We estimated the mean of this normal distribution using the scores between 71 and 139.

(iii) We used this to estimate a mean score for children scoring below 71.

(iv) The children scoring 70 were included in the analysis but were given the mean score derived in (iii)

(20) We are grateful to Keith Hope at Nuffield College, Oxford whose comments on an earlier draft of this section of the paper helped us clear our ideas on the general form of this fallacy. See Keith Hope, *Social Research: the Fifth Estate*.

For an extended discussion of the analysis of ecological data see Dogan and Rokkan, *Quantitive Ecological Analysis in the Social Sciences*.

(21) The table below shows how the child index was created. The source of the measures was in every case but one the data collected in the Literacy Survey. The verbal reasoning scores were added to the children's file at the time of their assessment for transfer to secondary school, two and half years after the first stage of the survey (see notes 13 and 18). Data not known were taken as at-risk.

Criteria	*Child counted as at-risk if*
1. Occupation of father	Father was a semi-skilled or unskilled manual worker, he was unemployed or his occupation was not known.
2. Family size	By adding together the number of parents and the number of siblings of school age and living at home, the family was six or more.
3. Cash Supplements to the family, Receipt of free school meals	The child received free school meals.
4. Handicapped Pupils, Low Verbal Reasoning	Child was in group 6 or 7 on the secondary school transfer profile (the lowest scoring 25 per cent). Children whose profile score was not known were included in the analysis presented in Tables 3 and 4A and 4B but excluded for Table 6 (see note 18).
5. Immigrant Pupils	The stated country of origin was other than the United Kingdom or the Republic of Ireland.
6. Teacher Turnover	He had been taught by more than one class teacher over the previous year.
7. Pupil Turnover	He had attended more than two schools to date.
8. Poor Attendance	Child was absent for more than one third of possible occasions.
CUMULATIVE INDEX OF RISK	Items on which a child was found to be "at-risk" were summed together. The higher the score achieved, the greater the chance of being disadvantaged.

(22) Teachers in this group of schools all received extra increments to their salary as part of the national programme of positive discrimination which followed the publication of the *Plowden Report*. See Chapter 3 of Halsey (ed.), *Educational Priority* for an account of the sequel to the publication of the Report. Schools receiving the salary allowances were seen to have been "nationally recognised as E.P.A.". In addition, the I.L.E.A. allowed these schools the maximum of extra resources available in its own attempts to help E.P.A. schools.

(23) The tables in the Appendix provide further data on the distribution of children. They show the numbers and proportions of English and West Indian immigrant children (by social class) in schools characterised by the proportion of immigrant and of unskilled and semi-skilled workers' children in them.

(24) We considered the possibility of constructing an index of "socialisation" based on

questions concerning the teacher's perceptions of a child's attitudes and relationships at school. For the reasons outlined in 13 above we abandoned this idea. We considered that any answers to such questions were probably too closely related to reading performance to be useful in forming an independent criterion measure.

(25) See the Schools Council Study of the *Aims of Primary Education*. Forthcoming.

(26) Children whose verbal reasoning rank position was unknown were dropped for this analysis (see note 18).

(27) Children were only included in the calculation of these mean scores—as for the regression analysis presented in Tables 8 to 12—if all four items of family characteristic were known: The occupational group of their family, their immigrant status, the family size and receipt of free school meals. The West Indian immigrant group was isolated because it was the only sufficient large, relatively homogeneous immigrant group; all other immigrant children were dropped from this analysis.

(28) Throughout the analysis we assume that the scores for any group are normally distributed. Given this assumption, it is simple to calculate what percentage of children in a group fall below any given score: see Blalock, *Social Statistics*.

(29) The Plowden Council considered recommending that measures of parental attitudes be used in addition to their "objective criteria". They rejected this on the grounds of difficulty and unreliability. It should be noted that the heterogeneity of disadvantaged circumstances we have identified is not revealed by adding more variables into the analysis, although clearly this is possible in principle.

(30) If we have two measurements X_1 and Y_1 for each of n individuals we may define a linear correlation between the two sets of measurements

$$r_{XY} = \frac{\sum (X_1 - \bar{X})(Y_1 - \bar{Y})}{(\text{Standard Deviation } X)(\text{Standard Deviation } Y)}$$

which varies between $+1$ and -1 and has the following properties

(i) If X is large when Y is large and vice versa r_{XY} will be close to $+1$.
(ii) If X is small when Y is large and vice versa r_{xy} will be close to -1.
(iii) If X and Y vary independently of each other r_{xy} will be close to zero.

(See Blalock, *Social Statistics*.)

The question arises, how are we to interpret a correlation which is close neither to zero nor ± 1? Unfortunately this is largely a matter of personal decision based on experience. Certainly there is no reason to say, for example, that a correlation of $0 \cdot 5$ indicates a relationship which is twice as strong as that indicated by a correlation of $0 \cdot 25$.

(31) But the verbal reasoning was dropped for the reasons outlined above (see notes 13 and 18).

(32) Whenever we have a battery of measurements on a group of subjects it is natural to attempt to construct a simplified model, in which variation among the subjects over the battery variables can reasonably be explained by their position on one or two, preferably independent, underlying 'dimensions': in the present case dimensions of deprivation. A Principal Component Analysis (see for example Hope, *Methods of Multivariate Analysis*) seeks systematically to construct such dimensions in order of their explanatory importance, i.e., the percentage of the original variation which can be attributed to each, by considering linear combinations of the original battery variables.

(33) See Coleman et al., *Equality of Educational Opportunity*.

(34) See Mosteller and Moynihan (eds.), *On Equality of Educational Opportunity*.

(35) See Coleman et al., *Equality of Educational Opportunity*, Chapter 3, *passim*. Two types of argument are presented to support this. The first shows that there are differences between black and white groups on entry into school, which persist over time spent in school. The second results from estimates of various school and family input factors derived from individual student-level correlation and regression analysis.

(36) See Marshall Smith in Mosteller and Moynihan (eds.) for an extended critique of the findings in Chapter 3 of the Coleman Report.

(37) See Coleman "Reply to Cain and Watts", *American Sociological Review*, Volume 35, Number 2, April 1970.

(38) Teacher mobility was one of the variables used in the index to identify I.L.E.A.'s disadvantaged Schools. See Little and Mabey in Shonfield and Shaw, *Social Indicators and Social Policy*.

(39) In effect, between the time of the first (S.R.A.) and second (S.R.B.) test times.

(40) See note 27. Only cell sizes greater than 100 were said to be reliable.
(41) For the purposes of regression analysis we assume a simple linear relationship between one variable (the reading ability of a child) and another (the deprivation score of his school), i.e.,

$$Y \text{ (child score)} = a + b \times X \text{ (school deprivation score)}$$

where a and b are two constants, which we select such that the equation is a "best fit" to the data, i.e., explains as much as possible of the total variation in scores.
From this equation we can see that a change of 1 unit in X produces a change of b units in Y. Similarly if X varies by 1 standard deviation, Y varies by:

$$b \times \text{(standard deviation of } X)$$

From correlation and regression theory it is easy to show that

$$b \times \text{(standard deviation of } X) = r_{xy} \times \text{(standard deviation of } Y)$$

and it is this quantity which we use in our subsequent calculations.
(42) See Jencks, *Inequality* for analysis which includes a far greater range of data on American schools and children than were available to us. It should be remembered that Jencks is concerned with individuals as his prime unit of analysis. We illustrate our findings in terms of their consequences for schools, groups and for individuals.
(43) See Little and Mabey in Donnison and Eversley (eds.), *London: Urban Patterns, Problems and Policies.*
(44) In order to estimate the maximum school effect on variations in reading score among individuals we established the maximum reduction in standard deviation that could be brought about by equalising the school effect. Thus

$$\text{Standard Deviation} = (\sqrt{1 - R^2xy}) \times (\text{Standard Deviation})$$
(after adjusting for the school effect) (before adjusting for the school effect)

where Rxy is the correlation between school disadvantage score and child reading score.
(45) In order to estimate the maximum school effect on the mean score for groups we considered the outcome of decreasing the school disadvantage score from its average value in the most disadvantaged 10 per cent of schools to its value in the average school. Suppose this involves a change of N standard deviations in school disadvantage score (i.e., of X — see note 41), then for the change in group average reading score (Y) we have:

$$\text{Change in } Y = N \times b_{yx} \times \text{Standard Deviation of } X \text{ for the group}$$

where b_{yx} is the regression coefficient of Y on X, or

$$\text{Change in } Y = N \times r_{xy} \times \text{Standard Deviation of } Y \text{ for the group}$$

(46) Although there are considerable difficulties in using regression techniques with classification level variables, we considered it very important to have comparable measures using the family background variables. We therefore produced estimates of R^2xy, the proportion of variance in reading score explained by these variables, and used these in the same way that we used the Rxy between school disadvantage score and reading score.
(47) See Coleman *et al.*, *Equality of Educational Opportunity.*
(48) See Douglas *et al.*, *All Our Future.*
(49) See I.L.E.A. *Literacy Survey*, 1972 Report.
(50) We took all children who had reading scores on both the 1968 and the 1971 test and calculated the change in score for each child. Unfortunately we were unable to say whether children had changed schools within the I.L.E.A. over this period.
(51) Unfortunately the 1968 reading test had been standardised by the teachers before the results were returned to the I.L.E.A. Although raw scores were available for the 1971 survey, this meant that we could not restandardise scores for those children who were in both surveys.

APPENDIX 1

DISTRIBUTION OF UNITED KINGDOM AND WEST INDIAN IMMIGRANT CHILDREN BY SOCIAL CLASS IN SCHOOLS

By low social class concentration in the school
By immigrant concentration in the school
By relative privilege score of the school
By schools grouped into thirds on their relative privilege scores

Table 1

Pupils in Schools with Varying Percentages of Low Social Class Children
United Kingdom Children

Social class	Percentage of low social class children in the school										Total (%)
	0–10	10–20	20–30	30–40	40–50	50–60	60–70	70–80	80–90	90–100	
a. By school											
1	49·4	25·4	16·3	10·7	6·6	5·4	3·2	1·9	1·6	—	8·5
2	30·0	29·8	23·4	17·1	16·3	14·4	13·3	9·9	8·1	4·1	16·5
3	16·5	31·7	39·1	44·2	40·6	34·0	28·0	21·7	11·9	2·0	34·7
4	3·4	7·8	13·6	16·2	20·6	26·0	28·1	31·7	35·0	32·7	21·7
5	0·8	5·3	7·7	11·9	15·9	20·2	27·4	34·7	43·3	61·2	18·7
Base (= 100%)	237	1,126	2,464	2,852	5,367	3,912	2,776	1,780	621	98	21,233

Social class	Percentage of low social class children in the school										Base (= 100%)
	0–10	10–20	20–30	30–40	40–50	50–60	60–70	70–80	80–90	90–100	
b. By social class											
1	6·5	15·8	22·2	16·8	19·5	12·0	4·9	1·8	0·6		1,805
2	2·0	9·6	16·4	13·9	25·0	16·0	10·5	5·0	1·4		3,509
3	0·5	4·8	13·1	17·1	29·6	18·0	10·5	5·3	1·0		7,370
4	0·2	1·9	7·3	10·0	24·0	22·1	16·9	12·3	4·7	0·7	4,607
5	0·1	1·5	4·8	8·6	21·6	20·0	19·3	15·7	6·8	1·5	3,942
Total	1·1	5·3	11·6	13·4	25·3	18·4	13·1	8·4	2·9	0·5	21,233

Table 2

Pupils in Schools with Varying Percentages of Low Social Class Children West Indian Immigrant Children

a. By school by social class
b. By social class by school

Social class	Percentage of low social class children in the school										Total (%)
	0–10	10–20	20–30	30–40	40–50	50–60	60–70	70–80	80–90	90–100	
a. By school											
1			3·2	2·4	1·9	1·2	0·5	—			1·4
2			8·1	9·7	4·0	4·7	7·9	3·6			5·7
3			41·9	39·4	34·5	26·9	19·3	19·1			27·5
4			30·6	23·0	32·8	31·5	34·8	29·4			31·8
5			16·1	25·5	26·7	35·7	37·6	47·9			33·6
Base (= 100%)	1	10	124	165	475	591	420	194	73	17	2,070
b. By social class											Base (= 100%)
1		3·6	14·3	14·3	32·1	25·0	7·1	—	3·6	0·9	28
2		0·9	8·5	13·6	16·1	23·7	28·0	5·9	2·5	0·4	118
3		1·1	9·1	11·4	28·8	27·9	14·2	6·5	0·7	1·1	570
4	0·2	0·3	5·7	5·8	23·7	28·1	22·2	8·7	4·3	1·0	659
5			2·9	6·1	18·3	30·4	22·7	13·4	5·3		695
Total	0·1	0·5	6·0	8·0	23·0	28·6	20·3	9·4	3·5	0·8	2,070

Table 3
Pupils in Schools with Varying Percentages of Immigrant Children United Kingdom Children

a. By school by social class
b. By social class by school

Social class	Percentages of immigrant children in the school										
	0-10	10-20	20-30	30-40	40-50	50-60	60-70	70-80	80-90	90-100	Total (%)
a. By school											
1	10·5	6·9	6·2	4·0	6·2	3·6	—	—			8·5
2	16·7	15·7	14·5	18·8	19·6	16·9	—	—			16·5
3	33·7	36·2	36·0	36·3	37·1	35·6	—	—			34·7
4	21·0	21·9	24·0	23·3	19·8	28·4	—	—			21·7
5	18·1	19·3	19·3	17·5	17·3	15·6	—	—			18·7
Base (= 100%)	14,019	3,887	1,789	1,003	469	225	28	4			21,424
b. By social class											Base (= 100%)
1	76·2	14·0	5·8	2·1	1·5	0·4	0·1	—			1,924
2	66·3	17·2	7·3	5·3	2·6	1·1	0·1	—			3,534
3	63·8	19·0	8·7	4·9	2·4	1·1	0·2				7,402
4	63·6	18·5	9·3	5·1	2·0	1·4	0·2				4,623
5	64·6	19·0	8·8	4·5	2·1	0·9	0·2				3,941
Total	65·4	18·1	8·4	4·7	2·2	1·1	0·1	—			21,424

Table 4

Pupils in Schools with Varying Percentages of Immigrant Children
West Indian Immigrant Children

a. By school by social class
b. By social class by school

Social class		Percentage of immigrant children in the school									Total (%)
	0–10	10–20	20–30	30–40	40–50	50–60	60–70	70–80	80–90	90–100	
a. By school											
1	1·3	1·6	1·2	1·1	1·6	1·6	—	—			1·4
2	6·6	5·8	6·2	7·9	4·5	6·9	—	—			5·7
3	23·8	30·6	25·5	23·4	28·9	30·9	—	—			27·5
4	34·4	31·1	32·1	31·3	31·8	32·4	—	—			31·8
5	33·9	30·8	35·0	36·4	32·2	28·2	—	—			33·6
Base (= 100%)	227	428	420	368	374	188	51	24			2,080
b. By social class											Base (= 100%)
1	—	—	—	—	—	—	—				28
2	11·7	19·5	20·3	22·7	13·3	10·2	2·3	1·8			128
3	9·5	23·0	18·8	15·1	18·9	10·2	2·8	1·5			570
4	11·8	20·2	20·5	17·5	18·1	9·3	1·2	0·6			659
5	11·1	19·0	21·2	19·3	17·8	7·6	3·5				695
Total	10·9	20·6	20·2	17·7	18·0	9·0	2·5	1·2			2,080

Table 5

Pupils in Schools with Varying Scores on the Relative Privilege: Under Privilege Scale
United Kingdom Children

a. By school by social class
b. By social class by school

a. By school

Social class	privileged (%)									under privileged (%)					Total (%)
1	18·1	18·3	24·3	17·5	11·4	9·4	5·8	5·0	3·0	4·9	4·4	2·2	2·1	—	9·0
2	26·7	31·6	22·2	21·2	18·6	14·9	17·5	14·6	13·7	11·9	9·4	9·2	9·9	—	16·6
3	37·1	29·8	29·1	33·4	34·3	36·6	36·3	25·4	34·2	34·3	35·9	21·5	21·5	—	34·4
4	15·5	14·1	15·2	14·6	19·2	20·5	22·6	24·5	28·4	25·4	25·7	24·5	22·5	—	21·5
5	2·6	6·2	9·2	13·3	16·5	18·6	17·8	20·4	20·8	23·5	24·6	42·6	43·7	—	18·5
Base (=100%)	116	531	950	1793	3,509	2,982	3,293	3,271	1,648	1,210	855	404	142	19	20,723

b. By social class

Social class	privileged (%)									under privileged (%)					Base (= 100%)
1	1·1	5·2	12·5	16·9	21·5	15·1	10·2	8·9	2·6	3·2	2·0	0·5	0·2	0·1	1,855
2	0·9	4·9	6·1	11·0	19·0	12·9	16·7	13·2	6·5	4·2	2·3	1·1	0·4	0·1	3,444
3	0·6	2·2	3·9	8·4	16·9	15·3	16·8	16·2	7·9	5·8	4·3	1·2	0·4	0·1	7,138
4	0·4	1·7	3·2	5·9	15·1	13·7	16·7	18·0	10·5	6·9	4·9	2·2	0·7	0·1	4,455
5	0·1	0·9	2·3	6·2	15·1	14·5	15·3	17·4	9·0	7·4	5·5	4·5	1·6	0·2	3,831
Total	0·6	2·6	4·6	8·7	16·9	14·4	15·9	15·8	8·0	5·8	4·1	2·0	0·7	0·1	20,723

285

Table 6

Pupils in schools with Varying Scores on the Relative Privilege: Under Privilege Scale West Indian Immigrant Children

a. By school by social class
b. By social class by school

Social class	privileged (%)												under privileged (%)	Total (%)
							a. By school							
1			—	3·6	3·8	1·9	1·4		0·7	1·1				1·3
2		—	—	4·3	6·2	3·8	6·1	5·3	6·9	5·7	4·8	—		5·5
3	—	—	—	30·2	28·5	29·3	24·4	27·7	27·5	32·2	21·9	—		27·6
4	—	—	—	37·4	28·5	30·3	30·5	34·4	35·5	30·5	15·2	—		31·8
5		—	—	24·5	33·1	34·7	37·6	32·5	29·3	30·5	58·1	—		33·8
Base (= 100%)	— 4	15	40	139	130	314	423	375	276	174	105	25	—	2,020
							b. By social class							Base (= 100%)
1			—	—	—	—	—	—	—	—				27
2		0·9	2·7	5·4	7·2	10·8	23·4	18·0	17·1	9·0	4·5	0·9		111
3	0·4	0·5	2·5	7·5	6·6	16·5	18·5	18·7	13·6	10·1	4·1	0·9		557
4	0·3	1·1	1·9	8·1	5·8	14·8	20·1	20·1	8·2	8·2	2·5	2·0		643
5		0·6	1·5	5·0	6·3	16·0	23·3	17·9	11·9	7·8	8·9	0·9		682
Total	0·2	0·7	2·0	6·9	6·4	15·5	20·9	18·6	13·7	8·6	5·2	1·2		2,020

Table 7

Pupils in Schools Groups into the Most Privileged and Least Privileged Thirds of Score

United Kingdom children
a. By school group by social class
b. By social class by school group

West Indian immigrant children
a. By school group by social class
b. By social class by school group

By school group

Social class	United Kingdom children				West Indian immigrant children			
	Most privileged (%)		Least privileged (%)	Total (%)	Most privileged (%)		Least privileged (%)	Total (%)
1	19·6	7·4	4·1	9·0	1·6	—	0·7	1·3
2	23·3	16·2	10·5	16·6	5·2	—	6·0	5·5
3	31·7	35·5	32·2	34·2	27·3	—	27·6	27·6
4	14·7	22·4	25·1	21·5	32·0	—	31·0	31·8
5	10·7	18·6	28·0	18·5	33·8	—	34·7	33·8
Base (= 100%)	3,390	14,703	2,630	20,723	1,381	59	580	2,020

By social class

Social class	United Kingdom children				West Indian immigrant children			
	Most privileged (%)		Least privileged (%)	Base (= 100%)	Most privileged (%)		Least privileged (%)	Base (= 100%)
1	35·7	58·4	5·9	1,855	—	—	—	27
2	22·9	69·0	8·0	3,444	64·9	3·6	31·5	111
3	15·1	73·0	11·9	7,138	67·9	3·4	28·7	557
4	11·2	74·0	14·8	4,455	68·7	3·3	28·0	643
5	9·4	71·3	19·2	3,831	68·5	2·1	29·5	682
Total	16·4	71·0	12·7	20,723	68·4	2·9	28·7	2,020

BIBLIOGRAPHY

Benn, C. and Simon, B., *Half way there: a report on the British comprehensive school reform*, Second edition, Harmondsworth, Penguin Education, 1972.

Blalock H. M., *Social statistics*, Second edition, New York, McGraw-Hill, 1972.

Coleman, J. S. and others, *Equality of educational opportunity*, Washington, D.C., U.S. Government Printing Office, 1966.

Coleman, J. S. and others, *Equal educational opportunity*, Cambridge, Mass., Harvard University Press, 1969. (An expansion of the Winter 1968, special issue of *Harvard Educational Review*.)

Coleman, J. S., "Reply to Cain and Watts", *American Sociological Review*, April 1970, vol. 35, no. 2, pp. 242–252.

Dogan, M. and Rokkan, S., *Quantitative ecological analysis in the social sciences*, Cambridge, Mass., MIT Press, 1969.

Donnison, D. and Eversley, D., (ed.), *London: urban patterns, problems and policies*, London, Heinemann, 1973.

Douglas, J. W. B. and others, *All our future: A longitudinal study of secondary education*. London. Peter Davies, 1968.

Evetts, J., "Equality of educational opportunity: the recent history of a concept." *British Journal of Sociology*, December 1970, vol. 21, pp. 425–430.

Goodacre, E. J., *Teachers and their pupils' home backgrounds: and investigation into teachers' attitudes and expectations in relation to their estimates and records of pupils' abilities, attributes and reading attainment*, Slough, National Foundation for Educational Research in England and Wales, 1969.

Halsey, A. H., *Educational priority: E.P.A. problems and policies*, vol. 1, London, H.M.S.O., 1972.

Hope, K., *Methods of multivariate analysis*, London, University of London Press, 1969.

Hope, K., "Social Research, the Fifth Estate," Unpublished lecture given to the Sociology Section of the British Association meeting at Leicester 1972.

Inner London Education Authority, *Literacy survey, 1971 follow-up*, Preliminary report, Report to the Education Committee, I.L.E.A. 203. December 1972.

Jencks, Christopher and others, *Inequality: a reassessment of the effect of family and schooling in America*, New York, Basic Books, 1972.

Lunn, J. Barker, *Streaming in the primary school: a longitudinal study of children in streamed and non-streamed junior schools*, Slough, National Foundation for Educational Research in England and Wales, 1970.

Mosteller, F. and Moynihan, D. P., *On equality of educational opportunity*. Papers deriving from the Harvard University Faculty Seminar on the Coleman Report, New York, Random House, 1972.

Passow, A. H., *Urban education in the 1970's: reflections and a look ahead*, New York, Teachers College Press, 1971.

Plowden, Lady B. (chairman), *Children and their primary schools.* A report of the Central Advisory Council for Education (England), London, H.M.S.O., 1967.

Robbins, Lord (chairman), *Report of the Committee on Higher Education,* London, H.M.S.O., 1963 (Cmnd 2154). Especially Appendix 2.

Rubinstein, David and Simon, B., *The Evolution of the Comprehensive School 1926–1972,* London, Routledge and Kegan Paul, 1973.

Schools Council, *Aims of primary education.* Forthcoming.

Shonfield, A. and Shaw, S. (ed.), *Social indicators and social policy,* London, Heinemann Educational Book, 1973.

Smith, George and Little, A. N., *Strategies for compensation, a review of educational projects for the disadvantaged in the United States,* Paris, O.E.C.D., 1971.

Westergaard, J. and Little, A. N., "The trend of class differentials in educational opportunity in England and Wales," *British Journal of Sociology,* December 1964, vol. 15, no. 4, pp. 301–316.

Printed in England for Her Majesty's Stationery Office by
McCorquodale Printers Ltd., London
Dd 288660 K120 1/75.